MW00835530

Hands-On Python D
Learning for the Web

Integrating neural network architectures to build smart web apps with Flask, Django, and TensorFlow

Anubhav Singh
Sayak Paul

BIRMINGHAM - MUMBAI

Hands-On Python Deep Learning for the Web

Copyright © 2020 Packt Publishing

All rights reserved. No part of this book may be reproduced, stored in a retrieval system, or transmitted in any form or by any means, without the prior written permission of the publisher, except in the case of brief quotations embedded in critical articles or reviews.

Every effort has been made in the preparation of this book to ensure the accuracy of the information presented. However, the information contained in this book is sold without warranty, either express or implied. Neither the authors, nor Packt Publishing or its dealers and distributors, will be held liable for any damages caused or alleged to have been caused directly or indirectly by this book.

Packt Publishing has endeavored to provide trademark information about all of the companies and products mentioned in this book by the appropriate use of capitals. However, Packt Publishing cannot guarantee the accuracy of this information.

Commissioning Editor: Sunith Shetty
Acquisition Editor: Ali Abidi
Content Development Editor: Pratik Andrade
Senior Editor: Ayaan Hoda
Technical Editor: Sarvesh Jaywant
Copy Editor: Safis Editing
Project Coordinator: Neil Dmello
Proofreader: Safis Editing
Indexer: Manju Arasan
Production Designer: Alishon Mendonsa

First published: May 2020

Production reference: 1150520

Published by Packt Publishing Ltd.
Livery Place
35 Livery Street
Birmingham
B3 2PB, UK.

ISBN 978-1-78995-608-5

www.packt.com

`Packt.com`

Subscribe to our online digital library for full access to over 7,000 books and videos, as well as industry leading tools to help you plan your personal development and advance your career. For more information, please visit our website.

Why subscribe?

- Spend less time learning and more time coding with practical eBooks and Videos from over 4,000 industry professionals

- Improve your learning with Skill Plans built especially for you

- Get a free eBook or video every month

- Fully searchable for easy access to vital information

- Copy and paste, print, and bookmark content

Did you know that Packt offers eBook versions of every book published, with PDF and ePub files available? You can upgrade to the eBook version at `www.packt.com` and as a print book customer, you are entitled to a discount on the eBook copy. Get in touch with us at `customercare@packtpub.com` for more details.

At `www.packt.com`, you can also read a collection of free technical articles, sign up for a range of free newsletters, and receive exclusive discounts and offers on Packt books and eBooks.

About the authors

Anubhav Singh, a web developer since before Bootstrap was launched, is an explorer of technologies, often pulling off crazy combinations of uncommon tech. An international rank holder in the Cyber Olympiad, he started off by developing his own social network and search engine as his first projects at the age of 15, which stood among the top 500 websites of India during their operational years. He's continuously developing software for the community in domains with roads less walked on. You can often catch him guiding students on how to approach ML or the web, or both together. He's also the founder of The Code Foundation, an AI-focused start-up. Anubhav is a Venkat Panchapakesan Memorial Scholarship awardee and an Intel Software Innovator.

My thanks go out to everyone who pushed me toward the completion of this book – my parents, who kept asking me about it on every call; my friends and professors, who were lenient on me so I could focus on the book; and the team at Packt, who patiently kept motivating us throughout the process. A huge thanks to my coauthor, Sayak Paul, who believed in me and invited me to work with him on this book.

Sayak Paul is currently with PyImageSearch, where he applies deep learning to solve real-world problems in computer vision and bring solutions to edge devices. He is responsible for providing Q&A support to PyImageSearch readers. His areas of interest include computer vision, generative modeling, and more. Previously at DataCamp, Sayak developed projects and practice pools. Prior to DataCamp, Sayak worked at TCS Research and Innovation (TRDDC) on data privacy. There, he was a part of TCS's critically acclaimed GDPR solution called Crystal Ball. Outside of work, Sayak loves to write technical articles and speak at developer meetups and conferences.

I would like to, first and foremost, thank my parents, Baby Paul and Tapas Kumar Paul, for their continued support, patience, and encouragement throughout the long process of writing this book. Thanks to my coauthor Anubhav too, he has been very patient with my little suggestions and he has tried his best to match them.

About the reviewer

Karan Bhanot is a computer science graduate from Punjab Engineering College, India. He is a machine learning and data science enthusiast. He has worked on numerous projects involving Python, Jupiter Notebook, NumPy, pandas, Matplotlib, Flask, Flask-RESTPlus, neural networks (Keras and TensorFlow), R, Shiny, Leaflet, and ggplot. As a frontend developer, he has also worked on HTML, CSS, and JavaScript. He is currently pursuing a PhD in computer science with a research focus on data science and machine learning. He is active on GitHub and blogs his ideas and learnings on online blogging websites such as Medium.

I would like to thank my sister, Ms. Naina Bhanot, and my parents, Mr. Arvind Bhanot and Mrs. Savita Bhanot, for always supporting me in all my endeavors.

Packt is searching for authors like you

If you're interested in becoming an author for Packt, please visit authors.packtpub.com and apply today. We have worked with thousands of developers and tech professionals, just like you, to help them share their insight with the global tech community. You can make a general application, apply for a specific hot topic that we are recruiting an author for, or submit your own idea.

To my father, Shiv Bahadur Singh, who is a teacher and taught me the beauty of sharing knowledge, and to my mother, Nirmala Singh, who never let me stray from my focus in the face of adversities.

– Anubhav Singh

To my mother, Baby Paul, and my father, Tapas Kumar Paul, who have always encouraged me to pursue the things I love and care about. To all my university juniors, who have supported me tremendously in all of my honest endeavors.

– Sayak Paul

Preface

Deep learning techniques can be used to develop intelligent web apps. Over the last few years, tremendous growth in the number of companies adopting deep learning techniques in their products and businesses has been observed. There has been a significant surge in the number of start-ups providing AI and deep learning-based solutions for niche problems. This book introduces numerous tools and technological practices used to implement deep learning in web development using Python.

To start with, you will learn about the fundamentals of machine learning, with a focus on deep learning and the basics of neural networks, along with their common variants, such as convolutional neural networks, and how you can integrate them into websites with frontends built with different standard web tech stacks. You will create your deep learning-enabled web application using Python libraries such as Django and Flask by creating REST APIs for custom models. You will set up a cloud environment for deep learning-based web deployments on Google Cloud and AWS, and get guidance on how to use their battle-tested deep learning APIs. Further, you will use Microsoft's Intelligent Emotion API, which can detect human emotions from a picture of a face. You will also get to grips with deploying real-world websites, and you will get great insights into securing those websites using reCaptcha and Cloudflare for a robust experience. Finally, you will use natural language processing to recommend restaurants from user reviews and to integrate a voice UX on your web pages through Dialogflow.

By the end of this book, you'll be able to deploy your intelligent web apps and websites with the help of the best tools and practices.

Who this book is for

This book is for data scientists, machine learning practitioners, and deep learning engineers who are looking to perform deep learning techniques and methodologies on the web. This book will also be ideal for web developers who want to use smart techniques in the browser to make it more interactive. You will gain deep insights into browser data using this handy guide.

Having a working knowledge of the Python programming language and fundamental machine learning techniques (as covered in the Machine Learning Crash Course by Google, available at `https://developers.google.com/machine-learning/crash-course`) will be beneficial for reading this book.

What this book covers

Chapter 1, *Demystifying Artificial Intelligence and Fundamentals of Machine Learning*, briefly introduces machine learning, deep learning, and other forms of artificial intelligence methodologies related to web development. This chapter quickly goes over fundamental topics of the machine learning pipeline, such as exploratory data analysis, data preprocessing, feature engineering, training and testing, models of evaluation, and more. Toward the end, a comparison between the interactivity and user experience offered by websites before AI became popular and how they are in the modern day is presented. We also study the usage of AI on the web by some of the biggest firms and how AI has revolutionized their products.

Chapter 2, *Getting Started with Deep Learning Using Python*, introduces basic concepts and terminologies related to deep learning and how to use deep learning to build a simple web app with different deep learning libraries in Python.

Chapter 3, *Creating Your First Deep Learning Web Application*, discusses several important concepts regarding the structure of web applications specifically for leveraging deep learning. It then proceeds to discuss the approaches to understanding a dataset. The chapter also shows how to implement and improve a simple neural network and how it can be wrapped into an API for the development of a simple web application. We then proceed to showcase how the API can be implemented using different standard web tech stacks.

Chapter 4, *Getting Started with TensorFlow.js*, introduces the most popular JavaScript library for deep learning—TensorFlow.js (Tf.js). It gives a brief overview of what TensorFlow.js is and the things it is capable of doing in a browser. Furthermore, this chapter shows how you can use pre-trained models using TensorFlow.js and build a simple web application with it.

Chapter 5, *Deep Learning through APIs*, introduces the concept of APIs and their importance in software development. Further, the chapter proceeds to show examples of different deep learning APIs. Toward the very end, the chapter presents an approach to choosing deep learning API providers to suit particular use cases. The deep learning APIs covered are the Vision API, the Text API, and others.

Chapter 6, *Deep Learning on Google Cloud Platform Using Python*, introduces the offerings by Google Cloud Platform for web developers to integrate into their websites. The focus is on Dialogflow, which can be used to make chatbots and conversational AIs; the Cloud Inference API, which can be used to build a good recommendation system; and also the Translation API, which is used to provide users in different locales with website content in their languages. The chapter discusses their applications at length and also demonstrates a basic how-to for using them with Python.

Chapter 7, *DL on AWS Using Python: Object Detection and Home Automation,* introduces Amazon Web Services and talks briefly about the various offerings, including the Alexa API and the Rekognition API. The Alexa API can be used to build home automation web apps and other interactive interfaces, while the Rekognition API can be used to detect people and objects in photos and videos.

Chapter 8, *Deep Learning on Microsoft Azure Using Python,* introduces Microsoft Azure Cloud Services, focusing on the Cognitive Toolkit, which is Microsoft's alternative to TensorFlow's Emotion API, which can be used to determine the emotion of a person from a photograph of their face, and the Text-to-Speech API, which can be used to generate natural-sounding voice from text.

Chapter 9, *A General Production Framework for Deep Learning-Enabled Websites,* introduces the general framework to be set up for the efficient deployment of deep learning on the web in a production environment. Strategies for reducing computing resources, converting raw datasets to datasets for training deep learning models, and how to make models available for usage on the web in a minimally resource-intensive way are covered.

Chapter 10, *Securing Web Apps with Deep Learning,* discusses several tricks and techniques for securing websites with deep learning with Python. We present reCaptcha and Cloudflare and discuss how they are used to enhance the security of websites. We also show how to implement security mechanisms to detect malicious users on websites using deep learning on the Python backend.

Chapter 11, *DIY – A Web DL Production Environment,* discusses the methods by which we update models in production and how we can choose the right method according to requirements. We begin with a brief overview and then demonstrate some famous tools for creating deep learning data flows. Finally, we implement a demo of online learning, or incremental learning, to establish a method of model update in production.

Chapter 12, *Creating an E2E Web App Using DL APIs and Customer Support Chatbot,* introduces natural language processing and discusses how to create a chatbot for resolving general customer support queries using Dialogflow and integrate it into a Django and Flask website. We explore ways of implementing bot personalities and how to make such system resources effective. We also introduce a method for implementing a text-to-speech and speech-to-text-based user interface with Python.

Appendix, *Success Stories and Emerging Areas in Deep Learning on the Web,* illustrates some of the most famous websites whose products are based heavily upon leveraging the power of deep learning. This chapter also discusses some key research areas in web development that could be enhanced using deep learning. This will help you to delve even deeper into the fusion of web technologies and deep learning and will motivate you to come up with your own intelligent web applications.

To get the most out of this book

This book assumes an understanding of the Python language, specifically Python 3.6 and above. It is strongly recommended to have the Anaconda distribution of Python installed on your local systems. Any Anaconda distribution with support for Python 3.6 and above is good for running the examples in this book.

In terms of hardware, this book assumes the availability of a microphone, speaker, and webcam on your computer.

Software/Hardware covered in the book	OS Requirements
Anaconda distribution of Python and other Python packages	1 GB RAM minimum, 8 GB recommended 15 GB disk space
Code editor of your choice (Sublime Text 3 recommended)	2 GB RAM

If you are using the digital version of this book, we advise you to type the code yourself or access the code via the GitHub repository (link available in the next section). Doing so will help you avoid any potential errors related to the copying and pasting of code.

It is expected that you will try to implement the samples present in this book by yourself. In case you run into problems, you can reach out to us by emailing the authors – Sayak Paul (spsayakpaul@gmail.com) and Anubhav Singh (xprilion@gmail.com). In case you are unable to run the samples provided in the code repo of the book, you can raise issues on the repo and we'll get back to you there!

Download the example code files

You can download the example code files for this book from your account at www.packt.com. If you purchased this book elsewhere, you can visit www.packtpub.com/support and register to have the files emailed directly to you.

You can download the code files by following these steps:

1. Log in or register at www.packt.com.
2. Select the **Support** tab.
3. Click on **Code Downloads**.
4. Enter the name of the book in the **Search** box and follow the onscreen instructions.

Once the file is downloaded, please make sure that you unzip or extract the folder using the latest version of:

- WinRAR/7-Zip for Windows
- Zipeg/iZip/UnRarX for Mac
- 7-Zip/PeaZip for Linux

The code bundle for the book is also hosted on GitHub at `https://github.com/PacktPublishing/Hands-On-Python-Deep-Learning-for-Web`. In case there's an update to the code, it will be updated on the existing GitHub repository.

We also have other code bundles from our rich catalog of books and videos available at `https://github.com/PacktPublishing/`. Check them out!

Download the color images

We also provide a PDF file that has color images of the screenshots/diagrams used in this book. You can download it here: `http://www.packtpub.com/sites/default/files/downloads/9781789956085_ColorImages.pdf`.

Conventions used

There are a number of text conventions used throughout this book.

`CodeInText`: Indicates code words in text, database table names, folder names, filenames, file extensions, pathnames, dummy URLs, user input, and Twitter handles. Here is an example: "We now need to import the saved model and weights from the model training step. Once we do so, we need to recompile the model and make its `predict` function using the `make_predict_fuction()` method."

A block of code is set as follows:

```
def remove_digits(s: str) -> str:
    remove_digits = str.maketrans('', '', digits)
    res = s.translate(remove_digits)
    return res
```

Any command-line input or output is written as follows:

```
python main.py
```

Bold: Indicates a new term, an important word, or words that you see onscreen. For example, words in menus or dialog boxes appear in the text like this. Here is an example: "Fill up the entries and click on **Continue**."

 Warnings or important notes appear like this.

 Tips and tricks appear like this.

Get in touch

Feedback from our readers is always welcome.

General feedback: If you have questions about any aspect of this book, mention the book title in the subject of your message and email us at customercare@packtpub.com.

Errata: Although we have taken every care to ensure the accuracy of our content, mistakes do happen. If you have found a mistake in this book, we would be grateful if you would report this to us. Please visit www.packtpub.com/support/errata, selecting your book, clicking on the Errata Submission Form link, and entering the details.

Piracy: If you come across any illegal copies of our works in any form on the Internet, we would be grateful if you would provide us with the location address or website name. Please contact us at copyright@packt.com with a link to the material.

If you are interested in becoming an author: If there is a topic that you have expertise in and you are interested in either writing or contributing to a book, please visit authors.packtpub.com.

Reviews

Please leave a review. Once you have read and used this book, why not leave a review on the site that you purchased it from? Potential readers can then see and use your unbiased opinion to make purchase decisions, we at Packt can understand what you think about our products, and our authors can see your feedback on their book. Thank you!

For more information about Packt, please visit packt.com.

Table of Contents

Section 4: Deep Learning in Production (Intelligent Web Apps)

Chapter 9: A General Production Framework for Deep Learning-Enabled Websites

Artificial Intelligence on the Web

This section introduces the definition of **Artificial Intelligence** (**AI**) and shows how AI is having an effect on the web to a great extent. It also discusses the fundamentals of machine learning in brief.

This section comprises the following chapters:

- Chapter 1, *Demystifying Artificial Intelligence and Fundamentals of Machine Learning*

1

Demystifying Artificial Intelligence and Fundamentals of Machine Learning

"Just as electricity transformed almost everything 100 years ago, today I actually have a hard time thinking of an industry that I don't think AI will transform in the next several years."

- Andrew Ng

This quote may appear extremely familiar and it's needless to say that, as a statement, it is really strongly resonant with respect to the current technological disruption. Over the recent course of time, **Artificial Intelligence** (**AI**) has been a great area of interest to almost every industry. Be it an educational company, a telecommunications firm, or an organization working in healthcare —all of them have incorporated AI to enhance their businesses. This uncanny integration of AI and several other industries only promises to get better with time and solve critical real-world problems in intelligent ways. Today, our phones can make clinical appointments for us upon our instructions, our phone cameras can tell us several human-perceived attributes of the images they capture, and our car alarm systems can detect our driving gestures and can save us from possible accidents. The examples will only get better and better and will grow as intelligent as possible with advancements in research, technology, and the democratization of computing power.

As we step into the era of Software 2.0, it is extremely important to understand why a technology that has existed since the 1950s is making most of the headlines in recent times. Yes! Artificial intelligence was born in the 1950s when a handful of computer scientists and mathematicians such as **Alan Turing** started to think about whether machines could think and whether they could be empowered with intelligence so that they can answer questions on their own without being explicitly programmed.

Soon after this inception, the term **artificial intelligence** was first coined by **John McCarthy** in 1956 in an academic conference. From the question "**Can machines think?**" (proposed by Turing in his paper, entitled *Computing Machinery and Intelligence*) around 1950 to the current day in the 21st century, the world of AI has shown some never-seen-before results that we could never have even thought of.

Today, it is almost impossible to think of a day without using **the web.** It has easily become one of our fundamental necessities. Our favorite search engines can directly answer our questions rather than give us a list of relevant links. They can analyze online text and detect their intent and summarize their content. All of this is possible because of AI.

This book aims to be a hands-on guide to the readers on how they can use AI techniques such as **deep learning** to make intelligent web applications based on **computer vision**, **natural language processing, security**, and lots more. This chapter provides the readers with a quick refresher on AI and its different types and the basic concepts of ML, and introduces some of the biggest names in the industry and what they are doing by fusing AI and web technologies. We will be covering the following aspects:

- Introduction to AI and its different types
- **Machine Learning** (**ML**): The most popular AI
- A brief introduction to **Deep Learning** (**DL**)
- The relationship between AI, ML, and DL
- Fundamentals of ML
- The web before and after AI
- The biggest web-AI players and what they are doing

Introduction to artificial intelligence and its types

In a simpler sense, artificial intelligence is all about giving machines the ability to perform intelligently. For example, many of us can play chess. Essentially, we do this first by *learning* the fundamentals of playing the game and then we engage ourselves in actually playing the game with others. But can machines do this? Can machines learn on their own and play the game of chess with us?

AI attempts to make this possible by giving us the power to synthesize what we call *intelligence* in terms of some rules and instill it into machines. **Machines** as mentioned here can be anything that can compute. For example, it could be software or a robot.

There are actually several types of AI. The popular ones are the following:

- Fuzzy systems
- Expert systems
- ML systems

The final type sounds the most familiar here. We will get to it in the next section. But before we proceed with it, it is a good time to take a look at some of the points that enable the AI advancements we are witnessing today.

Factors responsible for AI propulsion

The major factors that are driving the AI force are the following:

- Data
- Algorithmic advancements
- Computer hardware advancements
- The democratization of high-performance computing

Data

The amount of data we have today is enormous—as **Hal Varian**, Chief Economist at Google, put it in 2016:

> *"Between the dawn of civilization and 2003, we only created five exabytes; now we're creating that amount every two days. By 2020, that figure is predicted to sit at 53 zettabytes (53 trillion gigabytes)—an increase of 50 times."*

That's a lot of data. As the number of digital devices grows, this volume of data will only continue to grow exponentially. Gone are the times when a running car only displayed the speed on the speedometer. We're in an age where every part of the car can be made to produce logs at every split second, enabling us to entirely reconstruct any moment of the car's life.

The more a person gets to learn from life, the wiser the person becomes, and the better they can predict outcomes of events in the future. Analogically with machines, the greater the amount of (quality) data that a piece of software gets to train upon, the better it gets at predicting future unseen data.

In the last few years, the availability of data has grown manifold due to various factors:

- Cheaper storage
- Higher data transmission rates
- Availability of cloud-based storage solutions
- Advanced sensors
- The Internet of Things
- An increase in the various forms of digital electronic devices
- Increased usage of websites and native apps

There are more digital devices now than ever. They are all equipped with systems that can generate logs at all times and transmit them over the internet to the companies that manufacture them or any other vendor that buys that data. Also, a lot of logs are created by the websites or apps people use. All of these are easily stored in cloud-based storage solutions or in physical storage of high storage capacity, which are now cheaper than before.

If you look around yourself, you will probably be able to see a laptop on which you regularly use several pieces of software and websites—all of which may be collecting data on every action you perform on them. Similarly, your phone acts as such a data-generating device. With a television with several channels provided by your television service provider—both the service provider and the channel provider are collecting data about you to serve you better and to improve their products. You can only imagine the massive amount of data a single person generates on a daily basis, and there are billions of us on this planet!

Advancements in algorithms

An algorithm is an unambiguous sequence of steps that leads to the solution of a given problem. Over time, with the expansion of science and human understanding of the laws of nature by the aid of mathematics, algorithms have seen improvements. More often than not, nature has inspired solutions to complex problems. A neural network is probably the most talked-about, nature-inspired algorithm in the present day.

When computer logic began with multiple if-else ladders, no one would ever have thought that one day we'd have computer programs that would learn to produce results similar to the if-else ladder without the need to write conditions manually. What's more, we have computer programs today that generate other programs that can simulate AI!

Surely, with each passing day, algorithms developed by humans and now, by machines too, are getting smarter and more powerful at performing their tasks. This has directly impacted the rise of neural networks, which, in their rudimentary form, seem to be a time-consuming super-nesting of loops to solve matrices and vector arithmetic problems.

Advancements in hardware

When Intel revealed its first Dynamic RAM module in 1970, it was capable of holding 1 KB of data. Approximately 50 years later, we've 128 GB RAM modules available in the market. That's nearly 1.28×10^8 times as much memory space.

A similar trend has been exhibited by hard disks. With the first hard disk for personal computers being able to store a precious 5 megabytes, 2016 saw Seagate announcing a 60-terabyte storage on a solid-state drive. That's a 1.2×10^7 fold increase.

But we've only yet talked about direct individual computing comparisons, without considering the effect of technological growth since the first computers were introduced. Today, with the advent of cloud computing, it's become common to hear someone talking about **unlimited cloud storage**.

AI has greatly benefited from this exponential increase in computing speed and data storage.

The democratization of high-performance computing

With the reducing costs of commodity hardware and their increasing performance capabilities, high-performance computing is not something exclusive to tech giants these days. Today, it is very easily possible for any single person to set up for their personal use a network of computing devices to facilitate high-performance computing if they're not already satisfied with the exceptional performance that can be delivered through single devices. However, investing in hardware is not the only way of availing high-performance computing. The emergence of cloud-based computing solutions has resulted in very high-speed computing infrastructure available with click-deploy methods. Users can, at any moment, launch a cloud-based instance over the network and run their performance-intensive software on it at minimal charges.

With high-performance computing becoming readily available to individual developers, the development of AI solutions has come into the hands of a wide community of developers. This has led to a boom in the number of creative and research-based applications of AI.

Let's now unravel the most popular form of AI as of the time of writing and discuss some important concepts regarding it.

ML – the most popular form of AI

Without taking any mathematical notations or too many theoretical details, let's try to approach the term **Machine Learning** (**ML**) from an intuitive perspective. For doing this, we will have to take a look at how we actually learn. Do you recollect, at school, when we were taught to identify the parts of speech in a sentence? We were presented with a set of rules to identify the part of the speeches in a sentence. We were given many examples and our teachers in the first place used to identify the parts of speeches in sentences for us to *train* us effectively so that we could use this learning experience to identify the parts of speeches in sentences that were not taught to us. Moreover, this learning process is fundamentally applicable to anything that we learn.

What if we could similarly train the machines? What if we could program them in such a way that they could learn from experiences and could start answering questions based on this knowledge? Well, this has already been done, and, knowingly or unknowingly, we are all taking the benefits yielded by this. And this is exactly what ML is when discussed intuitively. For a more formal, standard understanding, let's take a look at the following definition by Tom Mitchell in his book, *Machine Learning*:

> *"A computer program is said to learn from experience E with respect to some task T and some performance measure P, if its performance on T, as measured by P, improves with experience E."*

The preceding definition is a more precise version of what we just discussed about ML from an intuitive perspective. It is important to note here that most AI wizardry that we see today is possible due to this form of AI.

We now have a fair idea of what ML is. Now, we will move to the next section, which discusses the most powerful subfield of ML—DL. We will not go into the bone-breaking mathematical details. Instead, we will break it down intuitively, as in this section.

What is DL?

Now comes the most exciting part and probably the hottest technical term of this century. Reality apart, we now understand the **learning** to some extent, so let's get to the first part of the term *deep learning*—**deep**.

DL is a type of machine learning but it is purely based on **neural networks**. We will take a look at neural networks too but in the next chapter. The basic objective of any machine learning system is to *learn useful representations of the data* given to it. But what makes DL different? It turns out that DL systems treat data as a representation of layers. For example, an image can be treated as a representation of layers of varying properties such as edges, contours, orientation, texture, and gradients. The following diagram from the book, *Deep Learning with Python*, by François Chollet captures this idea nicely:

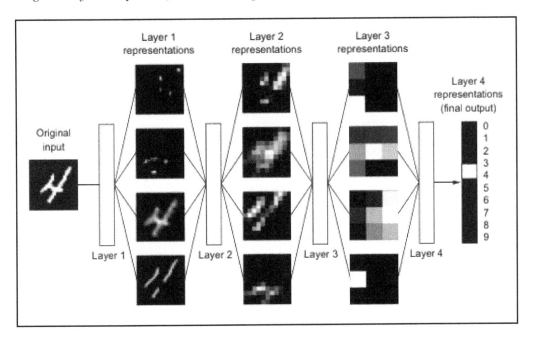

In the preceding diagram, a DL system is being employed to classify an image of a hand-written digit. The system takes the image of the handwritten digit as its input and tries to learn its underlying representations. In the first layer, the system learns generic features such as strokes and lines. As the layers increase, it learns about the features that are more specific to the given image. The more the number of layers, the *deeper* the system gets. Let's take a look at the following definition, which is given by François Chollet in his book, *Deep Learning with Python*:

> *"The **deep** in deep learning isn't a reference to any kind of deeper understanding achieved by the approach; rather, it stands for this idea of successive layers of representations. How many layers contribute to a model of the data is called the depth of the model. [...] In deep learning, these layered representations are (almost always) learned via models called neural networks, structured in literal layers stacked on top of each other."*

The definition quite aptly captures all of the necessary ingredients of DL and beautifully introduces the concept of treating data as a layered representation. So, a DL system, in a broad sense, breaks down the data into simple representations in a layered fashion, and to learn these representations, it often makes use of many layers (which is referred to as *deep*). We will now take a look at the big picture, which tells us how AI, ML, and DL are related to each other.

The relation between AI, ML, and DL

To make sure that our basics are clear regarding the distinction between AI, ML, and DL, let's refer to the following diagram, which elegantly captures the relationship between these three big names:

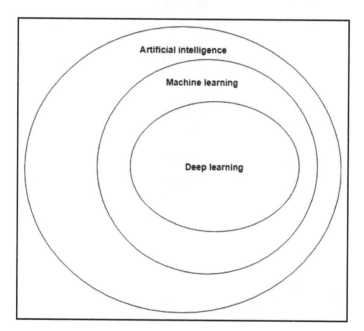

The diagram is quite self-explanatory and it has been referred to in many books in the field of DL. Let's try drawing an interesting conclusion from this diagram.

 All DL systems are ML systems and therefore all DL systems are AI systems as well. But the converse is not true—not all AI systems are DL systems.

The statement may appear slightly confusing at first glance, but if we got our basics right, then this captures the distinction between AI, ML, and DL beautifully. We will proceed toward revisiting some of the necessary ML terminologies and concepts that will be required in the latter parts of this book.

Revisiting the fundamentals of ML

We have already seen what is meant by ML. In this section, we will focus on several terminologies such as supervised learning and unsupervised learning, and we will be taking a look at the steps involved in a standard ML workflow. But you may ask: why ML? We are supposed to learn about the applications of *DL* in this book. We just learned that DL is a type of ML only. Therefore, a quick overview of the basic ML-related concepts will certainly help. Let's start with several types of ML and how they differ from each other.

Types of ML

ML encompasses a multitude of algorithms and topics. While every such algorithm that makes up an ML model is nothing but a mathematical computation on given data, the form of data that is provided and the manner of the task to be performed on it might hugely vary. Sometimes, you might want your ML model to predict future house prices based on the data of previous house prices with respect to details of the house such as the number of rooms and number of stories it has, and at other times, you might want your ML model to learn how to play computer games against you. You can easily expect the input data for the first task to be in tabular format, but for the second example, you might not be able to come up with the same. Hence, ML algorithms branch into three major categories and another form that derives from them, based on the input data they receive and the kind of output they are supposed to produce, namely, the following:

- Supervised learning
- Unsupervised learning
- Reinforcement learning
- Semi-supervised learning

The following diagram captures the three major types of ML, along with the hybrid form as a fourth type, and a very brief summary on each type:

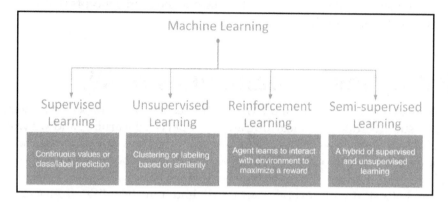

You may have heard of the fourth form of ML—semi-supervised learning, which fuses both the worlds of supervised and unsupervised learning.

Let's now understand these types of ML in greater depth, according to how they function and the types of problems they can be used to solve.

Supervised learning

In this form of ML, the algorithm is presented with a huge number of training samples, which contain information about all of the parameters, or *features*, that would be used to determine an output feature. This output feature could be a continuous range of values or a discrete collection of labels. Based on this, supervised ML algorithms are divided into two parts:

- **Classification**: Algorithms that produce discrete labels in the output feature, such as *normal* and *not normal* or a set of news categories
- **Regression**: When the output feature has real values, for example, the number of votes a political party might receive in an election, or the temperature of a material at which it is predicted to reach its melting point

Most ML enthusiasts, when they begin their study of machine learning, tend to familiarize themselves with supervised learning first due to its intuitive simplicity. It has some of the simplest algorithms, which are easy to understand without a deep knowledge of mathematics and are even derived from what mathematics students learn in their final years at schools. Some of the most well known supervised learning algorithms are linear regression, logistic regression, support vector machines, and k-nearest neighbors.

Unsupervised learning

Unsupervised learning presents itself in scenarios where the training samples do not carry with them output feature(s). You could wonder then, what are we supposed to learn or predict in such situations? The answer is similarity. In more elaborate terms, when we have a dataset for unsupervised learning, we're usually trying to learn the similarity between the training samples and then to assign classes or *labels* to them.

Consider a crowd of people standing in a large field. All of them have features such as age, gender, marital status, salary range, and education level. Now, we wish to group them based on their similarities. We decide to form three groups and see that they arrange themselves in a manner of gender—a group of females, a group of males, and a group of people who identify with other genders. We again ask them to form subgroups within those groups and see what people make groups based on their age ranges—children, teenagers, adults, and senior citizens. This gives us a total of 12 such subgroups. We could make further smaller subgroups based on the similarity any two individuals exhibit. Also, the manner of grouping discussed in the preceding example is just one among several manners of forming groups. Now, say we have 10 new members joining the crowd. Since we already have our groups defined, we can easily sort these new members into those groups. Hence, we can successfully apply group labels to them.

The preceding example demonstrates just one form of unsupervised learning, which can be divided into two types:

- **Clustering**: This is to form groups of training samples based on the similarity of their features.
- **Association**: This is to find abstract associations or rules exhibited between features or training samples. For example, on analyzing a shop's sales logs, it was found that customers buy beer mostly after 7 p.m.

K-means clustering, DBSCAN, and the Apriori algorithm are some of the best-known algorithms used for unsupervised learning.

Reinforcement learning

Reinforcement learning (RL), is a form of ML wherein a virtual agent tries to learn how to interact with its surroundings in such a way that it can achieve the maximum reward from it for a certain set of actions.

Let's try to understand this with a small example—say you build a robot that plays darts. Now, the robot will get a maximum reward only when it hits the center of the dartboard. It begins with a random throw of dart and lands on the outermost ring. It gets a certain amount of points, say x1. It now knows that throwing near that area will yield it an expected value of x1. So, in the next throw, it makes a very slight change of angle and luckily lands in the second outermost right, fetching it x2 points. Since x2 is greater than x1, the robot has achieved a better result and it will learn to throw nearby this area in the future. If the dart had landed even further out than the outermost ring, the robot would keep throwing it near the first throw that it made until it got a better result.

Over several such trials, the robot keeps learning the better places to throw and makes small detours from those positions until it gets the next better place to throw at. Eventually, it finds the bull's eye and meets the highest points every time.

In the preceding example, your robot is the agent who is trying to throw a dart at the dartboard, which is the environment. Throwing the dart is the action the agent performs on the environment. The points the agent gets act as the reward. The agent, over multiple trials, tries to maximize the reward that it gets by performing the actions.

Some well-known RL algorithms are Monte Carlo, Q-learning, and SARSA.

Semi-supervised learning

While we have discussed the three major types of ML, there exists yet another type, which is semi-supervised learning. By the name of the term, you could guess that it would have to do something with a mix of labeled and unlabeled training samples. In most cases, the number of unlabeled training samples exceeds the number of labeled samples.

Semi-supervised learning has been used successfully to produce more efficient results when some labeled samples are added to a problem entirely belonging to unsupervised learning. Also, since only a few samples are labeled, the complexity of supervised learning is avoided. With this approach, we can produce better results than we would get from a purely unsupervised learning system and incur lesser computational cost than a pure supervised learning system.

Necessary terminologies

We have made ourselves familiar with different types of ML systems. Now, we will learn about some extremely important terminologies related to ML that will help us in the later chapters of this book.

Train, test, and validation sets

Any ML system is to be given **data**. Without data, it is practically impossible to design an ML system. We are not concerned about the quantity of the data as of now, but it is important to keep in mind that we need data to devise an ML system. Once we have that data, we use it for *training* our ML systems so that they can be used to *predict something* on the new data (*something* is a broad term here and it varies from problem to problem). So, the data that is used for training purposes is known as a **train set** and the data on which the systems are tested is known as a **test set**. Also, before actually employing the model on the test data, we tend to validate its performance on another set of data, which is called a **validation set**. Sometimes, we don't get the data in these nice partitions; we just get the data in a raw unfathomable format, which we further process and make these partitions with accordingly.

Technically, all of the instances in these three different sets are supposed to vary from each other while the distribution in the data is supposed to be the same. Nowadays, many researchers have found critical issues regarding these assumptions and have come up with something called **adversarial training**, which is out of the scope of this book.

Bias and variance

Bias and variance are very intrinsic to any ML model. Having a good understanding of them really helps in the further assessment of the models. The *trade-off* between the two is actually used by the practitioners to assess the performance of machine learning systems.

You are encouraged to see this lecture by Andrew Ng to learn more about this trade-off, at `https://www.youtube.com/watch?v=fDQkUN9yw44t=293s`.

Bias is the set of assumptions that an ML algorithm makes to learn the representations underlying the given data. When the bias is high, it means that the corresponding algorithm is making more assumptions about the data and in the case of low bias, an algorithm makes as little an amount of assumptions as possible. An ML model is said to have a low bias when it performs well on the train set. Some examples of low-bias ML algorithms are k-nearest neighbors and support vector machines while algorithms such as logistic regression and naive Bayes are generally high-bias algorithms.

Variance in an ML context concerns the information present in the data. Therefore, high variance refers to the quality of how well an ML model has been able to capture the overall information present in the data given to it. Low variance conveys just the opposite. Algorithms such as support vector machines are generally high on variance and algorithms such as naive Bayes are low on variance.

Overfitting and underfitting

When an ML model performs very well on the training data but poorly on the data from either the test set or validation set, the phenomenon is referred to as **overfitting**. There can be several reasons for this; the following are the most common ones:

- The model is very complex with respect to the data. A decision tree with very high levels and a neural network with many layers are good examples of model complexity in this case.
- The data has lots of features but very few instances of the population.

In ML literature, the problem of overfitting is also treated as a problem of *high variance*. **Regularization** is the most widely used approach to prevent overfitting.

We have already discussed the concept of bias. A model has a low bias if it performs well on the training data, that is, the model is not making too many assumptions on the data to infer its representation. If the model fails miserably on the training data, it is said that the model has a high bias and the model is **underfitting**. There can be many reasons for underfitting as well. The following are the most common ones in this case:

- The model is too simple to learn the underlying representation of the data given to it.
- The features of the data have not been engineered well before feeding them to the ML model. The engineering part is very popularly known as feature engineering.

 Based on this discussion, we can draw a very useful conclusion: an ML model that is overfitting might be suffering from the issue of high variance whereas an underfitting model might be suffering from the issue of high bias.

The discussion of overfitting and underfitting remains incomplete without the following diagram (shown by Andrew Ng during his flagship course, *Machine Learning*):

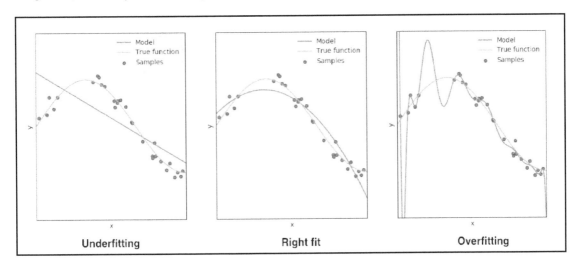

The preceding diagram beautifully illustrates underfitting and overfitting in terms of curvea fitting through the data points. It also gives us an idea of a model that **generalizes** well, that is, performs well on both the train and test sets. The model prediction line in blue is way off the samples, leading to underfitting, while in the case of overfitting, the model captures all points in the training data but does not yield a model that would perform well on data outside training data.

 Often, the idea of learning representations of the data is treated as a problem of approximating a function that best describes the data. And a function can easily be plotted graphically like the previous one, hence, the idea of **curve fitting**. The sweet spot between underfitting and overfitting where a model generalizes well is called a good fit.

Training error and generalization error

The mistakes that a model makes while predicting during its training phase are collectively referred to as its **training error**. The mistakes that model makes when tested on either the validation set or the test set are referred to as its **generalization error**.

If we were to draw a relationship between these two types of error and bias and variance (and eventually overfitting and underfitting), this would look something like the following (although the relationship may not be linear every time as depicted in the diagrams):

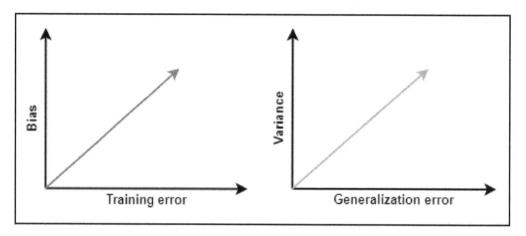

 If an ML model is underfitting (high bias), then its training error has to be high. On the other hand, if the model is overfitting (high variance), then its generalization error is high.

We will look at a standard ML workflow in the following section.

A standard ML workflow

Any project starts with a problem in mind and ML projects are no exception. Before starting an ML project, it is very important to have a clear understanding of the problem that you are trying to solve using ML. Therefore, problem formulation and mapping with respect to the standard ML workflow serve as good starting points in an ML project. But what is meant by an **ML workflow**? This section is all about that.

Designing ML systems and employing them to solve complex problems requires a set of skills other than just ML. It is good to know that ML requires knowledge of several things such as statistics, domain knowledge, software engineering, feature engineering, and basic high-school mathematics in varying proportions. To be able to design such systems, certain steps are fundamental to almost any ML workflow and each of these steps requires a certain skill set. In this section, we are going to take a look at these steps and discuss them briefly.

This workflow is inspired by **CRISP-DM**, which stands for **Cross Industry Standard Process for Data Mining** and is extremely widely used across many industries pertaining to data mining and analytics.

Data retrieval

As mentioned earlier in this chapter, ML systems need data for functioning. It is not available all of the time, in fact, most of the time, the data itself is not available in a format with which we can actually start training ML models. But what if there is no standard dataset for a particular problem that we are trying to solve using ML? Welcome to reality! This happens for most real-life ML projects. For example, let's say we are trying to analyze the sentiments of tweets regarding the New Year resolutions of 2018 and trying to estimate the most meaningful ones. This is actually a problem for which there is no standard dataset available. We will have to scrape it from Twitter using its APIs. Another great example is business logs. Business logs are treasures of knowledge. If effectively mined and modeled, they can help in many decision-making processes. But often, logs are not available directly to the ML engineer. So, the ML engineer needs to spend a considerable amount of time figuring out the structure of the logs and they might write a script so that the logs are captured as required. All of these processes are collectively called **data retrieval** or **data collection**.

Data preparation

After the data collection phase, we tend to prepare the data to feed it to the ML systems and this is known as **data preparation**. It is worth mentioning that this is the most time-consuming part of an ML workflow/pipeline. Data preparation includes a series of steps and they are as follows:

- Exploratory data analysis
- Data processing and wrangling
- Feature engineering and extraction
- Feature scaling and selection

 This is one of the most time-consuming parts of an ML project. When we take a broader look at the process, we find that data identification and collection are also sometimes really important aspects as the correct format, as mentioned previously, might not always be available.

Exploratory Data Analysis (EDA)

After the data is collected, the first step in the data preparation stage is **Exploratory Data Analysis**, which is very popularly known as **EDA**. EDA techniques allow us to know the data in a detailed manner for better understanding. This is an extremely vital step in the overall ML pipeline because without good knowledge about the data itself, if we blindly fit an ML model to the data, it most likely will not produce good results. EDA gives us a direction in which to proceed and helps us to decide further steps in the pipeline. EDA involves many things such as calculating useful statistics about the data and determining whether the data suffers from any outliers. It also comprises effective data visualization, which helps us to interpret the data graphically and therefore helps us to communicate vital facts about the data in a meaningful way.

 In short, EDA is all about getting to know about the data better.

Data processing and wrangling

We have performed some statistical analyses on the data. Now what? Most of the time, the data that is collected from several data sources is present in its raw form, which cannot be fed to an ML model, hence the need for further data processing.

 But you might ask, why not collect the data in a way so that it gets retrieved with all of the necessary processing done? This is typically not a good practice as it breaks the modularity of the workflow.

This is why to make the data consumable in the later steps in the workflow, we need to clean, transform, and persist it. This includes several things such as data normalization, data standardization, missing value imputation, encoding from one value to another, and outlier treatment. All of these are collectively named **data wrangling**.

Feature engineering and extraction/selection

Consider a situation where an employee from an analytics firm is given the company's billing data and is asked by their manager to build a machine learning system with it so the company's overall financial budget could be optimized. Now, this data is not in a format that can be given directly to an ML model since ML models expect data in the form of numeric vectors.

Although the data might be in good shape, the employee will still have to do *something* to convert that data into a favorable form. Given that the data is already wrangled, they still need to decide what features he is they are going to include in the final dataset. Practically, anything measurable can be a feature here. This is where good domain knowledge comes. This knowledge can help the employee to choose the features that have *high predictive power*. It may sound a bit light-weight, but it requires a lot of skills and it is definitely a challenging task. This is a classic example of **feature engineering**.

Sometimes, we employ several techniques that help us in the automatic extraction of the most meaningful features from a given dataset. This is particularly useful when the data is very high dimensional and the features are hard to interpret. This is known as **feature selection**. Feature selection not only helps to develop an ML model with the data that has the most relevant features but it also helps to enhance the model's predictive performance and to reduce its computation time.

Apart from feature selection, we might want to reduce the dimensionality of the data to better visualize it. Besides, **dimensionality reduction** is also employed to capture a representative set of features from the complete set of data features. **Principal Component Analysis** (**PCA**) is one such very popular dimensionality reduction technique.

> It is important to keep in mind that feature selection and dimensionality reduction are not the same.

Modeling

We have finally come to the step that appears to be the most exciting one—the **ML modeling** part. But it is worth noting here that a good ML project is not just about this part. All of the previously mentioned parts contribute equally to the standard of the project. In fact, it matters a lot how the data is being collected for the project, and for this, we are helped by powerful data engineers. For now, let's leave that part aside.

We already have the data in pretty good shape by now. In the process of modeling the data, we feed the training data to ML models for training them, we monitor their training progress and tune different hyperparameters so their performance is optimized, and we evaluate the model on the test set. *Model comparison* is also a part of this phase. It is indeed an *iterative* process and involves *trial and error* to some extent.

The main objective here is to come up with an ML model that best represents the data, that is, it *generalizes* well. Computation time is another factor we must consider here because we want a model that performs well but within a feasible time frame and thereby optimizing a certain business outcome.

Following are the parts that constitute the core of modeling:

- Model training
- Model evaluation
- Model tuning

Model training

This is the fundamental part of modeling as we introduce the data to different ML models and **train** the model so that it can learn the representations of the data holistically. We can see how a model is making progress during its training using *training error*. We often bring *validation error* (which means we validate the model training simultaneously) into this picture as well, which is a standard practice. Most of the modern libraries today allow us to do this and we will see it in the upcoming chapters of this book. We will now discuss some of the most commonly used error metrics.

Model evaluation

We have trained an ML model but how well will the model perform on the data it has never seen before? We answer this question using **model evaluation**.

Different machine learning algorithms call for different evaluation metrics.

For supervised learning methods, we usually use the following:

- The confusion matrix, which is a matrix consisting of four values: True Positive, False Positive, True Negative, and False Negative
- Accuracy, precision, recall, and F1-score (these are all byproducts of the confusion matrix)
- The **Receiver Operator Characteristic** (**ROC**) curve and the **Area Under Curve** (**AUC**) metric
- R-square (coefficient of determination), **Root Mean Square Error** (**RMSE**), F-statistic, **Akaike Information Criterion** (**AIC**), and p-values specifically for regression models

Throughout this book, we will be incorporating these metrics to evaluate our models. Although these are the most common evaluation metrics, be it for ML or DL, there are more specific evaluation metrics that correspond to different domains. We will get to that as well as we go along.

It worth mentioning here that we often tend to fall into the trap of the *accuracy paradox* in the case of *classification* problems where the data is *imbalanced*. In these cases, classification accuracy only tells one part of the story, that is, it gives the percentage of correct predictions made out of the total number of predictions made. This system fails miserably in the case of imbalanced datasets because accuracy does not capture how well a model is performing at predicting the negative instances of the dataset (which is originally the problem—predicting the uncommon class(es)).

Following are the most commonly used metrics for evaluating unsupervised methods such as clustering:

- Silhouette coefficients
- Sum of squared errors
- Homogeneity, completeness, and the V-measure
- The Calinski-Harabasz index

The evaluation metrics/error metrics remain the same for a train set, a test set, or a validation set. We cannot just jump to a conclusion just by looking at the performance of a model on the train set.

Model tuning

By this phase, we should have a baseline model with which we can go further for **tuning the model** to make it perform even better. Model tuning corresponds to **hyperparameter tuning/optimization**.

ML models come with different *hyperparameters* that cannot be learned from model training. Their values are set by the practitioners. You can compare the hyperparameter values to the knobs of an audio equalizer where we manually adjust the knobs to have the perfect aural experience. We will see how hyperparameter tuning can drastically enhance the performance of a model in later chapters.

There are several techniques for tuning hyperparameters and the most popularly incorporated are the following:

- Grid searching
- Random searching
- Bayesian optimization
- Gradient-based optimization
- Evolutionary optimization

Model comparison and selection

After we are done with the model tuning part, we would definitely want to repeat the whole *modeling* part for models other than the current one in the hope that we might get better results. As ML practitioners, it is our job to ensure that the model we have finally come up with is better than the other ones (obviously in various aspects). Naturally, comparing different ML models is a time-consuming task and we may not be able to always afford to do this when we need to meet short deadlines. In cases like this, we incorporate the following aspects of an ML model:

- Explainability, which answers a given question (how interpretable is the model and how easily it can be explained and communicated?)
- In-memory versus out-of-memory modeling
- The number of features and instances in the dataset
- Categorical versus numerical features
- The nonlinearity of the data
- Training speed
- Prediction speed

These metrics are the most popular ones but it hugely depends on the problem at hand. When these metrics do not apply, a good rule of thumb is to see how a model is performing on the validation set.

Deployment and monitoring

After a machine learning model is built, it is merged with the other components of an application and is taken into production. This phase is referred to as **model deployment**. The true performance of the developed ML model is evaluated after it is deployed into real systems. This phase also involves thorough monitoring of the model to figure out the areas where the model is not performing well and which aspects of the model can be improved further. Monitoring is extremely crucial as it provides the means to enhance the model's performance and thereby enhance the performance of the overall application.

So, that was a kind of a primer of the most important terminologies/concepts required for an ML project.

 For a more rigorous study of the basics of ML, you are encouraged to go through these resources: *Machine Learning Crash Course* by Google (`https://developers.google.com/machine-learning/crash-course/`) and *Python Machine Learning* by Sebastian Raschka (`https://india.packtpub.com/in/big-data-and-business-intelligence/python-machine-learning`).

For easy reference, you may refer to the following diagram as given in the book, *Hands-on Transfer Learning with Python* (by Dipanjan et. al), which depicts all of the preceding steps pictorially:

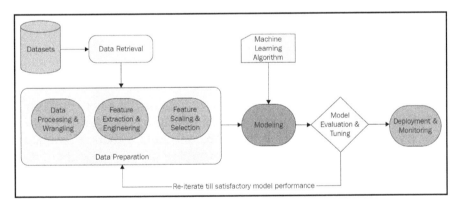

Practically, ML has brought about a lot of enhancements across a wide range of sectors and almost none are left to be impacted by it. This book is focused on building *intelligent web applications*. Therefore, we will start the next section by discussing the web in general and how it has changed since the advent of AI from a before-and-after perspective. Eventually, we will study some big names and how they are facilitating AI for building world-class web applications that are not only intelligent but also solve some real problems.

The web before and after AI

If you have been a regular user of the World Wide Web since 2014, you'd agree to a visible rapid flurry of changes in websites. From solving *ReCaptcha* challenges of increasingly illegible writing to being automatically marked as *human* in the background, web development has been one of the forerunners in the display of the wealth of artificial intelligence that has been created over the last two decades.

Sir Tim Berners-Lee, attributed as the inventor of the internet, has put forward his views on a Semantic Web:

> *"I have a dream for the Web [in which computers] become capable of analyzing all the data on the Web – the content, links, and transactions between people and computers. A "Semantic Web", which makes this possible, has yet to emerge, but when it does, the day-to-day mechanisms of trade, bureaucracy, and our daily lives will be handled by machines talking to machines. The "intelligent agents" people have touted for ages will finally materialize."*

From serving static pages with tons of information visible in them and links that permanently take you to related resources, the web is now an ever-changing portal of information generated dynamically. You might never see the same view of a web page again if you refresh it.

Let's understand some of the most important shifts in web development that have come about due to the rise of AI.

Chatbots

If you have ever wondered how some web pages provide 24/7 live help through chat on their websites, the answer would almost always be a chatbot is answering your queries from the other end. When in 1966 Joseph Weizenbaum's ELIZA chatbot created waves across the world by beating the Turing Test, we would never have thought of the impact chatbots would create in the World Wide Web (a reason for this, though, could be that ARPANET was itself only created in 1969).

Today, chatbots are everywhere. Many Fortune 500 companies are pursuing research in the domain and have come out with implementations of chatbots for their products and services. In a recent survey done by Oracle, featuring responses from 800 top executives of several companies and startups, it was found that nearly 80% of them said they had already used or were planning to use a chatbot in their customer-facing products by 2020.

Before AI began powering chatbots, as in the case with ELIZA (and its successor ALICE), chatbots were mostly about a fixed set of responses mapped to several input patterns. Coming across the word *mother* or *father* in a sentence entered by the user would almost certainly produce a response asking about the family of the user or their well-being. This clearly wasn't the response desired if the user wrote something like "I do not want to talk about XYZ's family".

And then, there is the famous "sorry, I did not get that" response of such rule-based chatbots, which made them appear quite stupid at times. The advent of neural-network-based algorithms saw chatbots being able to understand and customize responses based on user emotion and the context of the user input. Also, some chatbots scrape online data in case of encountering any new query and build up answers in real time about the topics mentioned in the new, unknown queries. Apart from that, chatbots have been used to provide alternative interfaces to business portals. It is now possible to book hotels or flights over a chatbot platform provided by WhatsApp.

Facebook Messenger's bot platform saw over 100,000 bots created in the first 17 months of its being opened to the public. Hundreds of pages on the social networking giant today have automated responses for users who send messages to their pages. Several bots are running on Twitter that can create content, closely mimicking a human user, and can respond to messages or comments made on their posts.

 You can chat with an online version of ELIZA at `eliza.botlibre.com`.

Web analytics

In the early years of the internet, many websites carried odometer-style counters embedded in them. These were simple counts of the number of hits the website or a particular page had received. Then, they grew in their available formats—plain counters, counters per day/week/month, and even geolocation-based counters.

The collection of data, which is essentially the logs of the interactions of users and how they interact with a web-based application, processing this data to produce performance indicators, and then finally to identify measures that can be taken by a company to improve their web application is collectively known as web analytics.

Since the invention of the internet, web applications today generate a huge amount of logs every moment. Even leaving your mouse pointer idle on a web page might be getting reported to a Google Analytics dashboard, from where the webmaster would be able to see which pages are being viewed by users and how much time they are spending on the pages. Also, the flow users take between pages would be a very interesting metric.

While the earliest web analytics tools would merely measure page hits, being able to create a map of how many times a given page was visited and how many times it was a unique user, they could hardly provide anything about the visiting patterns of users, unless they were specifically hardcoded, which would be presented in very generalized manners and were never website specific. The same form of analytics was being provided to a company doing e-commerce as was being provided to a personal website.

With the revolution that AI brought around in the web analytics domain, tools today that deploy the power of artificial intelligence can come up with future predictions of website performance and even suggest removing or adding specific content on a web page to improve user engagement with that page.

Spam filtering

When half the emails being sent across the world are marked spam, it's an issue. While at first thought, we associate fraudulent and unnecessary emails promoting businesses and products as spam, that's only a part of the definition. It is important to realize that even good, quality content when posted on the same document several times over is spam. Furthermore, the web has evolved since the term *spam* was first used in Usenet groups. What was initially an activity performed with the intention of annoying people, or driving in messages forcefully to certain target users, spam today is much more evolved and potentially a lot more dangerous—from being able to track your browser activity to identity theft, there is a lot of malicious spam on the internet today that compromises user security and privacy.

Today, we have spam of various kinds—instant messenger spam, website spam, advertisement spam, SMS spam, social media spam, and many other forms.

Apart from a few, most types of spam are exhibited on the internet. It is hence critical to be able to filter spam and take protective measures against it. While the most initial spam-fighting began as early as the 1990s with identifying the IP addresses that were sending out spam emails, it was soon realized to be a highly inefficient method to do so as the blacklist grew large and its distribution and maintenance became a pain.

In the early 2000s, when Paul Graham published a paper titled *A Plan for Spam*, for the first time, an ML model—Bayesian filtering—was deployed to fight spam. Soon, several spam-fighting tools were spun from the paper and proved to be efficient.

Such was the impact of Bayesian filtering method against spam that, at the *World Economic Forum* in 2004, the founder of Microsoft, Bill Gates went forward to say that:

> *"Two years from now, spam will be solved."*

Bill Gates, however, as we know today, could not have been more wrong in this one prediction. Spam evolved, with spammers studying Bayesian filtering and finding out ways to avoid being marked as spam in the detection phase. Today, neural networks are deployed on large scale, continuously scanning new emails and taking decisions on determining spam or non-spam content, which could not have been logically reached by a human by merely studying logs of email spam.

Search

One of the most strongly impacted domains by the rise of AI has been web search. From its humble beginnings of having to know the exact wording of the particular web page's title that you wished to visit, to search engines being able to identify songs that are audible in your environment, the domain has been entirely transformed due to AI.

When in 1991, Tim Berners-Lee set up the World Wide Web Virtual Library, it looked something like this:

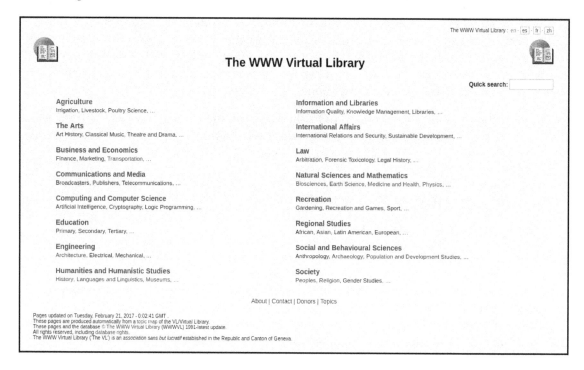

It was a collection of manually listed web pages, filterable by the search box, which appeared at the right-top. Clearly, instead of trying to predict what the user was intending to find, the user himself/herself had to decide the category to which their search term would belong to.

The current face of the web search engines was introduced by Johnathan Fletcher in December 1993, when he created JumpStation, the first search engine to use the modern-day concepts of crawling, indexing, and searching. The appearance used by JumpStation was how we see the leading search providers such as Google and Bing today, and made Johnathan the "Father of the search engine".

Two years later, in December 1995, when AltaVista was launched, it brought a radical shift in search technology—unlimited bandwidth, search tips, and even allowing natural language queries—a feature brought in more strongly by Ask Jeeves in 1997.

Google came around in 1998. And it brought with itself the technology of PageRank. However, several contenders were present in the market, and Google didn't dominate the search engine game right then. Five years later, when Google filed its patent for using neural networks to customize search results based on users' previous search history and record of visited websites, the game shifted very quickly toward Google becoming the strongest provider in the search domain.

Today, a huge code base, deploying several deep neural networks working in coherence, powers Google Search. Natural language processing, which majorly deploys neural networks, has allowed Google to determine the content relevancy of web pages, and machine vision thanks to **Convolutional Neural Networks** (**CNNs**) has been able to produce accurate results visible to us in the Google Image Search. It should not come as a surprise that John Ginnandrea led Google Search and introduced the Knowledge Graph (the answers Google sometimes comes up with on certain questions such as queries); he's one of the most sought-after specialists in AI and has now been recruited by Apple, to improve Siri, which is again a neural network product.

Biggest web-AI players and what are they doing with AI

The growth spurt of AI saw several contenders running to make the most out of it. Over the last two decades, several individuals, start-ups, and even huge industrialists have sought to reap the benefits offered by the applications of AI. There are products in the market to whom artificial intelligence serves as the very heart of their business.

"War is 90% information."

- Napoleon Bonaparte, 18th Century A.D.

In the Second World War, the Allied forces deployed bomber aircraft. These were key to the strategies employed by the Allied forces. But somehow, these bombers failed to deliver due to them being shot down in large numbers when in enemy territory. It was clear that the bombers needed more armor. But due to the weight of armor, it was not possible to entirely cover the aircraft. Hence, it was decided that the most critical areas of the aircraft should be covered up with extra armor. Abraham Wald, a Jewish mathematician, was asked to come up with a way to determine which areas of the aircraft had to be armor-plated. He studied the aircraft that had come back from battle and made note of which areas carried the most bullet marks.

It was found that the wings, the nose, and tail were the parts that carried the highest number of bullet marks, and it was concluded that these were the parts that needed more armor, while the cockpit and the engines displayed the least bullet holes:

But surprisingly, going against the regular method of thought, Wald suggested that it was the cockpit and the engines that needed armor because it was those bombers that were not returning. Bullets in the tail, wings, and nose could not deal fatal damage to the aircraft and hence they returned successfully.

This is how, working with data and identifying the correct pattern, the entire course of the Second World War was changed by a mathematician. Data has been termed as the new oil. What makes it more interesting is that when you have oil, you burn it to produce electricity and energy, to drive vehicles. But with data, you use it to improve business and make decisions, which, in the future, produce more data. The companies that realized this and took the most benefit out of the data available have seen huge growth in recent times. Let's explore what few of such companies are doing with all of the data available, using AI.

Google

A name that comes to almost every mind as soon as the term AI is mentioned, Google has revolutionized and pushed the edges of AI continuously.

> *"We are now witnessing a new shift in computing: the move from a mobile-first to an AI-first world."* -Sundar Pichai, CEO, Google

Google has been using AI across several of its products; let's go through some of them here.

Google Search

Searching for `who is the google ceo` on December 14, 2018 brought up a results page resembling the following screenshot:

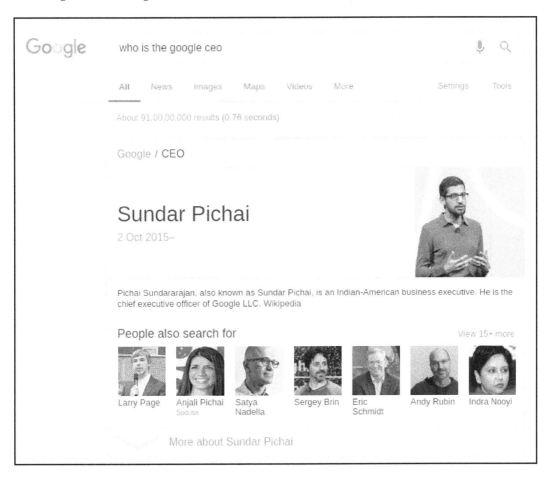

The preceding feature, which generates answers to commonly asked questions, is known as the *Google Knowledge Graph*, which we mentioned in an earlier section. Besides this one feature, Google Search has grown exponentially more powerful due to AI techniques such as natural language processing and information extraction.

The ability to come up with exact timings in a video that relate to a query made by the user is possible, all thanks to AI:

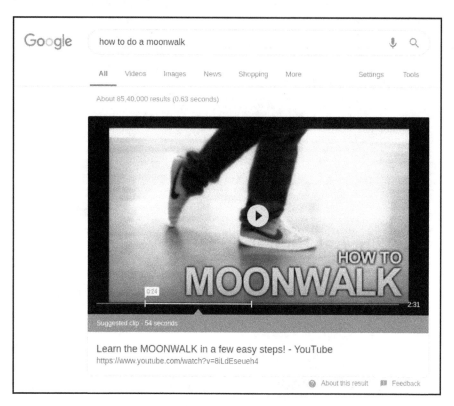

Next, we will look at Google Translate.

Google Translate

Supporting over 100 languages, Google Translate is probably the best translation tool publicly available on the internet. From being able to detect the language being fed into it to converting it into the desired language as set by the user, there's a deep mesh of neural networks running in the background to produce the best results. This algorithm, to which Google switched in November 2016, was named the *Google Neural Machine Translation* algorithm. It is available on the web as an API to web developers who wish to translate their website's content in real time to be able to cater to users of different locales. Also, the service is integrated with Google Chrome, the browser made by Google, and provides real-time translations of web pages as soon as the user visits them in the browser.

Google Assistant

One of the most recent ventures of Google, Google Assistant, is a competitor to Apple's Siri and Microsoft's Cortana and a successor of Google Now. It is an AI-powered virtual assistant available on mobile and smart home devices (branded as *Google Home*). Currently, it can make searches on the user's Google Drive data, produce results based on the user's preferences, provide reminders of notes given by the user, dial numbers, send text messages, and much more as directed by the user either by normal tap-input on touch screens or by voice input:

Next, we will look at other products.

Other products

AI is one of the primary technologies powering Google Ads. Click baiting or the problem of fake clicks was solved using neural networks. Further, determining which type of ads performed best down to the level of each single web page is efficiently facilitated by the use of AI. These technological advancements of Google's ad services made it rapidly grab the internet advertisement space from the preexisting advertising platforms.

Google projects such as Google Lens, self-driving cars, and many others have been primarily AI-based projects.

Facebook

Being the largest social networking platform on the internet with several profiles, Facebook generates a huge amount of data on a daily basis. Data of its users posting content, reports made by the users, logs of the various APIs provided by Facebook, and so on all add up to nearly 4 petabytes of data generated every day. Needless to say, the tech giant has capitalized on this data gold and come up with ways to make its platform safer for users and to boost user engagement.

Fake profiles

A primary issue faced by Facebook was the presence of *fake profiles* in huge numbers. To deal with them, Facebook deployed AI-based solutions to automatically mark and challenge such profiles to confirm their identity. In the first quarter of 2018 alone, Facebook disabled nearly 583 million fake or clone accounts.

Fake news and disturbing content

Another issue faced by Facebook and their acquired messaging service, WhatsApp, was the issue of fake news or misleading news. Also, adding to the degradation of user experience was the presence of visually and/or emotionally disturbing content on the platform. And finally, there was something that nearly all online platforms had to fight: spam. Facebook's AI algorithms over the years have become very good at identifying and removing spam. By the application of computer vision solutions facilitated by the usage of CNNs, Facebook has been able to come up with a feature that covers/blurs visually disturbing images and videos and asks for user consent before allowing users to view them.

Work on identifying and taking down fake news is currently under progress and is almost entirely being done by the application of AI.

Other uses

Facebook provides its own Messenger bot platform, which is hugely used by Facebook pages and developers to add rich interaction into the instant messaging service provided by the company.

Amazon

The leading e-commerce platform on the internet, Amazon has incorporated AI in almost all of its products and services. While a late-comer to the AI party being enjoyed by Google, Facebook, Microsoft, and IBM, Amazon quickly grew and attracted attention to the various uses it put AI to. Let's go through some of the major applications that Amazon came out with.

Alexa

The AI that powers all Alexa and Echo devices produced by the company, Alexa is the name given to the virtual assistant AI developed in direct competition with Google Home, which was powered by Google Assistant (formerly Google Now). Not debating on which is better, Alexa is a fairly advanced AI, being able to produce answers to questions that many users have found interesting and witty. Alexa products have recently seen a rise in adoption with Amazon's move to make Alexa Skills Studio available to developers publicly, who added greatly to the actions that Alexa can perform.

Amazon robotics

As soon as a user buys a product from the website, a robot sitting in the sprawling huge 855,000 square-foot fulfillment center at Kent, Washington (obviously, only for products available there) stirs up, lifts a large crate of products, and makes its way toward the site, carrying the very product sold on the platform, where a worker picks it up from the crates to further process it. Amazon recently equipped its Milwaukee fulfillment center with the same technology after a very successful run previously and plans to extend it to 10 other large centers soon.

DeepLens

An artificial intelligence-enabled video camera would have been the ultimate geek fantasy in the early 2000s. With the coming of Amazon's DeepLens, which is exactly that, the possibilities opened up are endless. Imagine a situation where you are a host to a party and you get notified of every guest who comes in, directly on your phone. Surprisingly enough, this has been achieved and experiments have even been done on equipping public places with CCTV cameras that can identify criminals and trigger alerts automatically.

Summary

In this chapter, we briefly introduced many important concepts and terminologies that are vital to execute an ML project in general. These are going to be helpful throughout this book.

We started with what AI is and its three major types. We took a look at the factors that are responsible for the AI explosion that is happening around us. We then took a quick tour of several components of ML and how they contribute to an ML project. We saw what DL is and how AI, ML, and DL are connected.

Toward the very end of this chapter, we saw some examples where AI is being merged with web technologies to make intelligent applications that promise to solve complex problems. Behind almost all of the AI-enabled applications sits DL.

In the next chapters, we are going to leverage DL to make smart web applications.

Using Deep Learning for Web Development

2

This section introduces the basic concepts and terminologies related to deep learning and covers how to use deep learning to build a simple web app with different deep learning libraries in Python.

This section comprises the following chapters:

- Chapter 2, *Getting Started with Deep Learning using Python*
- Chapter 3, *Creating Your First Deep Learning Web Application*
- Chapter 4, *Getting Started with TensorFlow.js*

2
Getting Started with Deep Learning Using Python

In the first chapter, we had a very close look at deep learning and how it is related to machine learning and artificial intelligence. In this chapter, we are going to delve deeper into this topic. We will start off by learning about what sits at the heart of deep learning—namely, neural networks and their fundamental components, such as neurons, activation units, backpropagation, and so on.

Note that this chapter is not going to be too math heavy, but at the same time, we are not going to cut short the most important formulas that are fundamental to the world of neural networks. For a more math-heavy study of the subject, readers are encouraged to read the book *Deep Learning* (`deeplearningbook.org`) by Goodfellow et al.

The following is an overview of what we are going to cover in this chapter:

- A whirlwind tour of neural networks and their related concepts
- Deep learning versus shallow learning
- Different types of neural networks
- Setting up a deep-learning-based cloud environment
- Exploring Jupyter Notebooks

Demystifying neural networks

Let's start this section by finding the answers to the question, "Why are neural networks called 'neural'?". What is the significance behind this term?

Our intuition says that it has something to do with our brains, which is correct, but only partially. Before we get to the reason why it is only partially correct, we need to have some familiarity with the structure of a brain. For this purpose, let's look at the anatomy of our own brains.

A human brain is composed of approximately 10 billion *neurons*, each connected to about 10,000 other neurons, which gives it a network-like structure. The inputs to the neurons are called *dendrites* and the outputs are called *axons*. The body of a neuron is called a *soma*. So, on a high level, a particular soma is connected to another soma. The word "neural" comes from the word "neuron," and in fact, neural is the adjective form of the word "neuron." In our brains, neurons are the most granular units that form this dense network we just discussed. We are slowly understanding the resemblance of an artificial neural network to the brain, and in order to continue our understanding of this similarity, we will briefly learn about the functionalities of a neuron.

 A network is nothing but a graph-like structure that contains a set of nodes and edges that are connected to each other. In the case of our brains, or any brain in general, neurons are referred to as nodes and the dendrites are referred to as the vertices.

A neuron receives inputs from other neurons via their dendrites. These inputs are electrochemical in nature. Not all the inputs are equally powerful. If the inputs are powerful enough, then the connected neurons are activated and continue the process of passing the input to the other neurons. Their power is determined by a predefined threshold that allows the activation process to be selective so that it does not activate all the neurons that are present in the network at the same time.

To summarize, neurons receive a collective sum of inputs from other neurons, this sum is compared to a threshold, and the neurons are activated accordingly. An **artificial neural network** (**ANN**), or simply a **neural network** (**NN**), is based on this important fact, hence the resemblance.

So, what makes a network a *neural* one? What does it take to form an NN?

The following quote from the book *Deep Learning For Computer Vision With Python* by Adrian Rosebrock answers this question in a very commendable way:

Each node performs a simple computation. Each connection then carries a signal (i.e., the output of the computation) from one node to another, labeled by a weight indicating the extent to which the signal is amplified or diminished. Some connections have large, positive weights that amplify the signal, indicating that the signal is very important when making a classification. Others have negative weights, diminishing the strength of the signal, thus specifying that the output of the node is less important in the final classification. We call such a system an Artificial Neural Network if it consists of a graph structure with connection weights that are modifiable using a learning algorithm.

We have learned about the resemblance of neural networks to brains. We will now take this information and learn more about the granular units of ANNs. Let's start by learning what a simple neuron has to do in an ANN.

Artificial neurons

Let's call the neurons that are used in ANNs artificial neurons. Broadly speaking, artificial neurons can be of two types:

- Linear neuron
- Nonlinear neuron

Anatomy of a linear neuron

A neuron is the most granular unit in a neural network. Let's look at the second word of "neural network." A network is nothing but a set of vertices (also called nodes) whose edges are connected to each other. In the case of a neural network, neurons serve as the nodes. Let's consider the following neural network architecture and try to dissect it piece by piece:

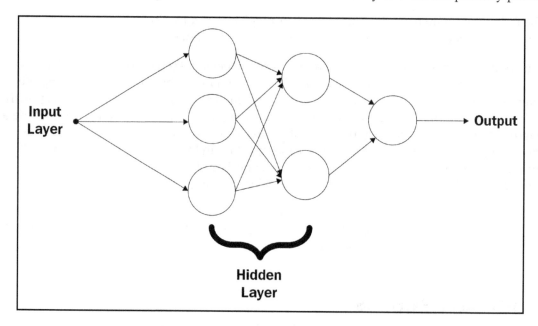

What we can see in the preceding diagram is a neural network with two hidden layers (in a neural network, a layer is a set of neurons) with a single output. In fact, this is called a two-layer neural network. The neural network consists of the following:

- One single input
- Two hidden layers, where the first hidden layer has three neurons and the second hidden layer contains two neurons
- One single output

There is no deeper psychological significance in calling the layers hidden they are called hidden simply because the neurons involved in these layers are neither parts of the input nor output. One thing that is very evident here is that there is a layer before the first hidden layer. Why are we not counting that layer? In the world of neural networks, that initial layer and output are not counted in the stack of layers. In simple words, if there are *n* hidden layers, it is an *n*-layer neural network.

The initial layer (also called an input layer) is used for receiving primary input to the neural network. After receiving the primary input, the neurons present in the input layer pass them to the next set of neurons that are present in the subsequent hidden layers. Before this propagation happens, the neurons add weights to the inputs and a bias term to the inputs. These inputs can be from various domains—for example, the inputs can be the raw pixels of an image, the frequencies of an audio signal, a collection of words, and so on. Generally, these inputs are given as feature vectors to the neural network. In this case, the input data has only one feature.

Now, what are the neurons from the next two layers doing here? This is an important question. We can consider the addition of weights and biases to the inputs as the first level/layer of learning (also called the decision making layer). The neurons in the initial hidden layer repeat this process, but before sending the calculated output to the neurons that are present in the next hidden layer, they compare this value to a threshold. If the threshold criteria are satisfied, then only the outputs are propagated to the next level. This part of the whole neural network learning process bears a solid resemblance to the biological process that we discussed earlier. This also supports the philosophy of learning complex things in a layered fashion.

A question that is raised here is, "What happens if no hidden layers are used?". It turns out that adding more levels of complexity (by adding more layers) in a neural network allows it to learn the underlying representations of the input data in a more concise manner than a network with just the input layer and the output. But how many layers would we need? We will get to that later.

Let's introduce some mathematical formulas here to formalize what we just studied.

We express the input features as x, the weights as w, and the bias term as b. The neural network model that we are currently trying to dissect builds upon the following rule:

$$\text{output} = \begin{cases} 0 & \text{if } w \cdot x + b \leq 0 \\ 1 & \text{if } w \cdot x + b > 0 \end{cases}$$

The rule says that after calculating the sum of weighted input and the bias, if the result is greater than 0, then the neuron is going to yield 1, and if the result is less than or equal to 0, then the neuron is simply going to produce 0 in other words, the neuron is not going to fire. In the case of multiple input features, the rule remains exactly the same and the multivariate version of the rule looks like the following:

$$\text{output} = \begin{cases} 0 & \text{if } \sum_i w_i x_i + b \leq 0 \\ 1 & \text{if } \sum_i w_i x_i + b > 0 \end{cases}$$

Here, *i* means that we have a total of *i* input features. The preceding rule can be broken down as follows:

- We take the features individually, and then we multiply them by the weights
- After finishing this process for all the individual input features, we take all of the weighted inputs and sum them and finally add the bias term.

 The preceding process is continued for the number of layers we have in our network. In this case, we have two hidden layers, so the output of one layer would be fed to the next.

The elements we just studied were proposed by Frank Rosenblatt in the 1960s. The idea of assigning 0 or 1 to the weighted sum of the inputs based on a certain threshold is also known as the **step-function**. There are many rules like this in the literature, these are called update rules.

The neurons we studied are **linear neurons** that are capable of learning linear functions. They are not suited for learning representations that are nonlinear in nature. Practically, almost all the inputs that neural networks are fed with are nonlinear in nature. In the next section, we are going to introduce another type of neuron that is capable of capturing the nonlinearities that may be present in the data.

 Some of you might be wondering whether this NN model is called an **MLP** (**multilayer perceptron**). Well, it is. In fact, Rosenblatt proposed this way back in the 1960s. Then what are neural networks? We are going to learn the answer to this shortly.

Anatomy of a nonlinear neuron

A nonlinear neuron means that it is capable of responding to the nonlinearities that may be present in the data. Nonlinearity in this context essentially means that for a given input, the output does not change in a linear way. Look at the following diagrams:

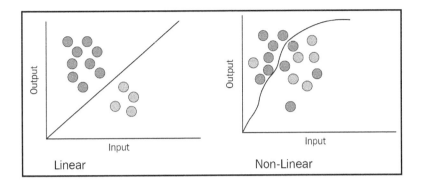

Both of the preceding figures depict the relationship between the inputs that are given to a neural network and the outputs that the network produces. From the first figure, it is clear that the input data is linearly separable, whereas the second figure tells us that the inputs cannot be linearly separated. In cases like this, a linear neuron will miserably fail, hence the need for nonlinear neurons.

 In the training process of a neural network, conditions can arise where a small change in the bias and weight values may affect the output of the neural network in a drastic way. Ideally, this should not happen. A small change to either the bias or weight values should cause only a small change in the output. When a step function is used, the changes in weight and bias terms can affect the output to a great extent, hence the need for something other than a step function.

Behind the operation of a neuron sits a function. In the case of the linear neuron, we saw that its operations were based on a step function. We have a bunch of functions that are capable of capturing the nonlinearities. The sigmoid function is such a function, and the neurons that use this function are often called sigmoid neurons. Unlike the step function, the output in the case of a sigmoid neuron is produced using the following rule:

$$\sigma(z) = \frac{1}{1 + e^{-z}}; z = \sum_i w_i x_i + b$$

So, our final, updated rule becomes the following:

$$\frac{1}{1 + \exp(-\sum_j w_j x_j - b)}$$

But why is the sigmoid function better than a step function in terms of capturing nonlinearities? Let's compare their performance in graphical to understand this:

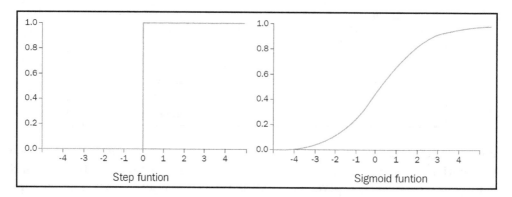

The preceding two figures give us a clear picture about the two functions regarding their intrinsic nature. It is absolutely clear that the sigmoid function is more sensitive to the nonlinearities than the step function.

Apart from the sigmoid function, the following are some widely known and used functions that are used to give a neuron a nonlinear character:

- Tanh
- ReLU
- Leaky ReLU

In the literature, these functions, along with the two that we have just studied, are called activation functions. Currently, ReLU and its variants are by far the most successful activation functions.

We are still left with a few other basic things related to artificial neural networks. Let's summarize what we have learned so far:

- Neurons and their two main types
- Layers
- Activation functions

We are now in a position to draw a line between MLPs and neural networks. Michael Nielson in his online book *Neural Networks and Deep Learning* describes this quite well:

> *Somewhat confusingly, and for historical reasons, such multiple layer networks are sometimes called multilayer perceptrons or MLPs, despite being made up of sigmoid neurons, not perceptrons.*

We are going to use the neural network and deep neural network terminologies throughout this book. We will now move forward and learn more about the input and output layers of a neural network.

A note on the input and output layers of a neural network

It is important to understand what can be given as inputs to a neural network. Do we feed raw images or raw text data to a neural network? Or are there other ways to provide input to a neural network? In this section, we will learn how a computer really interprets an image to show what exactly can be given as input to a neural network when it is dealing with images (yes, neural networks are pretty great at image processing). We will also learn the ways to show what it takes to feed a neural network with raw text data. But before that, we need to have a clear understanding of how a regular tabular dataset is given as an input to a neural network. Because tabular datasets are everywhere, in the form of SQL tables, server logs, and so on.

We will take the following toy dataset for this purpose:

x1	x2	y
1.0	2.0	0
2.0	4.0	1
3.0	2.0	0
4.0	8.0	0
5.0	4.0	1
6.0	3.0	1
7.0	5.0	0
8.0	4.5	1
9.0	5.5	0
10.0	2.4	0

Take note of the following points regarding this toy dataset:

- It has two predictor variables, $x1$ and $x2$, and these predictors are generally called input feature vectors.
- It is common to assign $x1$ and $x2$ to a vector, X (more on this later).
- The response variable is y.

- We have 10 instances (containing *x1*, *x2*, and *y* attributes) that are categorized into two classes, 0 and 1.
- Given *x1* and *x2*, our (neural network's) task is to predict *y*, which essentially makes this a classification task.

When we say that the neural network predicts something, we mean that it is supposed to learn the underlying representations of the input data that best approximate a certain function (we saw what function plotting look like a while ago).

Let's now see how this data is given as inputs to a neural network. As our data has two predictor variables (or two input vectors), the input layer of the neural network has to contain two neurons. We will use the following neural network architecture for this classification task:

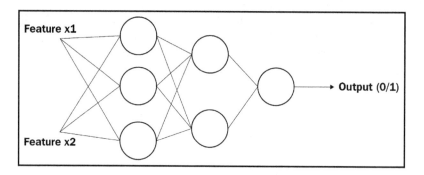

The architecture is quite identical to the one that we saw a while ago, but in this case, we have an added input feature vector. The rest is exactly the same.

To keep it simple, we are not considering the data preprocessing that might be needed before we feed the data to the network. Now, let's see how the data is combined with the weights and the bias term, and how the activation function is applied to them.

In this case, the feature vectors and the response variable (which is *y*) are interpreted separately by the neural network the response variable is used in the later stage in the network's training process. Most importantly, it is used for evaluating how the neural network is performing. The input data is organized as a matrix form, like the following:

$$
X = \begin{bmatrix} 1.0 & 2.0 \\ 2.0 & 4.0 \\ 3.0 & 2.0 \\ 4.0 & 8.0 \\ \dots & \dots \end{bmatrix} \quad y = \begin{bmatrix} 0 \\ 1 \\ 0 \\ 0 \\ \dots \end{bmatrix}
$$

The kind of NN architecture that we are using now is a fully connected architecture, which means that all of the neurons in a particular layer are connected to all the other neurons in the next layer.

The weight matrix is defined as follows:

$$W^1 = \begin{bmatrix} W^1_{11} & W^1_{12} & W^1_{13} \\ W^1_{21} & W^1_{22} & W^1_{23} \end{bmatrix}$$

For now, let's not bother about the weight values. The dimensions of the weight matrix is interpreted as the following:

- The number of rows equals the number of feature vectors (*x1* and *x2*, in our case).
- The number of columns equals the number of neurons in the first hidden layer.

There are some suffixes and superscripts associated with each of the weight values in the matrix. If we take the general form of the weight as W^l_{jk}, then it should be interpreted as follows:

- *l* denotes the layer from which the weight is coming. In this case, the weight matrix that we just saw is going to be associated with the input layer.
- *j* denotes the position of the neuron in l, whereas *k* denotes the position of the neuron in the next layer that the value is propagated to.

The weights are generally randomly initialized, which adds a *stochastic* character to the neural network. Let's randomly initialize a weight matrix for the input layer:

$$W^1 = \begin{bmatrix} 0.02 & 0.07 & 0.02 \\ 0.42 & 0.027 & 0.56 \end{bmatrix}$$

Now we calculate the values that are to be given to the first hidden layer of the NN. This is computed as follows:

$$Z^{(1)} = \begin{bmatrix} 1.0 & 2.0 \\ 2.0 & 4.0 \\ 3.0 & 2.0 \\ 4.0 & 8.0 \\ 5.0 & 4.0 \\ 6.0 & 3.0 \\ 7.0 & 5.0 \\ 8.0 & 4.5 \\ 9.0 & 5.5 \\ 10.0 & 2.4 \end{bmatrix} \cdot \begin{bmatrix} 0.02 & 0.07 & 0.02 \\ 0.42 & 0.027 & 0.56 \end{bmatrix}$$

The first matrix contains all the instances from the training set (without the response variable y) and the second matrix is the weight matrix that we just defined. The result of this multiplication is stored in a variable, $Z^{(1)}$ (this variable can be named anything, and the superscript denotes that it is related to the first hidden layer of the network).

We are still left with one more step before we send these results to the neurons in the next layer, where the activation functions will be applied. The sigmoid activation function and the final output from the input layer would look like the following:

$$a^{(1)} = sigmoid(Z^{(1)})$$

Here, $a^{(1)}$ is our final output for the next layer of neurons. Note that the sigmoid function is applied to each and every element of the $Z^{(1)}$ matrix. The final matrix will have a dimension of 10 X 3, where each row is for each instance from the training set and each column is for each neuron of the first hidden layer.

The whole calculation that we saw is without the bias term, b, that we initially talked about. Well, that is just a matter the of addition of another dimension to the picture. In that case, before we apply the sigmoid function to each of the elements of the $Z^{(1)}$ matrix, the matrix itself would be changed to something like this:

$$Z^{(1)} = \begin{bmatrix} 1.0 & 2.0 & 1 \\ 2.0 & 4.0 & 1 \\ 3.0 & 2.0 & 1 \\ 4.0 & 8.0 & 1 \\ 5.0 & 4.0 & 1 \\ 6.0 & 3.0 & 1 \\ 7.0 & 5.0 & 1 \\ 8.0 & 4.5 & 1 \\ 9.0 & 5.5 & 1 \\ 10.0 & 2.4 & 1 \end{bmatrix} \cdot \begin{bmatrix} 0.02 & 0.07 & 0.02 \\ 0.42 & 0.027 & 0.56 \\ 0.1 & 0.1 & 0.1 \end{bmatrix}$$

After this matrix multiplication process, the sigmoid function is applied and the output is sent to the neurons in the next layers, and this whole process repeats for each hidden layer and output layer that we have in the NN. As we proceed, we are supposed to get $a^{(3)}$ from the output layer.

The sigmoid activation function outputs values ranging from 0–1, but we are dealing with a binary classification problem, and we only want 0 or 1 as the final output from the NN. We can do this with a little tweak. We can define a threshold at the output layer of the NN—for the values that are less than 0.5 they should be identified as class 0 and the values that are greater than or equal to 0.5 should be identified as class 1. Note that this is called forward pass or forward propagation.

The NN we just saw is referred to as a feed-forward network with no further optimization in its learning process. But wait! What does the network even learn? Well, an NN typically learns the weights and bias terms so that the final output is as accurate as possible. And this happens with gradient descent and backpropagation.

Gradient descent and backpropagation

Before we start learning about what gradient descent and backpropagation have to do in the context of neural networks, let's learn what is meant by an optimization problem.

An optimization problem, briefly, corresponds to the following:

- Minimizing a certain cost
- Maximizing a certain profit

Let's now try to map this to a neural network. What happens if, after getting the output from a feed-forward neural network, we find that its performance is not up to the mark (which is the case almost all the time)? How are we going to enhance the performance of the NN? The answer is gradient descent and backpropagation.

We are going to optimize the learning process of the neural network with these two techniques. But what are we going to optimize? What are we going to minimize or maximize? We require a specific type of cost that we will attempt to minimize.

We will define the cost in terms of a function. Before we define a cost function for the NN model, we will have to decide the parameters of the cost function. In our case, the weights and the biases are the parameters of the function that the NN is trying to learn to give us accurate results (see the information box just before this section). In addition, we will have to calculate the amount of loss that the network is inculcating at each step of its training process.

For a binary classification problem, a loss function called a **cross-entropy** loss function (for a binary classification problem it is called a binary cross cross-entropy loss function) is widely used, and we are going to use it. So, what does this function look like?

$$L(\hat{y}, y) = -(y \log(\hat{y}) + (1 - y) \log(1 - \hat{y}))$$

Here, y denotes the ground truth or true label (remember the response variable, y, in the training set) of a given instance and $\hat{y}$ denotes the output as yielded by the NN model. This function is convex in nature, which is just perfect for convex optimizers such as gradient descent.

This is one of the reasons that we didn't pick up a simpler and nonconvex loss function. (Don't worry if you are not familiar with terms like convex and nonconvex.)

We have our loss function now. Keep in mind that this is just for one instance of the entire set of data this is not the function on which we are going to apply gradient descent. The preceding function is going to help us define the cost function that we will eventually optimize using gradient descent. Let's see what that cost function looks like.

$$J(w,b) = \frac{1}{m}\sum_{i=1}^{m} L(\hat{y}^i, y^i)$$

Here, w and b are the weights and biases that the network is trying to learn. The letter m represents the number of training instances, which is 10 in this case. The rest seems familiar. Let's put the original form of the function, $L()$, and see what $J()$ looks like:

$$J(w,b) = \frac{1}{m}\sum_{i=1}^{m} L(\hat{y}^i, y^i) = -\frac{1}{m}\sum_{i=1}^{m}[y^{(i)}\log(\hat{y}^{(i)}) + (1 - y^{(i)})\log(1 - \hat{y}^{(i)})]$$

The function may look a bit confusing, so just slow it down and make sure you understand it well.

We can finally move toward the optimization process. Broadly, gradient descent is trying to do the following:

- Give us a point where the cost function is as minimal as possible (this point is called the minima).
- Give us the right values of the weights and biases so that the cost function reaches that point.

To visualize this, let's take a simple convex function:

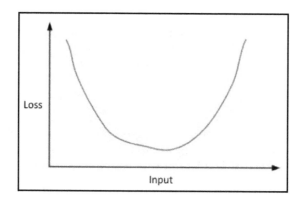

Now, say we start the journey at a random point, such as the following:

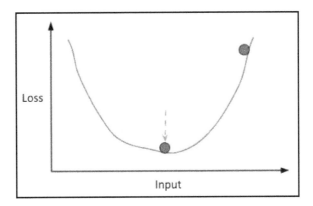

So, the point at the top right corner is the point at which we started. And the point (directed by the dotted arrow) is the point we wish to arrive at. So, how do we do this in terms of simple computations?

In order to arrive at this point the following update rule is used:

$$w := w - \alpha \frac{\partial J(w, b)}{\partial w}$$

Here, we are taking the partial derivative of J(w,b) with respect to the weights. We are taking a partial derivative because J(w,b) contains b as one of the parameters. **α** is the learning rate that speeds up this process. This update rule is applied multiple times to find the right values of the weights. But what about the bias values? The rule remains exactly the same only the equation is changed:

$$b := b - \alpha \frac{\partial J(w, b)}{\partial b}$$

These new assignments of weights and biases are essentially referred to as *backpropagation*, and it is done in conjunction with *gradient descent*. After computing the new values of the weights and the biases, the whole forward propagation process is repeated until the NN model generalizes well. Note that these rules are just for one single instance, provided that the instance has only one feature. Doing this for several instances that contain several features can be difficult, so we are going to skip that part however, those who are interested in seeing the fully fledged version of this may refer to a lecture online by Andrew Ng.

We have covered the necessary fundamental units of a standard neural network, and it was not easy at all. We started by defining neurons and we ended with backprop (the nerdy term of backpropagation). We have already laid the foundations of a deep neural network. Readers might be wondering whether that was a deep neural net that we just studied. As **Andriy Burkov** says (from his book titled *The Hundred Page Machine-Learning Book*):

> *Deep learning refers to training neural networks with more than two non-output layers. … the term "deep learning" refers to training neural networks using the modern algorithmic and mathematical toolkit independently of how deep the neural network is. In practice, many business problems can be solved with neural networks having 2-3 layers between the input and output layers.*

In the next sections, we will learn about the difference between deep learning and shallow learning. We will also take a look at two different types of neural networks—namely, convolutional neural networks and recurrent neural networks.

Different types of neural network

So far, we have learned what feed-forward neural networks look like and how techniques such as backpropagation and gradient descent are applied to it in order to optimize their training process. The binary classification problem we studied earlier appears to be too naive and too impractical, doesn't it?

Well, there are many problems that a simple NN model can solve well. But as the complexity of the problem increases, improvements to the basic NN model become necessary. These complex problems include object detection, object classification, image-caption generation, sentiment analysis, fake-news classification, sequence generation, speech translation, and so on. For problems like these, a basic NN model is not sufficient. It needs some architectural improvements so that it can solve these problems. In this section, we are going to study two of the most powerful and widely used NN models—convolutional neural networks and recurrent neural networks. At the heart of the stunning applications of deep learning that we see nowadays sit these NN models.

Convolutional neural networks

Have you ever uploaded a photo of your friends' group to Facebook? If yes, have you ever wondered how Facebook detects all the faces in the photo automatically just after the upload finishes? In short, the answer is **convolutional neural networks** (**CNNs**).

A feed-forward network generally consists of several fully connected layers, whereas a CNN consists of several layers of convolution, along with other types of sophisticated layers, including fully-connected layers. These fully-connected layers are generally placed towards the very end and are typically used for making predictions. But what kinds of predictions? In an image-processing and computer-vision context, a prediction task can encompass many use cases, such as identifying the type of object present in the image that is given to the network. But are CNNs only good for image-related tasks? CNNs were designed and proposed for image-processing tasks (such as object detection, object classification, and so on) but it has found its use in many text-processing tasks as well. We are going to learn about CNNs in an image-processing context because CNNs are most popular for the wonders they can work in the domains of image processing and computer vision. But before we move on to this topic, it would be useful to understand how an image can be represented in terms of numbers.

An image consists of numerous pixels and dimensions—height x width x depth. For a color image, the depth dimension is generally 3, and for a grayscale image, the dimension is 1. Let's dig a bit deeper into this. Consider the following image:

The dimension of the preceding image is 626 x 675 x 3, and numerically, it is nothing but a matrix. Each pixel represents a particular intensity of red, green, and blue (according to the RGB color system). The image contains a total of 422,550 pixels (675 x 626).

The pixels are denoted by a list of three values of red, green, and blue colors. Let's now see what a pixel (corresponding to the twentieth row and the hundredth column in the matrix of 422,550 pixels) looks like in coding terms:

12, 24, 10

Each value corresponds to a particular intensity of the colors red, green, and blue. For the purpose of understanding CNNs, we will look at a much smaller dimensional image in grayscale. Keep in mind that each pixel in a grayscale image is between 0 and 255, where 0 corresponds to black and 255 corresponds to white.

The following is a dummy matrix of pixels representing a grayscale image (we will refer to this as an image matrix):

120	121	91
127	109	98
114	108	79

Before we proceed, let's think intuitively about how can we train a CNN to learn the underlying representations of an image and make it perform some tasks. Images have a special property inherent to them: the pixels in an image that contain a similar type of information generally remain close to each other. Consider the image of a standard human face: the pixels denoting the hair are darker and are closely located on the image, whereas the pixels denoting the other parts of the face are generally lighter and also stay very close to each other. The intensities may vary from face to face, but you get the idea. We can use this spatial relationship of the pixels in an image and train a CNN to detect the similar pixels and the edges that they create in between them to distinguish between the several regions present in an image (in an image of a face, there are arbitrary edges in between the hair, eyebrows, and so on). Let's see how this can be done.

A CNN typically has the following components:

- Convolutional layer
- Activation layer
- Pooling layer
- Fully connected layer

At the heart of a CNN sits an operation called convolution (which is also known as cross relation in the literature of computer vision and image processing). Adrian Rosebrock of PyImageSearch describes the operation as follows:

> *In terms of deep learning, an (image) convolution is an element-wise multiplication of two matrices followed by a sum.*

This quote tells us how an (image) convolution operator works. The matrices mentioned in the quote are the image matrix itself and another matrix known as the kernel. The original image matrix can be higher than the kernel matrix and the convolution operation is performed on the image matrix in a left–right top–bottom direction. Here is an example of a convolution operation involving the preceding dummy matrix and a kernel of size 2 x 2:

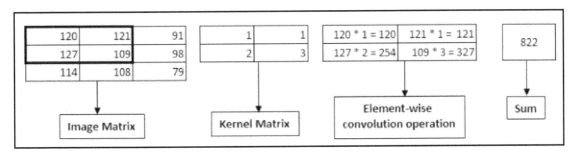

The kernel matrix actually serves as the weight matrix for the network, and to keep it simple, we ignore the bias term for now. It is also worth noting that our favorite image filters (sharpening, blurring, and so on) are nothing but outputs of certain kinds of convolution applied to the original images. A CNN actually learns these filter (kernel) values so that it can best capture the spatial representation of an image. These values can be further optimized using gradient descent and backpropagation. The following figure depicts four convolution operations applied to the image:

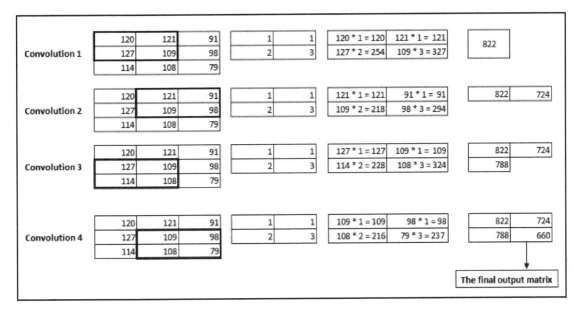

Note how the kernel is sliding and how the convoluted pixels are being calculated. But if we proceed like this, then the original dimensionality of the image gets lost. This can cause information loss. To prevent this, we apply a technique called padding and retain the dimensionality of the original image. There are many padding techniques, such as replicate padding, zero padding, wrap around, and so on. Zero padding is very popular in deep learning. We will now see how zero padding can be applied to the original image matrix so that the original dimensionality of the image is retained:

0	0	0	0	0
0	120	121	91	0
0	127	109	98	0
0	114	108	79	0
0	0	0	0	0

Zero padding means that the pixel value matrix will be padded by zero on all sides, as shown in the preceding image.

It is important to instruct the network how it should slide the image matrix. This is controlled using a parameter called stride. The choice of stride depends on the dataset and the correct use of stride 2 is standard practice in deep learning. Let's see how stride 1 differs from stride 2:

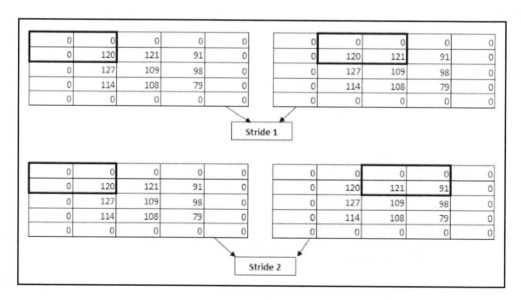

A convoluted image typically looks like the following:

The convoluted image largely depends on the kernel that is being used. The final output matrix is passed to an activation function and the function is applied to the matrix's elements. Another important operation in a CNN is pooling, but we will skip this for now. By now, you should have a good understanding of how a CNN works on a high level, which is sufficient for continuing to follow the book. If you want to have a deeper understanding of how a CNN works, then refer to the blog post at `https://www.` `pyimagesearch.com/2018/04/16/keras-and-convolutional-neural-networks-cnns/`.

Recurrent neural networks

Recurrent neural networks (RNNs) are another type of neural network, and are tremendously good at NLP tasks—for example, sentiment analysis, sequence prediction, speech-to-text translation, language-to-language translation, and so on. Consider an example: you open up Google and you start searching for recurrent neural networks. The moment you start typing a word, Google starts giving you a list of suggestions which is most likely to be topped by the complete word, or the most commonly searched phrase that begins with the letters you have typed by then. This is an example of sequence prediction where the task is to predict the next sequence of the given phrase.

Let's take another example: you are given a bunch of English sentences containing one blank per sentence. Your task is to appropriately fill the gaps with the correct words. Now, in order to do this, you will need to use your previous knowledge of the English language in general and make use of the context as much as possible. To use previously encountered information like this, you use your memory. But what about neural networks? Traditional neural networks cannot do this because they do not have any memory. This is exactly where RNNs come into the picture.

The question that we need to answer is how can we empower neural networks with memory? An absolutely naive idea would be to do the following:

- Feed a certain sequence into a neuron.
- Take the output of the neuron and feed it to the neuron again.

It turns out that this idea is not that naive, and in fact constitutes the foundation of the RNN. A single layer of an RNN actually looks like the following:

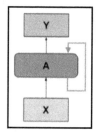

The loop seems to be a bit mysterious. You might already be thinking about what happens in each iteration of the loop:

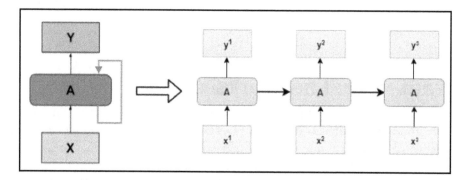

In the preceding diagram, an RNN (the figure on the left) is unrolled to show three simple feedforward networks. But what do these unrolled networks do? Let's find this out now.

Let's consider the task of sequence prediction. To keep it simple, we will look at how an RNN can learn to predict the next letter to complete a word. For example, if we train the network with a set of letters, *{w, h, a, t}*, and after giving the letters *w,h*, and *a* sequentially, the network should be able to predict that the letter should be *t* so that the meaningful word "what" is produced. Just like the feed-forward networks we saw earlier, X serves as the input vector to the network in RNN terminology, this vector is also referred to as the vocabulary of the network. The vocabulary of the network is, in this case, *{w, h, a, t}*.

The network is fed with the letters *w,h*, and *a* sequentially. Let's try to give indices to the letters:

- $w_{\rightarrow}(t-1)$
- $h_{\rightarrow}(t)$
- $a_{\rightarrow}(t+1)$

These indices are known as time-steps (the superscripts in the figure presenting the unrolling of an RNN). A recurrent layer makes use of the input that is given at previous time-steps, along with a function when operating on the current time-step. Let's see how the output is produced by this recurrent layer step by step.

Feeding the letters to the network

Before we see how a recurrent layer produces the output, it is important to learn how we can feed the set of letters to the networks. One-hot encoding lets us do this in a very efficient way:

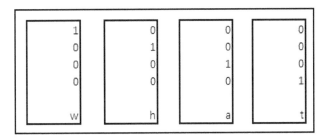

So, in one-hot encoding, our input vectors/vocabulary of letters are nothing but four 4 x 1 matrices, each denoting a particular letter. One-hot encoding is standard practice for these tasks. This step is actually a data-preprocessing step.

Initializing the weight matrix and more

When there are neural networks, there are weights. This is true, right? But before we start to deal with the weights for our RNN, let's see exactly where they are needed.

There are two different weight matrices in the case of an RNN—one for the input neuron (remember that we feed feature vectors only through neurons) and one for the recurrent neuron. A particular state in an RNN is produced using the following two equations:

1. $h_t = activation(W_{hh} h_{t-1} + W_{xh} x_t)$
2. $y_t = W_{hy} h_t$

To understand what each term means in the first equation, refer to the following image (don't worry, we will get to the second equation):

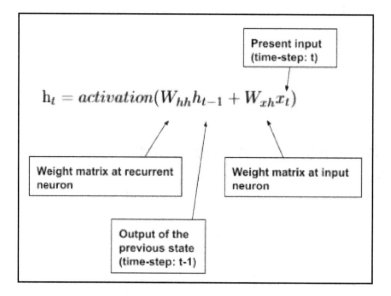

The first pass of the RNN x_1 is the letter w. We will randomly initialize the two weight matrices as present in the equation (1). Assume that the matrix W_{xh} after getting initialized looks like the following:

0.439572	0.960493	0.441548	0.702436
0.131675	0.61534	0.54317	0.356771
0.196245	0.092377	0.18735	0.514055

The W_{xh} matrix is 3 x 4:

- $x = 3$, as we have three recurrent neurons in the recurrent layer
- $h = 4$, as our vocabulary is 4

The matrix W_{hh} is a 1 x 1 matrix. Let's take its value as 0.35028053. Let's also introduce the bias term b here, which is also a 1 x 1 matrix, 0.6161462. In the next step, we will put these values together and determine the value of h_t. (We will deal with the second equation later.)

Putting the weight matrices together

Let's determine $W_{xh}x_1$ first. x_1 is a 4 x 1 matrix representing the letter w, which we defined earlier. The standard rules of matrix multiplication apply here:

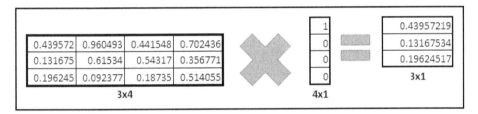

Now we will calculate the term $W_{hh}h_0 + b$. We will shortly see the significance of the bias term. Since w is the first letter that we are feeding to the network, it does not have any previous state therefore, we will take h_0 as a matrix of 3 x 1 consisting of zeros:

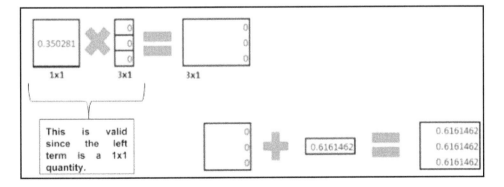

Note that if we didn't take the bias term, we would have got a matrix consisting of only zeros. We will now add these two matrices as per the equation (1). The result of this addition is a 3 x 1 matrix and is stored in h_t (which in this case is h_1):

$$(h_t =) W_{xh}x_1 + (W_{hh}h_0 + b) =$$

0.439572		0.616146		1.055718
0.131675	+	0.616146	=	0.747822
0.196245		0.616146		0.812391

Following the equation (1), all we need to do is apply the activation function to this matrix.

Applying activation functions and the final output

When it comes to RNNs, $tanh$ is a good choice as an activation function. So, after applying $tanh$, the matrix looks like the following:

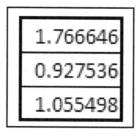

1.766646
0.927536
1.055498

We have got the result of h_t. h_t acts as h_{t-1} for the next time-step. We will now calculate the value of y_t using equation (2). We will require another weight matrix W_{hy} (of shape 4 x 3) that is randomly initialized:

0.50336705	0.193937	0.8673876
0.31384829	0.862868	0.4842808
0.80898295	0.314543	0.7916341
0.76527556	0.775302	0.2131228

After applying the second equation, the value of y_t becomes a 4 x 1 matrix:

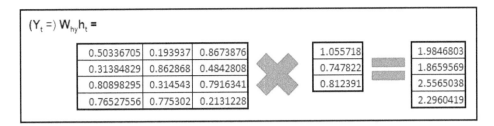

Now, in order to predict what might be the next letter that comes after w (remember, we started all our calculations with the letter w and we still left with the first pass of the RNN) to make a suitable word from the given vocabulary, we will apply the softmax function to y_t. This will output a set of probabilities for each of the letters from the vocabulary:

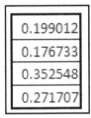

If anyone is curious about learning what a softmax function looks like, there is an extremely helpful article at http://bit.ly/softmaxfunc.

So, the RNN tells us that the next letter after w is more likely to be an a. With this, we finish the initial pass of the RNN. As an exercise, you can play around with the ht value we got from this pass and apply it (along with the next letter h) to the next pass of the RNN to see what happens.

Now, let's get to the most important question—what is the network learning? Again, weights and biases! You might have guessed the next sentence already. These weights are further optimized using backpropagation. Now, this backpropagation is a little bit different from what we have seen earlier. This version of backpropagation is referred to as **backpropagation through time**. We won't be learning about this. Before finishing off this section, let's summarize the steps (after one-hot encoding of the vocabulary) that were performed during the forward pass of the RNN:

- Initialize the weight matrices randomly.
- Calculate h_t using equation (1).

- Calculate y_t using equation (2).
- Apply the softmax function to y_t to get the probabilities of each of the letters in the vocabulary.

It is good to know that apart from CNNs and RNNs, there are other types of neural networks, such as auto-encoders, generative adversarial networks, capsule networks, and so on. In the previous two sections, we learned about two of the most powerful types of neural network in detail. But when we talk about cutting-edge deep-learning applications, are these networks good enough to be used? Or do we need more enhancements on top of these? It turns out that although these architectures perform well, they fail to scale, hence the need for more sophisticated architectures. We will get to some of these specialized architectures in the next chapters.

We have covered a good amount of theory since Chapter 1, *Demystifying Artificial Intelligence and Fundamentals of Machine Learning*. In the next few sections, we will be diving into some hands-on examples.

Exploring Jupyter Notebooks

While working on a project relating to deep learning, you must deal with a huge amount of variables of various types and arrays of various dimensions. Also, since the data contained in them is massive and keeps changing after nearly every step, we need a tool that helps us to observe the output produced by each step so that we can proceed accordingly. A Jupyter Notebook is one such tool. Jupyter Notebooks are known for their simplicity, and their wide support of features and platforms are currently the standard tool for developing deep-learning solutions. The reasons for their popularity can be understood by considering the fact that several of the top tech giants offer their own version of the tool, such as Google Colaboratory and Microsoft Azure Notebooks. Moreover, the popular code-hosting website GitHub has been providing a native rendering of Jupyter Notebook since 2016.

Installing Jupyter Notebook

Let's begin with the installation of Jupyter Notebook.

Installation using pip

If you already have Python installed on your system, you can install the Jupyter package from the `pip` repository to start using Jupyter Notebooks quickly.

For Python 3, use the following:

```
python3 -m pip install --upgrade pip
python3 -m pip install jupyter
```

For Python 2, use the following:

```
python -m pip install --upgrade pip
python -m pip install jupyter
```

 For Mac users, if the `pip` installation is not found, you can download the latest Python version, which carries `pip` bundled with it.

Installation using Anaconda

While it is possible to install Jupyter as a single package from `pip`, it is strongly recommended that you install the Anaconda distribution for Python, which automatically installs Python, Jupyter, and several other packages required for machine learning and data science. Anaconda makes it very easy to deal with the various package versions and update dependency packages or dependent packages.

Firstly, download the correct Anaconda distribution for your system and requirements from `https://www.anaconda.com/downloads` and then follow the corresponding installation steps given on the website.

Verifying the installation

To check whether Jupyter has correctly installed, run the following command in Command Prompt (Windows) or Terminal (Linux/Mac):

```
jupyter notebook
```

You will be able to see some logging output at the terminal (henceforth, the default term for Command Prompt on Windows and Terminal on Linux or Mac). After that, your default browser, will open up and you will be taken to a link on the browser which will resemble the following image:

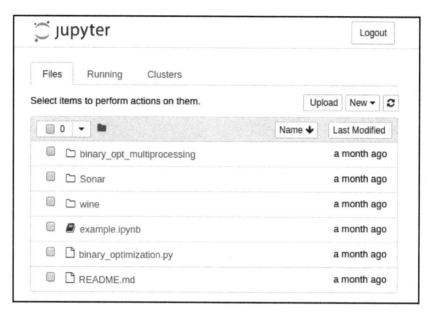

Under the **Files** tab, a basic file manager is provided that the user can use to create, upload, rename, delete, and move files.

The **Running** tab lists all the currently running Jupyter Notebooks, which can be shut down from the listing displayed.

The **Clusters** tab provides an overview of all the available IPython clusters. In order to use this feature, you are required to install the IPython Parallel extension for your Python environment.

Jupyter Notebooks

A Jupyter Notebook by default is identified by the `.ipynb` extension. Upon clicking on the name of once such notebook in the file manager provided by Jupyter, you'll be presented with a screen resembling the following:

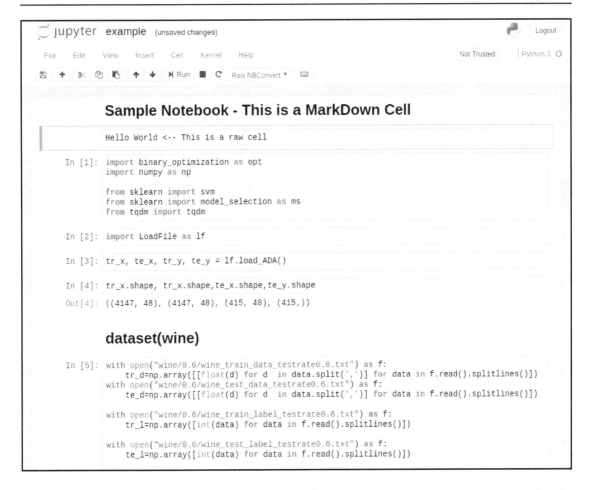

The topmost section, where you can see a menu bar, a toolbar, and the title of the notebook, is called the **header**. On the right side of the header you can see the environment in which the notebook is executing, and when any task is running, the white circle beside the environment language's name turns gray.

Below the header is the body of the notebook, which is composed of cells stacked vertically. Each cell in the body of the notebook is either a block of code, a markdown cell, or a raw cell. A code cell can have an output cell attached below it, which the user cannot edit manually. This holds the output produced by the code cell associated with it.

In a Jupyter Notebook, the keyboard behaves differently for different **modes** of a cell For this reason, these notebooks are called **modal**. There are two modes in which a notebook cell can operate: the **command** mode and the **editx** mode.

While a cell is in command mode, it has a gray border. In this mode, the cell contents cannot be changed. The keys of the keyboard in this mode are mapped to several shortcuts that can be used to modify the cell or the notebook as a whole.

While in command mode, if you press the *Enter* key on the keyboard, the cell mode changes to the edit mode. While in this mode, the contents of the cell can be changed and the basic keyboard shortcuts that are available in the usual textboxes in the browser can be invoked.

To exit the edit mode, the user can use the *Esc* key. To run the particular cell, the user has to input *Shift + Return*, which will do one of the following in each case:

- For a markdown cell, the rendered markdown shall be displayed.
- For a raw cell, the raw text as entered shall be visible.
- For a code cell, the code will be executed and if it produces some output, an output cell attached to the code cell will be created and the output will get displayed there. If the code in the cell asks for an input, an input field will appear and the cell's code execution stalls until the input is provided.

Jupyter also allows the manipulation of text files and Python script files using its in-built text editor. It is also possible to invoke the system terminal from within the Jupyter environment.

Setting up a deep-learning-based cloud environment

Before we begin setting up a cloud-based deep learning environment, we might wonder why would we need it or how a cloud-based deep learning environment would benefit us. Deep learning requires a massive amount of mathematical calculation. At every layer of the neural network, there is a mathematical matrix undergoing multiplication with another or several other such matrices. Furthermore, every data point itself can be a vector instead of a singular entity. Now, to train over several repetitions, such a deep learning model would require a lot of time just because of the number of mathematical operations involved.

A GPU-enabled machine would be much more efficient at executing these operations because a GPU is made specifically for high-speed mathematical calculations however, GPU-enabled machines are costly and may not be affordable to everyone. Furthermore, considering that multiple developers work on the same software in a work environment, it might be a very costly option to buy GPU-enabled machines for all the developers on the team. For these reasons, the idea of a GPU-enabled cloud computing environment has a strong appeal.

Companies nowadays are increasingly leaning towards the usage of GPU-enabled cloud environments for their development teams, which can lead to the creation of a common environment for all of the developers as well as the facilitation of high-speed computation.

Setting up an AWS EC2 GPU deep learning environment

In this section, we will learn how to set up a deep learning specific instance on AWS. Before you can begin working with AWS, you will need to create an account on the AWS console. To do so, go through the following steps:

1. Visit `https://console.aws.amazon.com` and you'll be presented with a login/sign up screen.
2. If you do not already have an AWS account, click on **Create a new AWS account** and follow the steps to create one, which might require you to enter your debit/credit card details to enable billing for your account.
3. Upon logging into your account, on the dashboard, click on **EC2** in the **All services** section, as shown in the following screenshot:

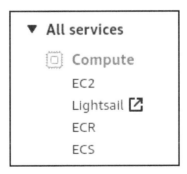

Once you have reached the EC2 management page within the AWS console, you'll need to go through the steps in the following sections to create an instance for your deep learning needs.

Step 1: Creating an EC2 GPU-enabled instance

First, select the Ubuntu 16.04 or 18.04 LTS AMI:

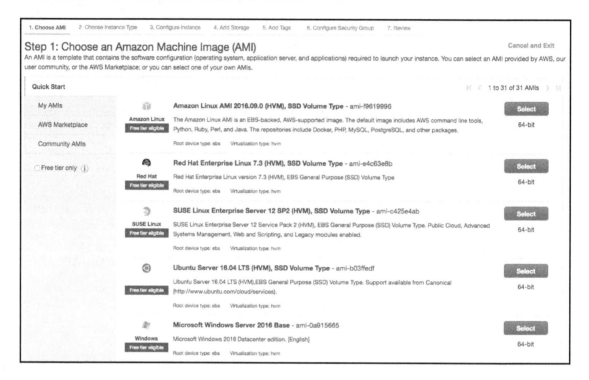

Then, choose a GPU-enabled instance configuration. The `g2.2xlarge` is a good choice for a starter deep learning environment:

	Compute optimized	c3.large	2	3.75	2 x 16 (SSD)	-	Moderate
	Compute optimized	c3.xlarge	4	7.5	2 x 40 (SSD)	Yes	Moderate
	Compute optimized	c3.2xlarge	8	15	2 x 80 (SSD)	Yes	High
	Compute optimized	c3.4xlarge	16	30	2 x 160 (SSD)	Yes	High
	Compute optimized	c3.8xlarge	32	60	2 x 320 (SSD)	-	10 Gigabit
■	GPU instances	g2.2xlarge	8	15	1 x 60 (SSD)	Yes	High
	GPU instances	g2.8xlarge	32	60	2 x 120 (SSD)	-	10 Gigabit
	Memory optimized	r4.large	2	15.25	EBS only	Yes	High
	Memory optimized	r4.xlarge	4	30.5	EBS only	Yes	High

Next, configure the required instance settings or leave them as their default and proceed to the storage step. Here, a recommended size of the volume is 30 GB. You can then proceed to launch the instance with the default options.

Assign an EC2 key pair to your instance so that you can access the instance's terminal over SSH from your system. If you name the key pair abc, then a file named abc.pem would download automatically to your browser's default download location.

Step 2: SSHing into your EC2 instance

Open up a terminal on your system and using cd, navigate to the directory that your abc.pem file is stored in.

If you're unfamiliar with the cd command, consider a scenario in which you are inside a folder named Folder1, which has the following contents:

```
Folder1 /
    - Folder2
    - Folder3
    - File1.jpg
    - File2.jpg
```

To access any files inside the folder named Folder2, you'll have to change your working directory to that folder. To do so, you can use the following example of the cd command:

```
cd Folder2
```

Note that this command only works when you're already inside Folder1, which can be reached with a similar usage of the cd command from anywhere on the system.

You can read more about the usage of any command on a Linux system by using the following command:

```
man <command>
```

For example, you can use the following:

```
man cd
```

Now, set the permissions required for SSH using the key file by entering the following:

```
$ chmod 400 abc.pem
```

Now, to SSH into your instance, you will need its public IP or instance public DNS. For example, if the public IP is `1.2.3.4`, then use the following command:

```
$ ssh -i abc.pem ubuntu@1.2.3.4
```

The public IP of the AWS instance can be found on the details panel below the list of running instances on the AWS console in the EC2 management page.

Step 3: Installing CUDA drivers on the GPU instance

First, update/install the NVIDIA graphics drivers:

```
$ sudo add-apt-repository ppa:graphics-drivers/ppa -y
$ sudo apt-get update
$ sudo apt-get install -y nvidia-xxx nvidia-settings
```

Here, `xxx` can be replaced with the graphics hardware version installed on your instance, which can be found in the instance details.

Next, download the CUDA deb file (this code is for the latest version at the time of writing, from Jan, 2019):

```
$ wget
https://developer.download.nvidia.com/compute/cuda/10.0/secure/Prod/local_i
nstallers/cuda-repo-ubuntu1804-10-0-local-10.0.130-410.48_1.0-1_amd64.deb
```

Then, proceed with the following commands:

```
$ sudo dpkg -i cuda-repo-ubuntu1804-10-0-
local-10.0.130-410.48_1.0-1_amd64.deb
$ sudo apt-key add /var/cuda-repo-<version>/7fa2af80.pub
$ sudo apt-get update
$ sudo apt-get install -y cuda nvidia-cuda-toolkit
```

To verify whether everything was installed successfully, run the following commands:

```
$ nvidia-smi
$ nvcc -version
```

If both the commands produce output without any warnings or errors, then the installation is successful.

Step 4: Installing the Anaconda distribution of Python

First, download the Anaconda installer script:

```
$ wget https://repo.continuum.io/archive/Anaconda3-2018.12-Linux-x86_64.sh
```

Next, set the script to executable:

```
$ chmod +x Anaconda*.sh
```

Then, run the installation script:

```
$ ./Anaconda3-2018.12-Linux-x86_64.sh
```

The installer will ask for several options. To verify successful installation, use the following command:

```
$ python3
```

The Python3 REPL loads into the terminal with a banner reflecting the Anaconda distribution version installed on your instance.

Step 5: Run Jupyter

Use the following command to get the Jupyter Notebook server started on the instance:

```
$ jupyter notebook
```

The output on the terminal will contain a URL on opening, with which you will be able to access the Jupyter Notebook running on your EC2 GPU instance.

Deep learning on Crestle

While a customized deep learning environment can be of use when you need greater control over the system—such as when you want to have third-party applications working along with your deep learning model—at other times, you may not have such needs, and you'll only be interested in performing deep learning on the cloud, quickly and in a collaborative manner. In such circumstances, paying the cost of an AWS `g2.2xlarge` instance would be much higher than that of paying only for computing time or GPU time used.

Crestle is a service that provides GPU-enabled Jupyter Notebooks online at very affordable pricing. To begin using Crestle, go through the following steps:

1. Log on to `www.crestle.com`.
2. Click on **Sign Up** and fill up the sign-up form that appears.
3. Check your email for an account confirmation link. Activate your account and sign in.
4. You'll be taken to the dashboard where you'll find a button reading **Start Jupyter**. You will have the option of using the GPU or keeping it disabled. Click on the **Start Jupyter** button with the GPU option enabled.

You will be presented with a Jupyter environment running on the cloud with GPU support. While the pricing is subject to change with the passage of time, it is one of the most affordable solutions available on the internet as of January 2020.

Other deep learning environments

As well as the aforementioned ways of performing GPU-enabled deep learning on the cloud, you can also, in certain circumstances, choose to use other platforms.

Google Colaboratory is a freely available Jupyter Notebook service that is accessible at `https://colab.research.google.com`. Colaboratory notebooks are stored on the user's Google Drive and so have a storage limit of 15 GB. It is possible to store large datasets on Google Drive and include them in the project with the help of the Google Drive Python API. By default, the GPU is disabled on Colaboratory and has to be manually turned on.

Kaggle is yet another platform that was specifically built to carry out contests on data science. It provides a Jupyter-Notebooks-like environment called a **kernel**. Each kernel is provided with a large amount of RAM and free GPU power however, there are more strict storage limits on Kaggle than on Google Colaboratory, and so it is an effective option when the computation is intensive but the data that is to be used and the output is not very large.

Exploring NumPy and pandas

NumPy and pandas are the backbone of nearly every data-science-related library available in the Python language. While pandas is built on top of NumPy, NumPy itself is a wrapping of Python around high-performance C code to facilitate superior mathematical computing in Python than Python itself in its pure form can provide.

Almost all deep learning software developed in Python in one way or another depends upon NumPy and pandas. It is therefore important to have a good understanding of both libraries and the features that they can provide.

NumPy

NumPy is an acronym for **Numerical Python**. Vanilla Python lacks the implementation of arrays, which are close analogs of the mathematical matrices used to develop machine learning models. NumPy brings to Python support for multidimensional arrays and high-performance computing features. It can be included into any Python code by using the following import statement:

```
import numpy as np
```

np is a commonly used convention for importing NumPy.

NumPy arrays

There are several methods to create arrays in NumPy. The following are some notable ones:

- np.array: To convert Python lists to NumPy arrays:

```
[10] array1 = np.array([[10,20,30], [40, 50, 60], [70, 80, 90]])
     array1

 ⊏→  array([[10, 20, 30],
            [40, 50, 60],
            [70, 80, 90]])
```

- `np.ones` or `np.zeros`: To create a NumPy array of all 1s or all 0s:

▼ **zero array**

```
[ ]   zero_arr1 = np.zeros(5)
      print(zero_arr1)

      print('\n*****************************************')

      zero_arr2 = np.zeros((4,4))
      print(zero_arr2)
```

```
[→  [0. 0. 0. 0. 0.]

    *****************************************
    [[0. 0. 0. 0.]
     [0. 0. 0. 0.]
     [0. 0. 0. 0.]
     [0. 0. 0. 0.]]
```

▼ **ones array**

```
[ ]   one_arr1 = np.ones(4)
      print(one_arr1)

      print('\n*****************************************')

      one_arr2 = np.ones((3,2), dtype = int)
      print(one_arr2)
```

```
[→  [1. 1. 1. 1.]

    *****************************************
    [[1 1]
     [1 1]
     [1 1]]
```

- `np.random.rand`: To generate an array of random numbers:

```
[ ]   rand_arr = np.random.rand(5,4)
      print(rand_arr)

 ⏵   [[0.37997193 0.71844568 0.07820339 0.55507054]
      [0.28035038 0.63730088 0.4725696  0.08614317]
      [0.94396988 0.12329078 0.39922435 0.02075598]
      [0.58262311 0.26633394 0.498427   0.09852439]
      [0.51260027 0.24621189 0.37022219 0.1738425 ]]
```

- `np.eye`: To generate an identity matrix of given square matrix dimensions:

```
[ ]   iden_arr1 = np.eye(4)
      print(iden_arr1)

      print('\n*************************************')

      iden_arr2 = np.eye(2, dtype = int)
      print(iden_arr2)

 ⏵   [[1. 0. 0. 0.]
      [0. 1. 0. 0.]
      [0. 0. 1. 0.]
      [0. 0. 0. 1.]]

      *************************************
      [[1 0]
      [0 1]]
```

Let's now look at basic NumPy array operations.

Basic NumPy array operations

NumPy arrays are Python analogues of mathematical matrices, and so they support the arithmetic manipulation of all basic types, such as addition, subtraction, division, and multiplication.

Let's declare two NumPy arrays and store them as `array1` and `array2`:

```
array1 = np.array([[10,20,30], [40, 50, 60], [70, 80, 90]])
array2 = np.array([[90, 80, 70], [60, 50, 40], [30, 20, 10]])
```

Now let's look at some examples of each arithmetic operation on these arrays:

- **Addition**:

```
[5]  array1 + array2

⊳   array([[100, 100, 100],
           [100, 100, 100],
           [100, 100, 100]])
```

- **Subtraction**:

```
[6]  array1 - array2

⊳   array([[-80, -60, -40],
           [-20,   0,  20],
           [ 40,  60,  80]])
```

- **Multiplication**:

```
[7]  array1 * array2

⊳   array([[ 900, 1600, 2100],
           [2400, 2500, 2400],
           [2100, 1600,  900]])
```

- **Division**:

```
[8]  array1 / array2

⊳   array([[0.11111111, 0.25      , 0.42857143],
           [0.66666667, 1.        , 1.5       ],
           [2.33333333, 4.        , 9.        ]])
```

Let's now compare NumPy arrays with Python lists.

NumPy arrays versus Python lists

Let's now see how NumPy arrays offer advantages over Python lists.

Array slicing over multiple rows and columns

While it is not possible to slice lists of lists in Python in such a way as to select a specific number of rows and columns in the list of lists, NumPy array slicing works according to the following syntax:

```
Array [ rowStartIndex : rowEndIndex, columnStartIndex : columnEndIndex
]
```

Here's an example:

```
[4]   a = np.arange(12).reshape(3, 4)
      a

⌐→  array([[ 0,  1,  2,  3],
           [ 4,  5,  6,  7],
           [ 8,  9, 10, 11]])


[5]   rows = np.array([False, True, True])


[6]   a[rows , : ]

⌐→  array([[ 4,  5,  6,  7],
           [ 8,  9, 10, 11]])
```

In the preceding example, we are able to select two rows and all elements of those rows in NumPy array a.

Assignment over slicing

While it is not possible to assign values to slices of Python lists, NumPy allows the assignment of values to NumPy arrays. For example, to assign 4 to the third to the fifth element of a NumPy one-dimensional array, we can use the following:

```
arr[2:5] = 4
```

Next, we will be looking at pandas.

Pandas

Built on top of NumPy, pandas is one of the most widely used libraries for data science using Python. It facilitates high-performance data structures and data-analysis methods. Pandas provides an in-memory two-dimensional table object called a DataFrame, which in turn is made of a one-dimensional, array-like structure called a series.

Each DataFrame in pandas is in the form of a spreadsheet-like table with row labels and column headers. It is possible to carry out row-based or column-based operations, or both together. Pandas strongly integrates with matplotlib to provide several intuitive visualizations of data that are often very useful when making presentations or during exploratory data analysis.

To import pandas into a Python project, use the following line of code:

```
import pandas as pd
```

Here, `pd` is a common name for importing pandas.

Pandas provides the following data structures:

- **Series**: One-dimensional array or vector, similar to a column in a table
- **DataFrames**: Two-dimensional table, with table headers and labels for the rows
- **Panels**: A dictionary of DataFrames, much like a MySQL database that contains several tables inside

A pandas series can be created using the `pd.Series( )` method, while a DataFrame can be created using the `pd.DataFrame( )` method—for example, in the following code, we create a pandas DataFrame object using multiple series objects:

```
import pandas as pd

employees = pd.DataFrame({ "weight": pd.Series([60, 80, 100],index=["Ram",
"Sam", "Max"]),"dob": pd.Series([1990, 1970, 1991], index=["Ram", "Max",
"Sam"], name="year"),"hobby": pd.Series(["Reading", "Singing"],
index=["Ram", "Max"]) })

employees
```

The output of the preceding code is as follows:

	dob	hobby	weight
Max	1970	Singing	100
Ram	1990	Reading	60
Sam	1991	NaN	80

Some of the most important methods available for a pandas DataFrame are as follows:

- `head(n)` or `tail(n)`: To display the top or bottom *n* rows of the DataFrame.
- `info( )`: To display information on all the columns, dimensions, and types of data in the columns of the DataFrame.
- `describe( )`: To display handy aggregate and statistical information about each of the columns in the DataFrame. Columns that are not numeric are omitted.

Summary

We covered a lot of different things in this chapter. We started by learning the basics of a neural network and then we gradually proceeded. We learned the two most powerful types of neural networks used today—CNNs and RNNs—and we also learned about them on a high level, but without skipping their foundational units. We learned that as the complexity in a neural network increases, it requires a lot of computational power, which standard computers may fail to cater for we saw how this problem can be overcome by configuring a deep learning development environment using two different providers—AWS and Crestle. We explored Jupyter Notebooks, a powerful tool for performing deep learning tasks. We learned about the usage of two very popular Python libraries—NumPy and pandas. Both of these libraries are extensively used when performing deep learning tasks.

In the next chapter, we will be building applications and integrating deep learning to make them perform intelligently. But before we did this, it was important for us to know the basics that were covered in this chapter. We are now in a good position to move on to the next chapter.

3
Creating Your First Deep Learning Web Application

After developing an understanding of neural networks and their setup for use in real-world projects, the natural next step is to develop a web-based deep learning application. This chapter is dedicated to creating a complete web application—albeit a very simplistic one—that, in a very simple way, demonstrates how the integration of deep learning in applications is done.

This chapter will introduce several terms that will be used throughout this book, and so it is a recommended read even for those of you who already have a basic understanding of deep learning web applications so that you are able to understand the terms used in future chapters. We will begin by structuring a deep learning web application and learning how to understand datasets. We will then implement a simple neural network using Python and create a Flask API to work with server-side Python.

In this chapter, the following topics will be covered:

- Structuring a deep learning web application
- Understanding datasets
- Implementing a simple neural network using Python
- Creating a Flask API that works with server-side Python
- Using cURL and the web client with Flask
- Improving the deep learning backend

Technical requirements

You can access the code used in this chapter at `https://github.com/PacktPublishing/`
`Hands-On-Python-Deep-Learning-for-web/tree/master/Chapter3`.

For this chapter, you'll need the following:

- Python 3.6+
- Flask 1.1.0+
- TensorFlow 2.0+

Structuring a deep learning web application

When solving a jigsaw puzzle, it is important that the parts fit, rather than them being forced together. Similarly, when developing a software solution, the parts of the solution must seamlessly work together and their interaction must be simple to understand. Good software requires proper software planning. Hence, providing a solid structure to the software is essential for its long-term use and for easy future maintenance.

Before we begin creating our first deep learning application that works on the web, we must chalk out a blueprint of the solution, keeping in mind the problems we wish to solve and the solutions to them. This is much like how we plan authentication systems or pass form values from one page to another during website development.

A general deep learning web solution would need the following components:

- A server that can store data and respond with queries
- A system that can use the stored data and process it to produce deep learning-based responses to queries
- A client that can send data to the server for storage, send queries with new data, and finally, accept and use the responses the server sends after querying the deep learning system

Let's try to visualize this structure using a diagram.

A structure diagram of a general deep learning web application

The following diagram depicts the interaction between the web client, web server, and the deep learning model:

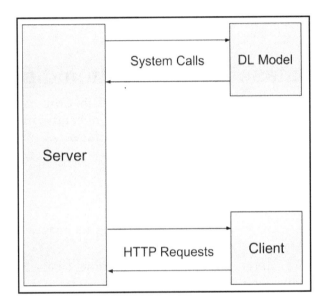

We will be creating three software parts—the client, the server, and the deep learning model—which will all work together. To do so, the client will make HTTP requests to the server and the server, in return, will produce output fetched from the separately trained deep learning model. This model may or may not be executed in the files present on the server that respond to the HTTP requests made by the client. In most cases, the deep learning model is separated from the file that handles the HTTP requests.

In the example presented in this chapter, we will present the server, the client, and the deep learning model in separate files. Our client will send simple HTTP requests to the server, such as a page-load request or a GET request for URLs, which will produce the output from the deep learning model based on the queries passed. However, it is very common practice for the client to communicate with the server via REST APIs.

Let's now move on to understanding the dataset that our application will work on.

Understanding datasets

It is of the utmost importance that we properly understand the dataset that we are working on in order to produce the best results—in terms of execution time and space for the data—with the most efficient code. The dataset we will be using here is probably the most popular dataset when it comes to using neural networks with images—the MNIST database of handwritten digits.

The MNIST dataset of handwritten digits

This dataset was created by a team made up of Yann LeCun, Corinna Cortes, and Christopher J.C. Burges. It is a large collection of images of handwritten digits, containing 60,000 training samples and 10,000 testing samples. The dataset is publicly available for download at `http://yann.lecun.com/exdb/mnist/` where it is present in the form of four `.gz` compressed files.

The four files are as follows:

- `train-images-idx3-ubyte.gz`: The training set images. These images will be used to train the neural network classifier.
- `train-labels-idx1-ubyte.gz`: The training set labels. Every image in the training set will have a label associated with it, which is the corresponding digit visible in that image.
- `t10k-images-idx3-ubyte.gz`: The test set images. We will use these images to test our neural network prediction accuracy.
- `t10k-labels-idx1-ubyte.gz`: The labels for the images in the test set. When our neural network makes predictions on the test set, we will compare them against these values to check our results.

The images stored in this dataset are not directly available for viewing due to their custom format. The developer working on the dataset is expected to create their own simple viewer for the images. Once you have done this, you will be able to see the images, which look something like this:

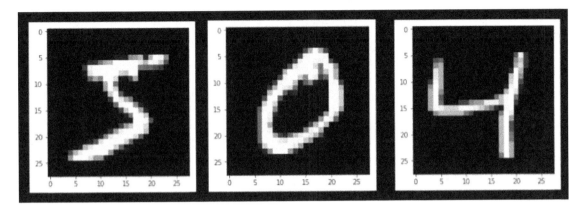

Let's talk about the images in a bit more depth. They are, as you can see, a little over the 25 pixels mark on both axes. To be exact, the images are all in the form of 28 x 28 pixels. Now, since the images are grayscale, it is possible for them to be stored in a single layer 28 x 28 matrix. Hence, we have a total of 784 values, ranging from 0 to 1, where 0 represents an entirely dark pixel and 1 represents a white pixel. Anything inside that range is a shade of black. In the MNIST dataset, these images are present in the form of a flattened array of 784 floating point numbers. In order to view these images, you need to convert the single dimension array into a two-dimensional array with a 28 x 28 shape and then plot the image using any self-developed or publicly available tools, such as Matplotlib or the Pillow library.

Let's discuss this method in the upcoming section.

Exploring the dataset

Let's begin by downloading all four files from the MNIST dataset web page, available at `http://yann.lecun.com/exdb/mnist`. Once downloaded, extract all the files and you should have folders that resemble the names in the following list:

- `train-images.idx3-ubyte`
- `train-labels.idx1-ubyte`
- `t10k-images.idx3-ubyte`
- `t10k-labels.idx1-ubyte`

Keep these files in your working directory. We will now create a Jupyter notebook to perform **exploratory data analysis** (**EDA**) on the dataset files we have extracted.

Open your Jupyter Notebook environment in your browser and create a new Python notebook. Let's begin by importing the necessary modules:

```
import numpy as np
import matplotlib.pyplot as plt
```

The preceding lines import the numpy module and matplotlib.pyplot to the project. The numpy module provides high-performance mathematical functions in Python while the matplotlib.pyplot module provides a simple interface to plot and visualize graphs and images. In order to view all the output from this library in the Jupyter notebook, add the following line of code:

```
%matplotlib inline
```

 If you are on Windows, to extract a .gz file you can use the 7-zip software, which is an excellent compression/decompression tool that is available to download for free at https://www.7-zip.org.

Creating functions to read the image files

As mentioned earlier, it is not possible to directly view the images in your downloaded image files. So, we will now create a function in Python that the matplotlib module will be able to use to display the images in the files:

```
def loadImageFile(fileimage):
  f = open(fileimage, "rb")

  f.read(16)
  pixels = 28*28
  images_arr = []
  while True:
    try:
      img = []
      for j in range(pixels):
        pix = ord(f.read(1))
        img.append(pix / 255)
      images_arr.append(img)
    except:
      break

  f.close()
  image_sets = np.array(images_arr)
  return image_sets
```

The preceding `loadImageFile` function takes a single parameter, which is the name of the file that contains the images. We have two such files available for us in our downloaded files folder: `train-images-idx3-ubyte` and `t10k-images-idx3-ubyte`. The output of the preceding function is a `numpy` array of images. We can store the result in a Python variable, as shown:

```
test_images = loadImageFile("t10k-images-idx3-ubyte")
```

Now, to view the images that are in the variable holding the `numpy` array of images, we can define another function that takes a single image's pixel array of 784 floating point numbers and plots them into a single image. The function can be defined as shown:

```
def gen_image(arr):
  two_d = (np.reshape(arr, (28, 28)) * 255).astype(np.uint8)
  plt.imshow(two_d, interpolation='nearest', cmap='gray')
  plt.show()
  return
```

Now, say we want to display the first of the test images; because we have stored the `numpy` array of images in the `test_images` variable, we can run the following code:

```
gen_image(test_images[0])
```

We are able to see the following output:

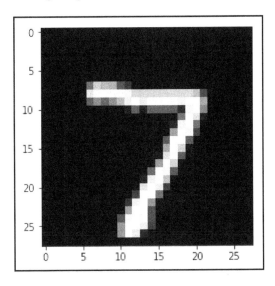

Now that we are able to view the images, we can proceed to building a function that will allow us to extract the corresponding digit from the labels.

Creating functions to read label files

There are two label files available to us in the MNIST dataset: `train-labels-idx1-ubyte` and `t10k-labels-idx1-ubyte`. To view these files, we can use the following function, which takes input of the filename as an argument and produces an array of one-hot-encoded labels:

```
def loadLabelFile(filelabel):
  f = open(filelabel, "rb")

  f.read(8)

  labels_arr = []

  while True:
    row = [0 for x in range(10)]
    try:
      label = ord(f.read(1))
      row[label] = 1
      labels_arr.append(row)
    except:
      break

  f.close()
  label_sets = np.array(labels_arr)
  return label_sets
```

This function returns a `numpy` array of labels in one-hot encoding, with the dimensions of the number of samples in the dataset times by 10. Let's observe a single entry in order to understand the nature of one-hot encoding. Run the following code, which essentially makes a print of the one-hot-encoded label set from the first sample in the test set:

```
test_labels = loadLabelFile("t10k-labels-idx1-ubyte")
print(test_labels[0])
```

We get the following output:

```
[0 0 0 0 0 0 0 1 0 0]
```

We can understand this by noting that since the digit at the seventh index is 1, the label of the first image in the test dataset is 7.

A summary of the dataset

After a very concise exploration of the available dataset, we are able to come up with the following results.

The training dataset contains 60,000 images with a dimension of 60,000 x 784, where each image is 28 x 28 pixels. The distribution of samples among the digits are as follows:

Digit	Number of Samples	Digit	Number of Samples
0	5,923	5	5,421
1	6,742	6	5,918
2	5,958	7	6,265
3	6,131	8	5,851
4	5,842	9	5,949

Observe that digit 5 has a smaller number of samples than digit 1. So, it is quite possible that a model that isn't finely trained will make mistakes in recognizing digit 5.

The summary of the number of labels present tells us that all 60,000 samples have their corresponding labels and none of their labels are missing.

Similarly, on the test dataset, we have 10,000 images and labels and the distribution of the number of samples is as follows:

Digit	Number of Samples	Digit	Number of Samples
0	980	5	892
1	1,135	6	958
2	1,032	7	1,028
3	1,010	8	974
4	982	9	1,009

The number of samples in the test dataset is quite evenly spread.

Implementing a simple neural network using Python

After doing a very basic data analysis, we can move on to coding our first neural network in Python. You can revise the concepts of neural networks in Chapter 2, *Getting Started With Deep Learning Using Python,* before moving on. We will now be creating a **convolutional neural network** (**CNN**), which will predict the handwritten digit labels.

We start by creating a new Jupyter notebook. You could name this Model.ipynb for convention. This notebook will be used to develop a **pickled** version of the deep learning model, which will later be put in a script that will generate predictions.

Importing the necessary modules

The modules that will be needed for Model.ipynb are imported as follows:

```
import numpy as np
import keras
from keras.models import Sequential
from keras.layers import Dense, Dropout, Flatten, Activation
from keras.layers import Conv2D, MaxPooling2D
from keras import backend as K
from keras.layers.normalization import BatchNormalization
```

The keras module is required to quickly implement high-performance neural networks with the TensorFlow backend. We have talked about Keras in earlier chapters. To install Keras, you can use the following command:

```
pip3 install keras
```

The preceding command will install Keras.

Reusing our functions to load the image and label files

Remember the `loadImageFile` and `loadLabelFile` functions we created during the exploration of the dataset? We will need them again and so we will copy those same functions into this notebook.

Together, they produce two cells of code for each of the functions:

- The `loadImageFile()` method
- The `loadLabelFile()` method

In a new code cell, we create the `loadImageFile()` function:

```
def loadImageFile(fileimage):
  f = open(fileimage, "rb")

  f.read(16)
  pixels = 28*28
  images_arr = []
  while True:
    try:
      img = []
      for j in range(pixels):
        pix = ord(f.read(1))
        img.append(pix / 255)
      images_arr.append(img)
    except:
      break

  f.close()
  image_sets = np.array(images_arr)
  return image_sets
```

In another new code cell, the `loadLabelFile()` function is created:

```
def loadLabelFile(filelabel):
  f = open(filelabel, "rb")
  f.read(8)

  labels_arr = []

  while True:
    row = [0 for x in range(10)]
    try:
      label = ord(f.read(1))
```

```
        row[label] = 1
        labels_arr.append(row)
    except:
        break

    f.close()
    label_sets = np.array(labels_arr)
    return label_sets
```

We can then import the images and label files in the form of numpy arrays by using the following lines of code:

```
train_images = loadImageFile("train-images-idx3-ubyte")
train_labels = loadLabelFile("train-labels-idx1-ubyte")

test_images = loadImageFile("t10k-images-dx3-ubyte")
test_labels = loadLabelFile("t10k-labels-idx1-ubyte")
```

This creates the `train_images`, `train_labels`, `test_images`, and `test_labels` NumPy arrays. We can observe their shape and we get the following output for `train_images`:

(60000, 784)

Next, we will learn how to reshape the arrays for processing with Keras.

Reshaping the arrays for processing with Keras

The current shape of the image arrays are not Keras-friendly. We must convert the image arrays into a shape of (60000, 28, 28, 1) and (10000, 28, 28, 1), respectively.

To do so, we use the following lines of code:

```
x_train = train_images.reshape(train_images.shape[0], 28, 28, 1)
x_test = test_images.reshape(test_images.shape[0], 28, 28, 1)
```

Now, if we observe the shape of x_train, we get an output as follows:

(60000, 28, 28, 1)

We have no changes to make in the labels arrays and so we directly assign them to
y_train and y_test:

```
y_train = train_labels
y_test = test_labels
```

Next, we will create a neural network using Keras.

Creating a neural network using Keras

Now, we are ready to proceed with the creation of the neural network:

1. We will first create a Sequential neural network model in Keras:

    ```
    model = Sequential()
    ```

2. To add a neuron layer to the network, we use the following code:

    ```
    model.add(Conv2D(32, (3, 3), input_shape=(28,28,1)))
    ```

    This adds a two-dimensional convolutional neuron layer to the network with an
    input shape that is the same as the shape of the images.

3. Now, let's add the activation layer with relu as the activation function:

    ```
    model.add(Activation('relu'))
    ```

4. After adding the activation layer, we can perform a batch normalization. During
    training, the data passes through several computational layers and may become
    too large or too small. This is known as the **covariate shift** and batch
    normalization helps bring back the data to a central region. This helps the neural
    network train faster:

    ```
    BatchNormalization(axis=-1)
    ```

5. Let's now add more hidden layers to the model:

    ```
    model.add(Conv2D(32, (3, 3)))
    model.add(Activation('relu'))
    model.add(MaxPooling2D(pool_size=(2,2)))

    BatchNormalization(axis=-1)
    model.add(Conv2D(64,(3, 3)))
    model.add(Activation('relu'))
    BatchNormalization(axis=-1)
    ```

```
model.add(Conv2D(64, (3, 3)))
model.add(Activation('relu'))
model.add(MaxPooling2D(pool_size=(2,2)))

model.add(Flatten())

BatchNormalization()
model.add(Dense(512))
model.add(Activation('relu'))
BatchNormalization()
model.add(Dropout(0.2))
```

6. At the last layer of the neural network, we need an output of 10 values, in the form of one-hot encoding, to denote the digit that has been predicted. To do this, we add a final layer of 10 neurons. This will hold 10 values in the continuous range of 0 to 1:

```
model.add(Dense(10))
```

7. Finally, to convert these 10 floating point values to a one-hot encoding, we use a softmax activation:

```
model.add(Activation('softmax'))
```

Let's now compile and train the Keras neural network.

Compiling and training a Keras neural network

We are now ready to compile and train the neural network. To compile the neural network, we use the following code:

```
model.compile(loss=keras.losses.categorical_crossentropy,
              optimizer=keras.optimizers.Adam(),
              metrics=['accuracy'])
```

In our model, which we compiled in the previous block of code, we have set categorical cross-entropy as the loss function; the optimizer function used is the Adam optimizer and the metric for evaluation is accuracy.

We then train the neural network with the `fit()` method of the Keras model object:

```
model.fit(x_train, y_train,
          batch_size=100,
          epochs=10,
          verbose=2,
          validation_split=0.2)
```

 It is recommended that you perform a split of the training data into further validation and training data, while leaving the test set untouched but for this dataset, it is fine.

The training is done for 10 batches and the batch size is of 100 samples.

Evaluating and storing the model

After training the model, we are now ready to evaluate its accuracy. To do so, we will use the following code:

```
score = model.evaluate(x_test, y_test, verbose=1)

print('Test loss:', score[0])
print('Test accuracy:', score[1])
```

We will get the following output for the preceding code:

```
10000/10000 [==============================] - 1s 56us/step
Test loss: 0.02411479307773807
Test accuracy: 0.9931
```

We get 99% accuracy, which is a very good accuracy score. Now, we can save the model, which will be used in the future to make predictions for user input through the web portal. We will split the model into two parts—the model structure and the model weights. To save the structure, we will use the JSON format, as shown:

```
model_json = model.to_json()
with open("model.json", "w") as json_file:
    json_file.write(model_json)
```

Now, to save the weights of the Keras model, we use the `save_weights()` method for the object:

```
model.save_weights('weights.h5')
```

Next, we will create a Flask API to work with server-side Python.

Creating a Flask API to work with server-side Python

We have completed our deep learning model and stored its structure in the `model.json` file and the weights for the model in the `weights.h5` file. We are now ready to wrap the model data in an API so that we can expose the model to web-based calls via the `GET` or `POST` methods. Here, we will be discussing the `POST` method. Let's begin with the required setup on the server.

Setting up the environment

In the server, we will require the Flask module—which will be service requests—which in turn will be running code that requires Keras (and so, TensorFlow), NumPy, and many other modules. In order to quickly set up the environment for our project, we follow these steps:

1. Install Anaconda.
2. Install TensorFlow and Keras.
3. Install Pillow.
4. Install Flask.

You can refer to the following block of commands to install TensorFlow, Keras, Pillow, and Flask:

```
pip3 install tensorflow keras pillow flask
```

We are now ready to start developing our API.

Uploading the model structure and weights

The model structure file, `model.json`, and the weights file, `weights.h5`, need to be present in the working directory. You can copy the files to a new folder—say, `flask_api`—or upload them to the correct path if you are using a remote server.

Creating our first Flask server

Create a new file in the working directory and name it `flask_app.py`. This file will be the one that handles all requests made to the server. Put the following code in the file:

```
from flask import Flask
app = Flask(__name__)
@app.route("/")
def index():
    return "Hello World!"
if __name__ == "__main__":
    app.run(host='0.0.0.0', port=80)
```

The preceding code first imports the necessary modules into the script. Then, it sets the app as the Flask server object and defines the `index` function with a directive of handling all the requests made to the `"/"` address, regardless of the type of request. At the end of the script, the `run()` method of the Flask object app is used to bind the script to a specified port on the system.

We can now deploy this simple *Hello World* Flask server. We run the following command in a Terminal:

```
python flask_app.py
```

Now, when we open the `http://localhost/` URL in the browser, we are greeted with a page presenting *Hello World*. The `index` function handles the requests made at the root of the server, since it's route is set to `"/"`. Let's now extend this example toward creating an API that can handle requests specifically for prediction.

Importing the necessary modules

In the preceding example, we will extend the `flask import` statement to import an additional method, `request`, which will allow us how to handle the `POST` requests made to the server. The line then looks as follows:

```
from flask import Flask, request
```

We then import the modules necessary for the reading and storing of the images. Also, the numpy module is imported as in the following code snippet:

```
from scipy.misc import imread, imresize
import numpy as np
```

Finally, we import the model_from_json() method of the Keras module to load the saved model files. We then import tensorflow, as Keras is dependent on it to execute:

```
from keras.models import model_from_json
import tensorflow as tf
```

Next, we load data into the script runtime.

Loading data into the script runtime and setting the model

Once we have imported the necessary modules, we load the saved model JSON and weights, as in the following code snippet:

```
json_file = open('model.json','r')
model_json = json_file.read()
json_file.close()
model = model_from_json(model_json)

model.load_weights("weights.h5")
model.compile(loss='categorical_crossentropy',optimizer='adam',metrics=['ac
curacy'])
graph = tf.get_default_graph()
```

Note that we have also created a default graph item for the session ahead. This was implicitly created during the model training but is not carried over in the saved model and weights files, so we must explicitly create it here.

Setting the app and index function

Now, we set the `app` variable to a Flask object and set the `"/"` route to be handled by the `index` function, which actually produces no meaningful output. This is because we will be using the `/predict` route to serve our prediction API as shown:

```
app = Flask(__name__)

@app.route('/')
def index():
    return "Oops, nothing here!"
```

We will cover the convert image function in the next section.

Converting the image function

We might sometimes get images in the form of `base64` encoded strings if the user makes an image `POST` request with a suitable setting. We can create a function to handle that:

```
import re
import base64

def stringToImage(img):
    imgstr = re.search(r'base64,(.*)', str(img)).group(1)
    with open('image.png', 'wb') as output:
        output.write(base64.b64decode(imgstr))
```

We use the `re` module for regex to determine whether the data passed is in the form of a `base64` string. The `base64` module is needed to decode the string and then the file is saved as `image.png`.

Prediction APIs

Now, let's define the `/predict` route, which will be our API to respond to the predicted digit with:

```
@app.route('/predict/', methods=['POST'])
def predict():
    global model, graph
    imgData = request.get_data()
    try:
        stringToImage(imgData)
    except:
```

```
        f = request.files['img']
        f.save('image.png')
    x = imread('image.png', mode='L')
    x = imresize(x, (28, 28))
    x = x.reshape(1, 28, 28, 1)

    with graph.as_default():
        prediction = model.predict(x)
        response = np.argmax(prediction, axis=1)
        return str(response[0])
```

Here, the `predict()` function takes in a `POST` method input, makes a check on the format that the file is passed in, and then saves it to the disk with the name of `image.png`. Then, the image is read into the program and resized to 28 x 28 dimensions. Next, the image array is reshaped, such that it can be put into the Keras model for prediction. Then, we use the `predict()` method of the Keras model and get a one-hot-encoded output with the predicted digit's index set to 1, while the rest remains as 0. We determine the digit and send it to the output of the API.

Now, we must, at the end of the file, add the code to bind the server to a port and set the required configuration:

```
if __name__ == "__main__":
    app.run(host='0.0.0.0', port=80)
    app.run(debug=True)
```

We have set the `debug=True` parameter in order to be able to see—in the server's console—whether any error occurs on the server. This is always a good idea during development but in production, this line of code can be skipped.

A final step before we run the application is to update the code for the `'/'` route. We will load the `index.html` item that we created whenever a person calls this route, as shown:

```
@app.route('/')
def index():
    return render_template("index.html")
```

We are now all set to start up the server and check whether it is working correctly. We use the same command as used previously to start up the server:

```
python flask_app.py
```

The preceding command will start up the server.

Using the API via cURL and creating a web client using Flask

With our server running, we can send `POST` requests to it with the image content and expect a predicted digit in the output. Two ways to test any API without any third-party tools are as follows:

- Use cURL.
- Develop a client to call the API.

We will be covering both of these methods.

Using the API via cURL

Before we develop a client to send `POST` requests to the API server, let's test the API via cURL, which is a command-line tool used to simulate `GET` and `POST` requests to URLs.

Use the following command in Terminal or Command Prompt to make a `curl` request to your prediction API:

```
curl -X POST -F img=@"path_to_file" http://localhost/predict/
```

Here, the `-F` flag is used to indicate that the `POST` request will contain files. The name of the `POST` variable that will hold the file is `img,path_to_file` should be replaced with the full path to the file that you wish to send to the server for the image that the prediction is to be made on.

Let's see how the API works with an example.

Say we have the following image with the `self2.png` filename and dimensions of 275 x 275:

Clearly, the image dimensions on the serverside must be adjusted. To make the request, we use the following command:

```
C:\WINDOWS\system32\cmd.exe

C:\Users\Training\Downloads>curl -X POST -F img=@self2.png http://localhost/predict/
```

The output of the API is a single integer—2. So, the API works successfully.

Creating a simple web client for the API

We will now be creating a bare-bones web Client to call the API. To do so, we must modify our current code. In `flask_app.py`, first change the `import` statement for Flask in order to extend it to another module—`render_template`—as shown:

```
from flask import Flask, request, render_template
```

Now, we create a folder, `templates`, in the working directory and add a file, `index.html`, to it with the following code:

```html
<!DOCTYPE html>
<html lang="en">
  <head>
    <title>MNIST CNN</title>
  </head>

  <body>
    <h1>MNIST Handwritten Digits Prediction</h1>

    <form>
      <input type="file" name="img"></input>
      <input type="submit"></input>
    </form>
    <hr>
    <h3>Prediction: <span id="result"></span></h3>

    <script
src='http://cdnjs.cloudflare.com/ajax/libs/jquery/2.1.3/jquery.min.js'></script>

    <script src="{{ url_for('static',filename='index.js') }}"></script>

  </body>
</html>
```

Essentially, all we do here is create a form with a single input element of the file type, called
`img`. We then add jQuery to the page and create a link to a static file, `index.js`, which is
served in the `static` folder of the server.

Let's create the `index.js` file. First, create a folder, `static`, in the root directory and then
create a new file, `index.js`, with the following code:

```
$("form").submit(function(evt){
    evt.preventDefault();
    var formData = new FormData($(this)[0]);
    $.ajax({
        url: '/predict/',
        type: 'POST',
        data: formData,
        async: false,
        cache: false,
        contentType: false,
        enctype: 'multipart/form-data',
        processData: false,
        success: function (response) {
            $('#result').empty().append(response);
        }
    });
    return false;
});
```

The preceding jQuery code makes a `POST` request to the `/predict/` route and then updates
the `result` divide on the page with the value that is returned from the server.

Let's take a sample run on this web client. First, we need to restart the Flask server. Then,
we open `http://localhost/` in the browser to get a web page that looks like this:

Say we choose a file named `mnist7.png`, which is essentially the first image of the test dataset and looks like this:

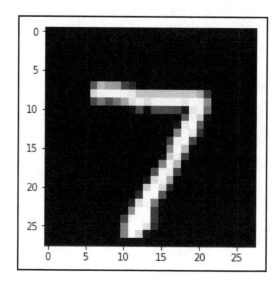

The expected output is 7. After clicking **Submit**, we get the following output on the page:

We can observe that that is the correct output and conclude that the web client works correctly.

Improving the deep learning backend

The simple model we have trained here is hardly one that we can claim is close to a perfect model. There are several methods that we can use to extend this model to make it better. For instance, some of the most basic steps that we can take to improve our deep learning model are as follows:

- **Increase training epochs**: We have only trained our model for 10 epochs, which is usually a very small value for any deep learning model. Increasing the number of training epochs can improve the accuracy of the model. However, it can also lead to overfitting and so the number of epochs must be experimented with.
- **More training samples**: Our web client currently doesn't do much more than show the predicted value. However, we could extend it to get feedback from the user on whether the prediction we made was correct. We can then add the user's input image to the training samples and train with the user-provided label for the image. We must, however, take caution against spammy user input images and labels and only provide this feature to trusted users or beta testers for our web app.
- **Create a deeper network**: We could increase the number of hidden layers in the network to make the predictions more accurate. Again, this method is susceptible to overfitting and must be carefully experimented with.

Summary

This chapter covered, in complete detail, how you can create a deep learning model and then facilitate its usage through an API via a web client or using cURL. The chapter began by discussing how deep learning web applications are structured, the various components of such applications, and how they interact with each other. Then, a short discussion and exploration of the MNIST handwritten digits dataset was presented. This led us on to the next section, where we built a deep learning model and stored it in files for future use. These files were then imported to the server API scripts and executed there whenever the API was called. Finally, the chapter presented a very basic client for the API and also instructed you on how to use the API over cURL through the command-line interface.

In the next chapter, we will discuss how deep learning can be performed within the browser window using TensorFlow.js.

4
Getting Started with TensorFlow.js

So far, we have gently introduced ourselves to the wonderful world of deep learning and we have got a fair sense of what deep learning has to offer in terms of making today's web applications more intelligent. In Chapter 1, *Demystifying Artificial Intelligence and Fundamentals of Machine Learning*, we saw a detailed overview of the web applications before and after AI breakout. In Chapter 3, *Creating Your First Deep Learning Web Application*, we built ourselves a simple image classifier-based web application using a simple neural network.

Web applications are all around us and they have easily become inseparable parts of our day-to-day lives. When it comes to building web applications, the use of JavaScript is too hard to ignore. So, what if we built an intelligent web application using JavaScript and no other scripting language? In this chapter, we are going to see how we can use a JavaScript library, called **TensorFlow.js** (**TF.js**), to build a deep learning-enabled web application—we are going to do all of this in a web browser.

In this chapter, we will cover the following topics:

- The fundamentals of TF.js and its offerings
- Developing a deep learning model with TF.js and making inferences
- Using the pretrained models directly in the browser
- Building a web application to recognize flower species
- Advantages and limitations of TF.js

Technical requirements

You can access the code used in this chapter at `https://github.com/PacktPublishing/Hands-On-Python-Deep-Learning-for-Web/tree/master/Chapter4`.

To work on this chapter, you'll need the following software:

- TF.js 0.15.1+
- The `@tensorflow/tfjs-node` 0.3.0+ package from the NPM repository

The fundamentals of TF.js

In this section, we are going to briefly review some of the fundamental concepts of TF.js. We will start off by introducing TensorFlow and then we will proceed to study different components of TF.js.

What is TensorFlow?

Before we can begin discussing TF.js, we must understand what TensorFlow is. TensorFlow is an open source library that is developed and maintained by Google. It is built on a data structure called tensors. Tensors are the generalized form of scalar and vector. TensorFlow provides a lot of efficient utilities for high-performance numerical computing across a wide range of scientific domains. TensorFlow also provides a very flexible suite of utilities for carrying out machine learning and deep learning development and research. You are encouraged to visit TensorFlow's official website at `https://www.tensorflow.org/` for more information.

What is TF.js?

TF.js is a JavaScript library that provides an ecosystem to build and deploy machine learning models. It offers the following functionalities:

- Developing machine learning models with JavaScript
- Using pretrained machine learning models
- Deploying machine learning models

TF.js provides you with all the elements required for a machine learning project. It has dedicated modules for data preprocessing, tensor handling, model building, model evaluation, and much more, but all in JavaScript. Before we move on to digging deeper into this, let's quickly understand the need for TF.js.

Why TF.js?

As we saw in the previous chapter, it is quite easy and intuitive to simply train and host a model online, wrap it up in a REST API, and then use the API on any frontend to display our results. Why, then, would the need to use TF.js arise?

A simple answer to this question would be if there is an AI in the browser! Think of a game that requires the use of an AI agent that learns from the human player's method of playing to become tougher or easier as the game progresses. Now, this would be overkill if, at every split second, the game kept sending requests to the server to transfer data to and from the game and the server. What's more, it might easily result in a **Denial of Service (DoS)** attack.

So, having an AI that can live and learn in the browser itself makes sense when the agent has to keep learning in real time. It could also be a hybrid in two ways:

- If a pretrained model is loaded during the rendering of the agent and, from there, it begins learning and updating the model on the server at intervals.
- If multiple versions of the AI agent run on several systems at once and they learn from interaction on the system on which they run. Also, if their collective learning is assimilated on the server and the agents fetch updates from the server at intervals.

So, using TF.js greatly reduces strong dependence on the page that the human user will interact with to communicate with the server at every step.

We can now build a mini project that shows the power of TF.js. Don't worry about the TF.js ecosystem for now—we will cover all the elements of the project as we go along.

The basic concepts of TF.js

The following are the components of TF.js that we will be using in our project:

- Tensors
- Variables

- Operations
- Models
- Layers

Let's look at each of them in detail.

Tensors

Like TensorFlow, the central data processing unit in TF.js is tensors. Goodfellow et al. (in their book on deep learning) make the following observation:

> *In the general case, an array of numbers arranged on a regular grid with a variable number of axes is known as a tensor.*

Simply described, a tensor is a container of one- or multi-dimensional arrays. The following are some examples of tensors that you may already know:

- Scalar (a rank zero tensor)
- Vector (a one-dimensional or rank-one tensor)
- Matrix (a two-dimensional or rank-two tensor)

We can create a tensor with respect to a given shape in TF.js as shown:

```
const shape = [2, 3]; // 2 rows, 3 columns
const a = tf.tensor([4.0, 2.0, 5.0, 15.0, 19.0, 27.0], shape);
```

a is a tensor that was created and its contents can be printed using the following command:

```
a.print()
```

The following output is printed:

```
Output: [[4 , 2 , 5 ],
        [15, 19, 27]]
```

a is a matrix (a rank-two tensor). TF.js also provides dedicated functions, such as tf.scalar, tf.tensor1d, tf.tensor2d, tf.tensor3d, and tf.tensor4d to create tensors of specific shapes without having to specify the shape argument explicitly. It also provides better readability. Tensors are immutable in TF.js.

Variables

Unlike tensors, variables are mutable in TF.js. Variables are particularly useful during the training of a neural network as they consist of lots of intermediate data stores and updates. The following is an example of how variables can be used in TF.js:

```
const initialValues = tf.ones([5]);
const weights = tf.variable(initialValues); // initialize weights
weights.print(); // output: [1, 1, 1, 1, 1]
const updatedValues = tf.tensor1d([0, 1, 0, 1, 0]);
weights.assign(updatedValues); // update values of weights
weights.print(); // output: [0, 1, 0, 1, 0]
```

Let's now look at operators.

Operators

Operators let you perform mathematical operations on data. TF.js provides various operations for manipulating tensors. As tensors are immutable in nature, operators don't change the data contained in the tensors—they return new tensors as results instead. You can perform binary operations, such as addition, multiplication, and subtraction, on tensors. You can even chain multiple operations. The following example shows the use of two different operators in TF.js using chaining:

```
const e = tf.tensor2d([[1.0, 2.0], [3.0, 4.0]]);
const f = tf.tensor2d([[3.0, 4.0], [5.0, 6.0]]);
const sq_sum = tf.square(tf.add(e, f));
sq_sum.print();
```

We first created two two-dimensional tensors and assigned them to e and f. We then added them and took their squares.

This produces the following output:

```
// Output: [[16 , 36],
// [64, 100]]
```

Next, we will cover models and layers.

Models and layers

In deep learning literature, a model refers to the neural network itself, specifically, the neural network architecture. As discussed in Chapter 2, *Getting Started With Deep Learning Using Python*, a neural network consists of basic components, such as layers, neurons, and connections, in between layers. TF.js provides two functions with which to create these models—tf.model and tf.sequential. tf.model helps you to get more sophisticated architectures, such as skipping certain layers, whereas tf.sequential provides a way to create linear stacks of layers without skipping, branching, and so on.

TF.js provides different types of dedicated layers for different types of tasks—tf.layers.dense, tf.layers.dropout, tf.layers.conv1d, tf.layers.simpleRNN, tf.layers.gru, and tf.layers.lstm. The following example demonstrates a simple neural network model with the help of tf.sequential and tf.layers.dense:

```
const model = tf.sequential();
model.add(tf.layers.dense({units: 4, inputShape: [4], activation:
'relu'}));
model.add(tf.layers.dense({units: 1, activation: sigmoid}));
```

The preceding example creates a simple neural network that has the following:

- Two layers (remember, we don't consider the input layer when counting the total number of layers). The network takes an input that has four features (the inputShape argument helps to specify that).
- The first layer contains four neurons (hence units: 4). The second layer (the output layer) has only one neuron.
- The relu activation function is used for the first layer, and the sigmoid activation function is used for the output layer.

 You are encouraged to go to https://js.tensorflow.org/api/latest/index.html to learn more about the preceding components of TF.js.

A case study using TF.js

We will follow all the steps that are typically involved in a machine learning project (which we discussed in Chapter 1, *Demystifying Artificial Intelligence and Fundamentals of Machine Learning*). A good project starts with a well-defined problem statement. So, let's quickly take a look at that and decide the subsequent steps accordingly.

A problem statement for our TF.js mini-project

The problem we will look at here is probably one of the most famous challenges you will come across when starting your journey in machine learning—classifying and predicting the type of an Iris flower by learning its features from the Iris flower dataset. Training, as well as the prediction, will be performed in the browser itself.

We have defined the problem statement for our project. What will follow is the data preparation step. The data is already available to us, so we don't need to collect it ourselves. But, before we prepare the data, it would be good to know a bit more about the data itself.

The Iris flower dataset

Introduced by Ronald Fisher, the statistician and biologist, in 1936, the Iris flower dataset contains 150 rows of data and about 3 different varieties of the Iris flower. The columns are as follows:

- Sepal length (cm)
- Sepal width (cm)
- Petal length (cm)
- Petal width (cm)
- Variety:
  - Setosa
  - Versicolour
  - Virginica

 You can get the raw dataset and learn more about it at http://archive.ics.uci.edu/ml/datasets/Iris.

Your first deep learning web application with TF.js

In this section, we are going to develop a web application with the help of TF.js. This application will include the steps for a standard, full stack, deep learning-enabled web project. We will begin by preparing the data, we will then study the project architecture briefly, and then, we will proceed toward building the required components as we go.

Preparing the dataset

The Iris flower dataset, in its original form, is a CSV file containing the data of 150 rows split into 5 columns in a comma-separated format, with each entry separated by a new line.

However, we will be using a JSON format of the data for easier operability with JavaScript. The dataset in JSON format can be downloaded from `https://gist.github.com/xprilion/33cc85952d317644c944274ee6071547`.

You can use simple functions in any language to convert a CSV file into a JSON file, with the column names changed as per the following conventions:

- Sepal length: `sepal_length`
- Sepal width: `sepal_width`
- Petal length: `petal_length`
- Petal width: `petal_width`
- Variety: `species`

We will use these property names in JSON while developing the tensors for model building.

Project architecture

We will be using Node.js in this project to create a server. This is done so that we get the benefits of faster computational performance of TF.js when used through the Node.js backend. We will create a very basic frontend that will be able to issue a command to perform the training of the neural network built using TF.js and another button to issue a command to predict the class of a hypothetical feature vector of an Iris flower based on input provided by the user.

The following diagram shows the components of the project, along with their interactions:

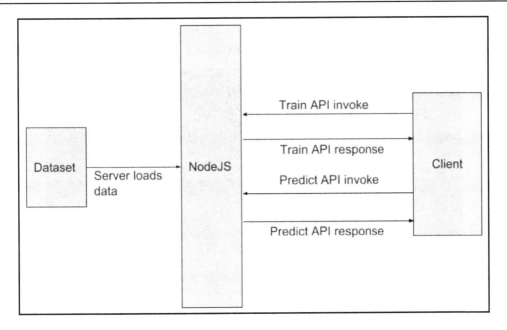

Now that we know about the architecture, let's start with the project.

Starting up the project

To start working on the project, you first need to install the latest versions of Node.js and **Node Package Manager** (**NPM**). While a standard way to do this would be to read the documentation provided on the Node.js website, we would suggest installing Node.js and NPM using **Node Version Manager** (**NVM**).

 The setup instructions and files can be found at `https://github.com/creationix/nvm`.

Once Node.js and NPM are installed, we're ready to start working on the project itself:

1. Create a folder called `tfjs-iris`.
2. Open up a Terminal and use the following command to initiate the package manager for this project:

    ```
    npm init -y
    ```

This should create a file, `package.json`, in your project directory. The output for the preceding command is as follows:

```
(base) xprilion@x1:~/projects/testrepo$ npm init -y
Wrote to /home/xprilion/projects/testrepo/package.json:

{
  "name": "testrepo",
  "version": "1.0.0",
  "description": "",
  "main": "index.js",
  "scripts": {
    "test": "echo \"Error: no test specified\" && exit 1"
  },
  "keywords": [],
  "author": "",
  "license": "ISC"
}
```

Notice that the output is in JSON format. The `main` key defines the file that will be the entry point for the program if it is imported as a module. The value for `main` in this project is set, by default, to `index.js`. However, this file is not yet created. Let's work on the `index.js` file.

We will be using the `express` module of Node.js to create our server. You can read more about `express` at https://expressjs.com.

3. To use `express`, we will need to add the module to our project. To do this, use the following code:

   ```
   npm install express --save
   ```

   This will add the `express` module dependency to the `package.json` file and install it in the `node_modules` directory inside the working directory of the project.

4. Create a file called `index.js` in the root directory of the project repository and add the following code:

   ```
   var express = require('express');
   var app = express();
   ```

This creates an express application object. We will now be adding TF.js to the project. The simplest way to do this is to install it via NPM. The complete setup instructions can be found at https://js.tensorflow.org/setup/.

5. Use the following command to install the TF.js module in the Terminal:

```
npm install @tensorflow/tfjs --save
```

6. We can now proceed to add the module to our index.js file:

```
const tf = require('@tensorflow/tfjs');
```

7. We will also require the body-parser module from Express.js to handle the incoming query data from the client side, which will be sent via AJAX POST requests. To do so, we use the following command:

```
npm install body-parser --save
```

8. We now create a body-parser object and bind it to the application using the following code:

```
var bodyParser = require('body-parser');
app.use(bodyParser.urlencoded({ extended: false }));
```

At this stage, package.json should contain the following snippet that lists the dependencies of your project:

```
"dependencies": {
    "@tensorflow/tfjs": "^0.15.1",
    "body-parser": "^1.18.3",
    "express": "^4.16.4"
}
```

Note that the preceding versions may change. We can now import the iris.json file, which we will be training our model on:

```
const iris = require('./iris.json');
```

With the initial setup done, we can now proceed to write the TF.js code to train on the available dataset.

Creating a TF.js model

Let's begin by reading the data we have stored in the `iris` variable to a `tensor2d` object:

1. In your `index.js` file, add the following code:

```
const trainingData = tf.tensor2d(iris.map(item=> [
    item.sepal_length, item.sepal_width, item.petal_length,
item.petal_width
]),[144,4])
```

We do not have any test data yet; this will be provided by the user.

2. Next, we create a one-hot encoding of the possible three varieties of flowers:

```
const outputData = tf.tensor2d(iris.map(item => [
    item.species === 'setosa' ? 1 : 0,
    item.species === 'virginica' ? 1 : 0,
    item.species === 'versicolor' ? 1 : 0
]), [144,3])
```

We are now ready to create the model for training. The following code might remind you of the code we used in the previous chapter when we were creating a model for the MNIST handwritten digits dataset. This is simply due to the fact that we are still using the concepts of TensorFlow, only in a different language!

3. We first declare a sequential TensorFlow model:

```
const model = tf.sequential();
```

4. Next, let's add a layer of neurons to the model:

```
model.add(tf.layers.dense({
    inputShape: 4,
    activation: 'sigmoid',
    units: 10
}));
```

The `inputShape` parameter indicates the shape of the input that will be added to this layer. The `units` parameter sets the number of neurons to be used in this layer. The `activation` function we are using is the `sigmoid` function.

5. Let's now add the output layer:

```
model.add(tf.layers.dense({
    inputShape: 10,
    units: 3,
```

```
    activation: 'softmax'
}));
```

Here, we will have 3 neurons in the output layer, and the input to be expected at this layer is 10, which matches the number of neurons in the previous layer.

 Apart from the input layer, we just have one hidden layer and the output layer. This is acceptable in this application because the dataset is small and the prediction is simple. Note that we used the `softmax` activation function here, which produces class probabilities as outputs.

This is particularly useful in our case as the problem is a multi-class classification problem.

6. With this done, we are now ready to compile our model. To do this, we use the following code:

```
model.compile({
    loss: "categoricalCrossentropy",
    optimizer: tf.train.adam()
});
```

Since we have a classification problem at hand where there are multiple possible labels, we use `categoricalCrossentropy` as the `loss` function. For optimization, the `adam` optimizer is used. You are encouraged to experiment with other hyperparameter values.

7. We can generate a summary of the model using the following code:

```
model.summary();
```

Next, we will train our TF.js model.

Training the TF.js model

We will now write an `async` function. The reason for doing this is so that the JavaScript on the client side that invokes our function doesn't get stuck waiting for the result. A function that will take time to complete in our program is the `train_data()` function. This function performs the training of the model:

```
async function train_data(){
    console.log("Training Started");
    for(let i=0;i<50;i++){
        let res = await model.fit(trainingData, outputData, {epochs: 50});
```

```
        console.log(`Iteration ${i}: ${res.history.loss[0]}`);
    }
    console.log("Training Complete");
}
```

The `train_data()` function can be run asynchronously. It also prints out the loss at every epoch of training to the console where we will run the server from. Let's now create an API that will invoke the `train_data()` function.

First, we create a *middleware* called `doTrain`, which will be run before the API for training and will return any data.

 You can read more about middlewares at `https://expressjs.com/en/guide/using-middleware.html`.

The `doTrain()` middleware accepts, in its arguments, the request made to the Node.js server, the variable for making the response, and the name of the function that will be used to forward the execution of the program after executing the block of code defined in the middleware:

```
var doTrain = async function (req, res, next) {
    await train_data();
    next();
}
```

The `doTrain` middleware calls the `train_data()` function and awaits its result. The `train_data()` function returns a *Promise* so that the execution continues without freezing. The `next()` function runs right after the `train_data()` function is complete and it merely passes the execution of the program to the function that is *chained* next to the middleware, as shown:

```
app.use(doTrain).post('/train', function(req, res) {
    res.send("1");
});
```

We now bind the `'/train'` route to the `express` app and then chain the `doTrain` middleware to it. Now, for every call made to the `'/train'` API, the middleware runs first and then the execution passes to the main block of code for the API. This block of code simply returns any arbitrary value to denote the completion of training.

Predicting using the TF.js model

After the training is done, we also need to create an API to invoke the prediction function and return the predicted result. We bind the API to the `'/predict'` route with a POST method to make a request to this API, as shown:

```
app.post('/predict', function(req, res) {
    var test = tf.tensor2d([parseFloat(req.body.sepLen),
parseFloat(req.body.sepWid),
parseFloat(req.body.petLen), parseFloat(req.body.petWid)], [1,4]);
    var out = model.predict(test);
    var maxIndex = 0;
    for (let i=1;i<out.size; i++){
        if (out.buffer().get(0, i) > out.buffer().get(0, maxIndex)){
            maxIndex = i;
        }
    }
    ans = "Undetermined";
    switch(maxIndex) {
        case 0:
            ans = "Setosa";
        break;
        case 1:
            ans = "Virginica";
        break;
        case 2:
            ans = "Versicolor";
        break;
    }
    console.log(ans);
    res.send(ans);
});
```

It is very simple to understand the code for the prediction API. Let's discuss it in parts:

```
app.post('/predict', function(req, res) {
```

This line binds the `'/predict'` route to the POST request method and opens the block of code for the statements that will handle requests made to this route:

```
    var test = tf.tensor2d([parseFloat(req.body.sepLen),
parseFloat(req.body.sepWid),
parseFloat(req.body.petLen), parseFloat(req.body.petWid)], [1,4]);
    var output = model.predict(test);
```

These lines create a TF.js `tensor2d` object from the data, which is received from the client side. It then runs the `predict` method on the model and stores the result in the output variable:

```
var maxIndex = 0;
for (let i=1;i<out.size; i++){
    if (out.buffer().get(0, i) > out.buffer().get(0, maxIndex)){
        maxIndex = i;
    }
}
```

This block of code merely finds the index that corresponds to the element in the `tensor2d` variable output that is highest. Remember that in a `softmax` activation output, the highest value corresponds to the predicted index.

After determining the maximum index from the output, we use a simple switch-case statement to decide what output is to be sent to the client from the API. The request data is also logged to the console visible on the server. Finally, we bind our Node.js application to listen to port 3000 using the following code:

```
app.listen(3000);
```

We will now create a simple client in the following section.

Creating a simple client

To handle the `'/'` route in our application, we add the following lines of code to `index.js`, which merely renders a static file, `index.html`, which is placed in the public folder:

```
app.use(express.static('./public')).get('/', function (req, res) {
    res.sendFile('./index.html');
});
```

Now, let's create the static `index.html` file by following these steps:

1. First, create a folder, `public`, and inside it, create `index.html`. Add the following code to the `index.html` file:

```
<html>
  <head>
    <title>TF.js Example - Iris Flower Classficiation</title>
  </head>
  <body>
```

```
<h1> TF.js Example - Iris Flower Classification </h1>
<hr>
<p>
    First, train the model. Then, use the text boxes to try any
dummy data.
</p>

<button id="train-btn">Train</button>

<hr><br>
<label for="sepLen">Sepal Length: </label>
<input type="number" id="sepLen" value="1" /><br>
<label for="sepWid">Sepal Width:  </label>
<input type="number" id="sepWid" value="1" /><br>
<label for="petLen">Petal Length: </label>
<input type="number" id="petLen" value="1" /><br>
<label for="petWid">Petal Width:  </label>
<input type="number" id="petWid" value="1" /><br>
<br>
<button id="send-btn" disabled"="true">Predict!</button>
<hr>
<h3> Result </h3>
<h4 id="res"></h4>

<script
src="https://cdnjs.cloudflare.com/ajax/libs/jquery/3.3.1/jquery.min
.js"></script>
```

2. After setting a simple UI to the client developed to call the APIs we have created using TF.js, we are ready to define the functions to deploy them from the client side. Notice that both the `"/train"` and `"/predict"` APIs will be called by a POST request:

```
<script>

  $('#train-btn').click(function(){
    $('#train-btn').prop('disabled', true);
    $('#train-btn').empty().append("Training...");
    $.ajax({
      type: 'POST',
      url: "/train",
      success: function(result) {
        console.log(result);
        $('#send-btn').prop('disabled', false);
        $('#train-btn').empty().append("Trained!");
      }
    });
  });
```

```
$('#send-btn').click(function(){
  var sepLen = $('#sepLen').val();
  var sepWid = $('#sepWid').val();
  var petLen = $('#petLen').val();
  var petWid = $('#petWid').val();
  $.ajax({
    type: 'POST',
    url: "/predict",
    data: {sepLen: sepLen, sepWid: sepWid, petLen: petLen, petWid:
petWid},
    success: function(result) {
      console.log(result);
      $('#res').empty().append(result);
    }
  });
});
</script>
</body>
</html>
```

Let's now run the TF.js web app.

Running the TF.js web app

With all the application coded, we are now ready to run our application. First, open a Terminal and make the tfjs-iris folder containing the package.json file as your working directory in it.

Run the following line of code to start the Node.js server:

```
node index.js
```

The command produces an output that resembles the following screenshot:

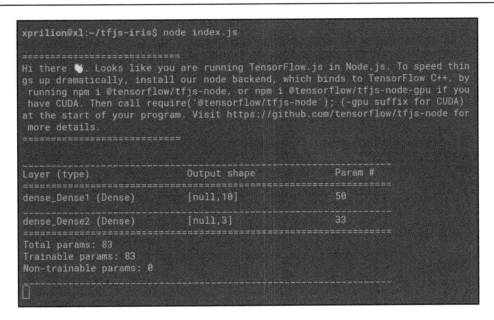

Now, along with this output, the server starts at port 3000 and we can view the same in the browser. Open a browser and type http://localhost:3000/ in the address bar to bring up the following output:

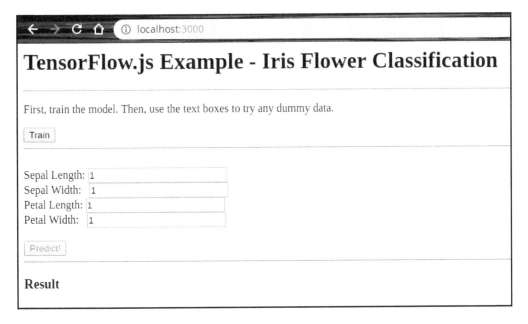

First, you must click on the **Train** button to invoke the `'/train'` API, which begins the training, and the button changes to a disabled state. Once the **Predict!** button is enabled, the training is complete and the user can send dummy data to the server to make predictions. Say we choose the 50th row of data from the dataset and send it to the server with an expected output of `Setosa`.

The following screenshot shows a small section of the final version of our project:

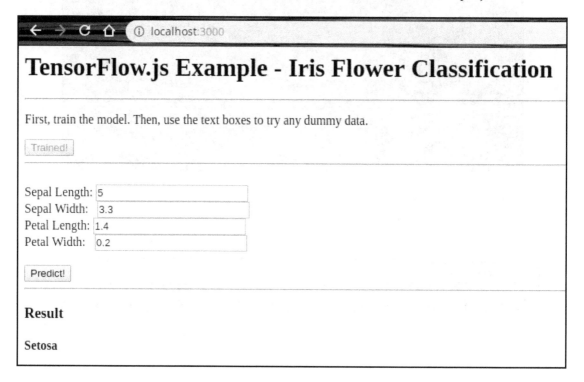

We see that the correct output is generated for the input provided.

Advantages and limitations of TF.js

Let's now summarize some of the advantages TF.js brings over TensorFlow, besides the ones we have already talked about in this chapter:

- **Automatic GPU support**: You don't need to install CUDA or GPU drivers separately with TF.js to benefit from the GPUs present on the system. This is because the browser itself implements GPU support.
- **Integration**: It is fairly simple to integrate TF.js into a web development project using Node.js and then import pretrained models to the project and run them in the browser.

However, it also has several disadvantages that have to be kept in mind whenever developing for production. Some of these are as follows:

- **Speed**: TF.js is suitable for small datasets. On large-scale datasets, the computation speed suffers heavily and is nearly 10x slower.
- **Lack of a tensor board**: This great tool, which enables TensorFlow models to be visualized, is missing in the JavaScript port of the framework since TF.js is only an API.
- **Incomplete support of APIs**: Not all of the TensorFlow APIs are available on TF.js, and so you might have to rethink the code logic or create your own functions to use certain features while developing with TF.js.

Summary

In this chapter, we learned how easy it is to create models with TF.js. You not only get the whole JavaScript ecosystem to work with, but you also get all the pretrained TensorFlow models within TF.js. We developed a simple web application using the Iris dataset and, along the way, we learned about several components that TF.js has to offer. By now, we have already built two simple end-to-end deep learning-based web applications.

Our progress is indeed apparent. In the upcoming chapters, we will be building our own deep learning APIs and using them to create intelligent web applications. But before that, let's make ourselves familiar with the whole concept of APIs in the next chapter.

3
Getting Started with Different Deep Learning APIs for Web Development

This section explains the usage of APIs in software development in general and shows how we can use different state-of-the-art deep learning APIs for building intelligent web applications. We'll cover areas including **Natural Language Processing** (**NLP**) and computer vision.

This section comprises the following chapters:

- Chapter 5, *Deep Learning through APIs*
- Chapter 6, *Deep Learning on Google Cloud Platform Using Python*
- Chapter 7, *DL on AWS Using Python: Object Detection and Home Automation*
- Chapter 8, *Deep Learning on Microsoft Azure Using Python*

Deep Learning through APIs

5

So far, we have become familiar with the basic pipeline that is followed in a deep learning project. We have completed two basic end-to-end projects in previous chapters using the Keras and TensorFlow.js libraries. We have become familiar with Python libraries such as NumPy, pandas, and Keras, and we have also seen how deep learning models can be developed using JavaScript. We have also used the Flask framework to create an API out of a deep learning model. In `chapter 4`, *Getting Started with TensorFlow.js*, we used third-party **Application Programming Interfaces** (**APIs**) to create a web application.

In this chapter, we are going to study the whole concept of APIs in detail. Starting with a more informal definition of APIs, we are going to take a look at all APIs that are relevant to deep learning. We will first look at some of the most widely known deep learning APIs, and then we will look at some lesser-known deep learning APIs. We will also learn how to choose a deep learning API provider.

In this chapter, we will be covering the following topics:

- What is an API?
- How an API is different from a library?
- Some widely known deep learning APIs
- Some lesser-known deep learning APIs
- Choosing a deep learning API provider

What is an API?

Let's first consider a problem scenario.

Imagine that you are working on a web application that needs an image recognition module to be integrated into it. But you are not into computer vision and deep learning. You have a very strict deadline to meet for the project. You cannot afford to commit to studying deep learning and then complete the project's image recognition module. What should you do now? Will your project be completed by the specified deadline?

It definitely won't! However, with the power of APIs, you will be able to easily integrate the image recognition module into your web application. Let's now discuss the concept of APIs in a bit more detail.

An API is a set of functions (although technically an API can consist of just one function) that can be integrated into an application to perform certain tasks. Often, as developers, there are specific utilities from our favorite websites that we wish to integrate into our own applications. For example, Twitter provides an API for retrieving tweets that match a certain keyword. We can use this API to collect data, analyze it, and eventually come up with interesting insights about data.

Companies such as Facebook, Google, Stack Overflow, and LinkedIn provide APIs for certain tasks, and it is really worth checking them out as a developer. APIs are virtually analogous to websites. When we click on something in a website, we are redirected to another page/section. In most cases, we get a web page as the output. But APIs generally do not produce a good-looking web page as their output. APIs are meant to be used from within the code, and the output of an API is generally in some popular data interchange format, such as JSON or XML. The output is then processed accordingly with respect to the application for which the API is used. An API lets you do the tasks you want to do by providing a suite of utilities or an ecosystem without you having to worry about the details.

You can test an API nowadays without having to write one bit of code. For example, you can use an API client such as Postman and test an open API that you really like, and no code is required to be written in order to do that.

What is even more magical about APIs is that you can write code, for example, in Java and use an API developed in Python. This is particularly useful when you are working in a team where people are very particular about the different programming languages they use. One of your teammates might be very comfortable working with Java while another teammate may be a Python expert. So, the whole concept of APIs really comes in handy in these situations.

We are going to discuss some of the deep learning APIs that are provided by Google AI, Facebook AI Research, and others shortly. We will see how these APIs can be used to develop intelligent web applications in the upcoming chapters.

The importance of using APIs

Besides saving you a lot of effort in creating and deploying your own deep learning model when you need a quick production or a minimal working product demo, APIs can provide several benefits, such as these:

- **A standard, stable model**:
    - APIs for deep learning are often created by an entire group of developers working together on industry-standard technology and research tools that may not be available to all developers. Also, the models deployed through commercial APIs are often very stable to use and provide state-of-the-art features, including scalability, customization, and accuracy. So, if you're facing accuracy issues, which is a common situation in the production of deep learning models, choosing an API is a good choice.

- **High-performance models**:
    - Commercial deep learning APIs often run on very powerful servers and are optimized to a great degree, such that they can perform their tasks very quickly. Therefore, such APIs are very handy if you wish to speed up the learning of your deep learning ecosystem.

- **A common platform for developers**:
  - While it is very simple to start coding anything from scratch, it becomes very tough when the person who coded it in the first place leaves without producing proper documentation and a new person has to pick up where they left off. Commercial APIs define a set standard of operations, and applications built with such APIs integrated into them are easy to maintain because API providers also always include extensive documentation, meaning developers can learn about the APIs beforehand.

- **Regular and seamless updates**:
  - It is often expensive for a nascent-stage company to afford development time to improve deep learning models once they have got a first version running, especially if their entire business model isn't particularly centered on artificial intelligence. Any such use case would benefit greatly from API usage because APIs are maintained by people who push regular updates and new features.

Considering all this, then, using an API provides the latest technology, high performance, and ever-evolving models that can be plugged into an application once and then be used for years without ever having to think about the APIs again.

Now, you may ask what the difference is between an API and a library. Let's find out in the next section.

How is an API different from a library?

Nowadays, the terms *library* and *API* are used interchangeably. There are many similarities between the two, but they are different in many aspects. Much like an API, a library also provides a collection of functions and classes that can be used as per your needs. The following are some pointers that will help you to distinguish between a library and an API:

- Libraries are generally specific to programming languages. For example, you cannot use the SciPy Python library if you are using a PHP programming environment. However, you can develop an API that uses SciPy and then consume the API using your PHP code.
- Developers do not have direct access to an API. APIs are consumed in different ways to how libraries are. Many APIs enforce some kind of authentication before a developer can actually use them. We do not see this very often when it comes to using a library. You can easily override and overload a library function or class and use it as you will.

- Libraries and APIs can be used in conjunction with each other. Many libraries use different APIs internally and vice versa.

These should give you some sense of the basic differences between a library and an API. However, if you are still finding it difficult to draw the line, don't worry about it: we will be looking at lots of examples, and by the time you are done with them, you will definitely be in a position to differentiate between APIs and libraries.

We will now introduce some of the APIs that are widely used for developing deep learning-enabled applications, some very widely known and some not that popular.

Some widely known deep learning APIs

In this section, we are going to take a look at some of the most widely used APIs, which are deployed for a variety of deep learning tasks, such as image recognition, sentiment detection from an image, sentiment classification, speech-to-text conversion, and so on. To limit our discussion in this section, we will divide deep learning tasks into two broad groups:

- Computer vision and image processing
- Natural language processing

We will then list some of the common tasks related to each of these groups and discuss the APIs that can be used to accomplish those tasks.

Let's now quickly list some common deep learning tasks and assign them to their categories:

- **Computer vision and image processing**:
    - **Image search**: Just like Google Search, image search engines allow us to search for images similar to a particular image.
    - **Image detection**: This is detecting what an image is about. It is also known as label detection.
    - **Object localization**: Given an image containing a set of different objects, this involves detecting a particular object in the image.
    - **Content moderation**: Given an image, this involves the detection of inappropriate content.
    - **Image attributing**: Given an image, this involves the extraction of different traits of the image.

- **Natural language processing**:
  - **Parts-of-speech tagging**: Given a piece of text, this involves the extraction of the parts of speech that the text contains.
  - **Topic summarization**: Given a piece of text, this involves determining the topic that the text is about.
  - **Sentiment classification**: Given some text, this involves predicting the sentiment that the text is conveying.
  - **Named entity recognition**: This involves the automatic recognition of different entities present in a given sentence.
  - **Speech-to-text conversion**: This involves the extraction of the text contained in a piece of speech.

All of the tasks listed here are extremely useful in our day-to-day lives and it is exciting to know that we can make applications that are able to do these tasks for us with the APIs that we are going to discuss now.

 There are other deep learning APIs for making casual inferences at scale, but for the time being, we can ignore them and focus on the two areas that are most impacted by deep learning.

The following table is a compilation of some of the most widely used deep learning APIs in the industry:

Provider	API	Group
Google	Vision API	Computer vision and image processing
	Video Intelligence API	
	Natural Language API	Natural language processing
	Speech-to-Text API	
	Text-to-Speech API	
	Translation API	
	Dialogflow API	
Facebook	DensePose	Computer vision and image processing
	Detectron	

Amazon	Amazon Rekognition	Computer vision and image processing
	Amazon Comprehend	Natural language processing
	Amazon Textract	
	Amazon Polly	
	Amazon Translate	
	Amazon Transcribe	
Microsoft	Computer Vision	Computer vision and image processing
	Video Indexer	
	Face	
	Content Moderator	
	Text Analytics	Natural language processing
	Bing Spell Check	
	Translator Text	
	Language Understanding	

The APIs shown in the preceding table are the most popular ones when it comes to using well-tested and scalable deep learning APIs. However, there are some other names that are yet to grow as popular as those. In the next section, we are going to take a look at them.

Some lesser-known deep learning APIs

The following table gives some details about a few lesser-known APIs:

Provider	API	Group
IBM Watson	Watson Virtual Recognition	Computer vision and image processing
	Watson Text to Speech	Natural language processing
	Watson Natural Language Classifier	
	Watson Conversation	
	Watson Natural Language Understanding	
AT&T	AT&T Speech	Natural language processing
Wit.ai	Speech	Natural language processing
	Message	
	Entities	

Now, among this ocean (well, almost) of APIs, how do you choose a particular provider for a specific task? It can be tricky and demands a discussion. In this section, we are going to discuss some of the strategies that can effectively help us to make these decisions.

Choosing a deep learning API provider

With the long list of API providers for deep learning that could be compiled, it can be a daunting task to decide which API you require. However, there are some simple rules that you can follow to come up with the most suitable API for your needs, and we'll be discussing a few of them in detail here:

- **Platforms**:
    - As simple as it sounds, this is probably the foremost factor that comes into play when you are choosing your API provider. Most of the time, if you are developing a product that runs on Google technologies, for instance, you might want to use the deep learning APIs that Google provides, simply because they would integrate seamlessly with the application development interface that you are working with.
    - More often than not, a development environment also offers templated solutions for using its deep learning APIs that are very simple to set up. Sometimes, the provider may also offer extra incentives for using their APIs to develop new products.
- **Performance**:
    - With access to multiple providers' APIs to perform a single task, you have the option of comparing their performance and then choosing. In such cases, it's up to you as to the metric to use when comparing and judging different APIs.
- **Cost**:
    - Different providers use different methods of costing, and this can play a huge role in deciding which provider you use. A certain provider may have a comfortable limit on the number of free API calls for experimentation and so might be a lucrative option for you. Often, experimenting developers and students choose to go with the provider that has the best offering in terms of cost.

Besides these three factors, there could be some other undeniable factors, such as a company requiring the usage of a certain API or your own inclination toward a certain API provider. However, unless on a large scale, it mostly matters very little which provider is used, since they all provide similar performance for small- to medium-scale usage.

Summary

In this chapter, we took a detailed look at the term API. In Chapter 3, *Creating Your First Deep Learning Web Application*, we saw how an API can be written in Python using Flask and we saw how to use that API in a web application. We now know how an API is different from a language library and how important it is to make use of APIs. We became familiar with a variety of deep learning APIs that are offered by some top-notch organizations.

As we progress through the upcoming chapters, we will see how to use these APIs to build powerful and intelligent web applications. We will start with the deep learning APIs provided by Google Cloud Platform in the next chapter.

6
Deep Learning on Google Cloud Platform Using Python

In the previous chapter, we saw a variety of deep learning APIs that are provided by various organizations. We also saw their applicability broadly grouped into two categories—the first was computer vision and image processing, and the second was natural language processing. We are going to continue exploring deep learning APIs in this chapter as well. This chapter introduces you to **Google Cloud Platform** (**GCP**) and three APIs offered by it in the area of deep learning.

In this chapter, we will cover the following topics:

- Setting up your GCP account
- Creating your first project on GCP
- Using the Dialogflow API in Python
- Using the Cloud Vision API in Python
- Using the Cloud Translation API in Python

Technical requirements

You can access the code for this chapter from `https://github.com/PacktPublishing/Hands-On-Python-Deep-Learning-for-Web/tree/master/Chapter6`.

To run the code in this chapter, you'll need to have Python 3.6+ on your system.

Other requisite installations will be introduced during the course of this chapter.

Setting up your GCP account

Before we proceed with using the APIs offered by GCP, you must set up your GCP account. Assuming that you already have a Google account—first, head to `https://cloud.google.com/`. GCP gives you $300 of credit (which you can use for a period of 12 months) if you are signing up to it for the first time; this credit is sufficient enough to accommodate many good projects and enable you to try out the offerings of GCP. Once this has been done, we can follow these steps:

1. At the top-right corner of GCP's home page, you should be able to locate a **Try free** button. Just click on it:

2. If you are not signed in to your Google account, you will be asked to sign in. Select your country accordingly and make sure you check the **Terms of service** box. After this, click on **AGREE AND CONTINUE**. You will see a page as in the following screenshot:

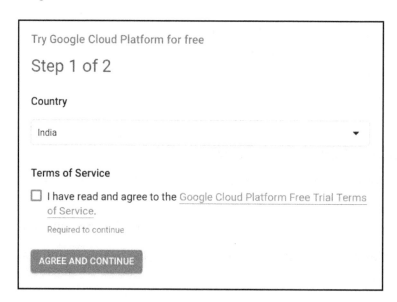

3. Then, you will be asked to enter the details for a payment method of your choice. Even if you have free credits, in order to use GCP's utilities, you need to set up a valid billing account. But don't worry, you will not be charged from your billing account unless you allow GCP to do so. During your free trial, all the billable utilities that you will use on GCP will be deducted from your free credit only. Once the limit for your free credit ends, GCP will send you a reminder.

Once your billing formalities are done, you should end up at GCP's console page, which looks like this:

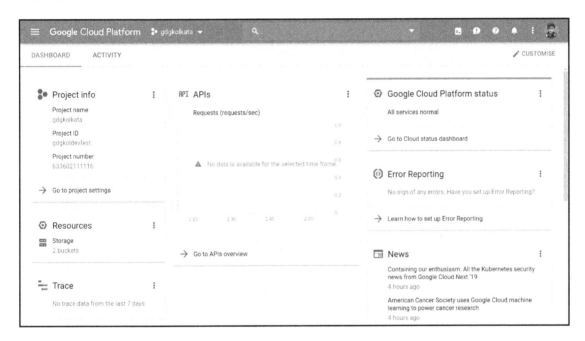

This is actually your GCP dashboard, which gives you an overall summary of your GCP usage. GCP also lets you customize the tags that appear on your GCP console.

You should now be done with the GCP account setup. To be able to use the utilities in GCP, you need to create a GCP project with a valid billing account tagged to it. In the next section, you will see how to do that.

Creating your first project on GCP

A project helps you organize all your GCP resources systematically. Creating a project on GCP can be done in just a matter of a few clicks:

1. After signing in to your Google account, open up your GCP console using `https://console.cloud.google.com`. In the top-left corner, you should see **Google Cloud Platform** and just beside that, you can see a drop-down list, as shown:

2. If you did create any projects while signing up for GCP or previously, then one of your projects will appear in the marked area (**fast-ai-exploration** and **gcp-api** are two projects that I created on GCP). Now, click on the down arrow and a popup should appear:

3. Click on **NEW PROJECT** to proceed. You should end up on a page, shown in the following screenshot, that will ask you to specify the project's name. GCP automatically generates an ID for the project that you are creating but it also lets you edit that ID according to your choices:

4. After you are done specifying the initial details of your project, just click on **CREATE** and the project will be created. Once the project is created, it should appear in the projects list. You can always navigate to this list using the handy dropdown that GCP provides on its console page. You can see this in the following screenshot:

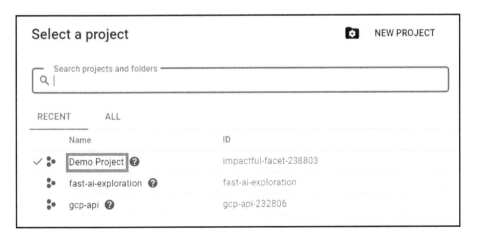

If you want to learn more about GCP projects, you can check the official documentation at `https://cloud.google.com/storage/docs/projects`. GCP is equipped with a wide suite of various utilities that can be found at `https://cloud.google.com/products/`. You are encouraged to take a look and explore them with respect to your interests.

GCP provides us with a wide range of APIs that can be used for a variety of tasks, including deep learning. In the next couple of sections, we will see how some of the most widely used deep learning APIs can be consumed using Python code. We will start with Dialogflow.

Using the Dialogflow API in Python

Before we start to learn how to use the Dialogflow API in Python, let's understand what Dialogflow is all about.

Dialogflow (formerly known as **api.ai**) provides a suite of utilities for building natural and rich conversational interfaces, such as voice assistants and chatbots. It is powered by deep learning and natural language processing and is used by a large number of companies. It seamlessly integrates with websites, mobile applications, and many popular platforms, such as Facebook Messenger, Amazon Alexa, and so on. Dialogflow provides us with three major components for building a conversational user interface:

- The best practices and processes that can easily be applied to any conversational user interface
- Functionalities to add any custom logic that might be required for building a conversational user interface
- Facilities to train agents so as to fine-tune the overall experience of the interface

Now, we will see how Dialogflow can be used to create a simple application in Python. You can refer to `https://dialogflow.com` to learn more about Dialogflow.

We will begin with the creation of a Dialogflow account.

Creating a Dialogflow account

Creating a Dialogflow account is simple and easy. The process involves the following steps:

1. Visit `https://console.dialogflow.com/api-client/#/login` and you will see the following screen:

2. After clicking the sign in with **Google** button, you'll be asked to choose which Google account you want to use with Dialogflow.
3. On selecting the account, you might be asked to allow **Account Permissions** for Diagflow and also to accept the Dialogflow terms and conditions.

Creating a new agent

After creating an account, you will be greeted with a dashboard that will either display your active Dialogflow projects or ask you to create a new agent to be displayed—but what is an **agent**?

An agent—in Dialogflow terminology—is a piece of software that performs the task of receiving input from users, which might be in the format of text, audio, image, or video. It then tries to determine the *intent* or the previously defined appropriate action corresponding to the input. The matched intent might perform an *action* or it may simply arrive on a hypertext response to the query made by the user input. Finally, the agent returns the results to the user.

To create a new agent, in the left-hand side navigation menu of the Dialogflow console, click on **Create Agent**.

You will be presented with a screen that looks like this:

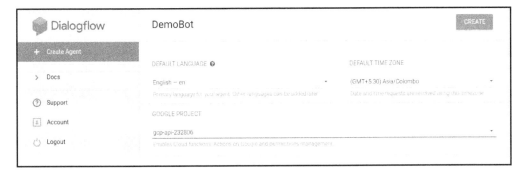

We have named our agent **DemoBot** and set the default language to **English**. Further, we had to select a Google project for the agent.

A Google project—or simply a **project**—is a term that you encounter in the study of GCP. A project encompasses the entire array of resources allocated toward any software project that uses those resources and is financed by a single billing account on GCP. No resources can be allocated without defining a project for them. Further, no project can be created without adding a valid billing option to it.

You will now be able to see a screen, as in the following screenshot, with certain default intents provided for your agent:

On the left, you can see the navigation menu, which provides all the various modules that can be brought together in your agent for better human-like interaction provided by the software. In the right-hand side panel, you have the option to test your agent at any moment with any input you provide. This will come in handy during the development of responses and when testing the matching of intents with input provided.

Creating a new intent

To create a new intent for our agent, follow these steps:

1. Click the **Create Intent** button at the top-right corner of the middle section.
2. You need to provide a name for this intent—let's say `Dummy Intent`.
3. We will then need to provide some training phrases that would trigger this intent. Let's say we provide three training phrases, as shown:

Now, we can expect this intent to be called on whenever the system encounters the phrases (or similar phrases) mentioned in the training.

4. We can now add some responses that our agent will make when this intent is invoked, as shown:

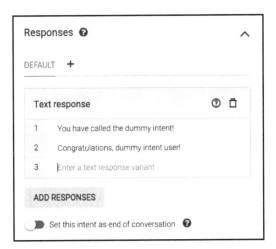

5. At the top-right corner of the middle section, click on the **SAVE** button to save the new intent and you will be notified that the agent training has started.

For a small agent, the training completes within seconds and you'll be presented with an **Agent training completed** notification.

We are now ready to test whether our agent is able to execute this intent.

Testing your agent

On the right-hand side section of your Dialogflow console, you'll be able to test your agent. In the top text field, enter your query. In our agent, to call Dummy Intent, we'll write Talk to the dummy.

If the intent matches correctly, you'll be able to see the response from Dummy Intent, as shown:

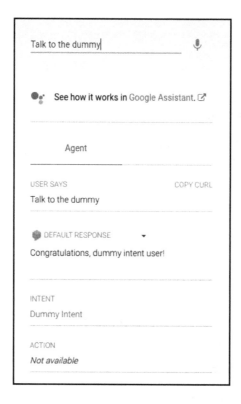

In the previous screenshot, you will observe that the input of the user is `Talk to the dummy` and the response generated is one of the two responses we defined in the responses for `Dummy Intent`. You can observe that the intent that was matched to the input was `Dummy Intent`.

We will now look at how we can invoke the agent using Python.

Installing the Dialogflow Python SDK

In this section, we will demonstrate how you can use the Dialogflow Python API V2 with your Dialogflow agent to bring interactivity to your application built using Python. Let's first understand how the several components of the DialogFlow ecosystem interact with the following diagram:

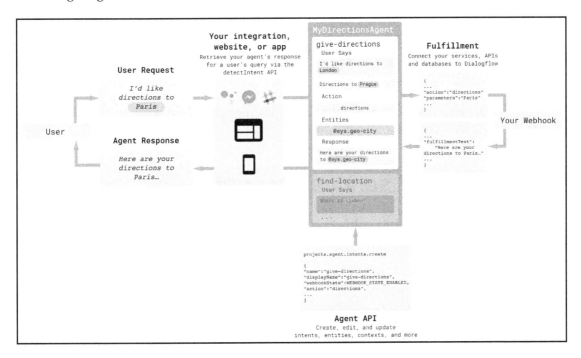

The user creates the input, which is sent to the agent via integration APIs, websites, or apps. The agent matches the user input to the available intents and produces a fulfillment of the **query**. The response is sent back to the user interface by the means of a webhook and the response is presented to the user.

It is quite possible for the integration APIs to include services other than Dialogflow. You could create an application that could propagate the same user query to multiple agents and consolidate their response.

Alternatively, the developer can introduce middleware handlers or integrations, which would preprocess or postprocess the user query and agent response:

1. To install the Dialogflow Python SDK, we use the following command in the terminal:

   pip install dialogflow

 It is highly recommended that you create a virtual environment using virtualenv before using the previous command to have clean and unbroken dependencies. To learn more about virtualenv, refer to https://virtualenv.pypa.io/en/latest/.

2. After the installation is complete, you will be able to import the Dialogflow API to your project by using the following import code:

   ```
   import dialogflow
   ```

We'll now create a GCP service account to authenticate our Python script in order to use the Dialogflow agent we created.

Creating a GCP service account

A GCP service account manages the permissions provided to access a GCP resource. The Dialogflow agent we created was a GCP resource and so to use it from the Python API, we'll need a service account:

1. In the GCP console, from the left-hand side navigation menu, go to **APIs** | **Services** | **Credentials**.
2. Click the **Create credentials** button to get the following options:

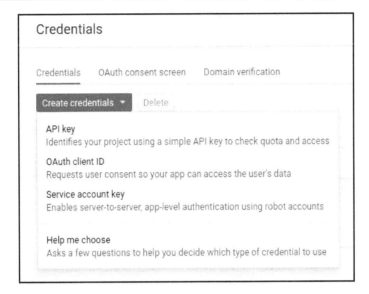

3. Click on **Service account key**. In the page that comes up next, select **Dialogflow Integrations** as the service account and **JSON** as the key type. After clicking **Create**, a JSON file is downloaded to your computer.

4. Note down the address of this JSON file—for example, `/home/user/Downloads/service-account-file.json`. The file name could differ, as it is provided by the GCP console when you download the file to your computer.

5. Open this file to obtain the project ID.

6. Now, use the following commands—with suitable replacements as present on your system—in the terminal to export the credentials to the environment variables:

- In Linux (Terminal):

```
export
GOOGLE_APPLICATION_CREDENTIALS="<your_service_account_file_location>"
export DIALOGFLOW_PROJECT_ID="<your_project_id>"
```

- In Windows (Command Prompt):

```
set GOOGLE_APPLICATION_CREDENTIALS=<your_service_account_file_location>
set DIALOGFLOW_PROJECT_ID=<your_project_id>
```

With this done, we are now ready to write the Python script that will call our Dialogflow agent.

Please note that the preceding commands only set the variables for the current session. You need to run the commands every time you restart the session.

Calling the Dialogflow agent using Python API

In this example, we'll be creating a simple Python-based API that calls to the agent we created in the Dialogflow console to invoke Dummy Intent, as shown:

1. Firstly, we must import the Dialogflow module to the project. To do so, use the following code:

   ```
   import dialogflow
   ```

2. To get the project ID into the script, we can fetch it from the runtime environment variables. To do so, use the following code:

   ```
   import os
   project_id = os.getenv("DIALOGFLOW_PROJECT_ID")
   ```

3. We will also declare a unique session ID to store the records of the conversations made in any single session with the user:

   ```
   session_id="any_random_unique_string"
   ```

4. We'll now create a handy function that will allow us to repeatedly perform a set of preprocessing statements required to call the Dialogflow agent:

   ```
   def detect_intent(project_id, session_id, text, language_code):

       session_client = dialogflow.SessionsClient()
       session = session_client.session_path(project_id, session_id)
       text_input = dialogflow.types.TextInput(text=text,
   language_code=language_code)
       query_input = dialogflow.types.QueryInput(text=text_input)
       response = session_client.detect_intent(session=session,
   query_input=query_input)
       return response.query_result.fulfillment_text
   ```

   In the preceding code, we will first initialize a SessionsClient object. A session records the complete interaction between the user and the Dialogflow agent during one uninterrupted conversation. Next, we must set the path of the session, which is the mapping of the project to a unique session ID.

The next two lines of the preceding function definition are used to create a Dialogflow `QueryInput` object that contains a Dialogflow `TextInput` object. The `query_input` variable holds the message the user inputs for the Dialogflow agent.

The next line invokes the `detect_intent()` method of the `SessionsClient` object. The `session ID-project ID` mapping, along with the input, is passed as the parameter to the method. The response of the Dialogflow agent is stored in the response variable. The function returns the fulfillment text response.

5. Let's now use this method. First, declare a message to pass to the Dialogflow agent. Recall the training phrases we provided to our Dialogflow agent for `Dummy Intent`. We'll pass a message that is similar to the training phrases:

```
message = "Can I talk to the dummy?"

fulfillment_text = detect_intent(project_id, session_id, message,
'en')

print(fulfillment_text)
```

We will get an output that is among the two responses we defined for `Dummy Intent`.

6. Generate the response variable in the `detect_intent()` method, which can be done by adding the following line of code in the `detect_intent()` function:

```
def detect_intent(project_id, session_id, text, language_code):
    ...
    response = session_client.detect_intent(session=session,
query_input=query_input)
    print(response) ### <--- ADD THIS LINE
    return response.query_result.fulfillment_text
```

You will get the following JSON:

```
response_id: "d1a7b2bf-0000-0000-0000-81161394cc24"
query_result {
  query_text: "talk to the dummy?"
  parameters {
  }
  all_required_params_present: true
  fulfillment_text: "Congratulations, dummy intent user!"
  fulfillment_messages {
    text {
      text: "Congratulations, dummy intent user!"
```

```
  }
}
intent {
  name: "projects/gcp-
api-232806/agent/intents/35e15aa5-0000-0000-0000-672d46bcefa7"
    display_name: "Dummy Intent"
}
intent_detection_confidence: 0.8199999928474426
language_code: "en"
}
```

You will observe that the name of the matched intent is Dummy Intent and the output that we had in this call of the agent is Congratulations, dummy intent user!.

There are several other ways of using the Dialogflow API using Python, including—but not limited to—audio-visual input and sensor-based inputs. The Dialogflow agents can be integrated with major platforms, such as Google Assistant, Facebook Messenger, Slack, Telegram, WhatsApp, and several others, as shown:

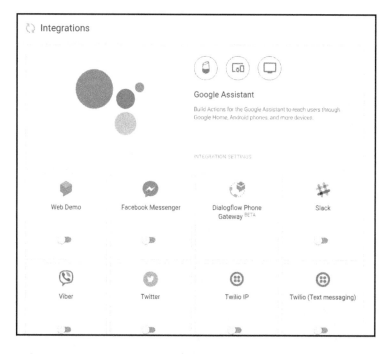

The Dialogflow ecosystem is rapidly introducing new features and is increasingly moving toward providing complete AI-based chatbots that can perform several tasks at the same time.

In the next section, we'll explore another GCP API that can be used to predict the contents of images and videos.

Using the Cloud Vision API in Python

Computer vision is the field of making computers understand images and make sense of them. Common computer vision tasks include image classification, image detection, image segmentation, and so on. As discussed in earlier chapters, the field of computer vision has been heavily affected by the effectiveness of deep learning in achieving human-level (and sometimes even better) performance.

The Cloud Vision API provides us with a lot of utilities for performing computer vision tasks. Cloud Vision allows us to use the pre-trained models as well as build our own custom production-ready models that cater to our needs (such as AutoML Vision Beta). Let's now briefly look at the features that are offered by the Cloud Vision API:

- Label detection
- Optical character recognition
- Handwriting recognition
- Landmark detection
- Object localization
- Image search
- Product search

Apart from the previously mentioned features, Cloud Vision also lets us extract different attributes of a given image. The following screenshot shows this utility:

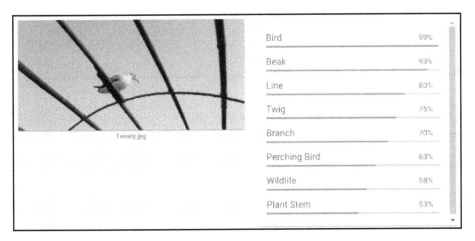

As we can see, when given an image, the Cloud Vision API automatically extracts its attributes. You can also try this by going to `https://cloud.google.com/vision/`.

We have been using the term **pre-trained models** from earlier chapters. We have also seen how the Cloud Vision API lets us incorporate the pre-trained models. It will be worth digging a bit deeper into the term pre-trained models in order to understand the importance of using them.

The importance of using pre-trained models

The use of pre-trained models is commonly referred to as **transfer learning**. Transfer learning is not something that is very fundamental to deep learning and it is just a methodology. It doesn't denote a particular deep learning model but its implications of transfer learning are very effective, especially in a deep learning context.

We human beings do not learn each and every task from scratch; we try to utilize our past experiences to do tasks that are similar in nature. This is transfer learning. We tend to transfer the knowledge of our past experiences to similar tasks that we are met with.

But how is this applicable to deep learning? Let's find out.

When a neural network is trained for a particular task, it tries to estimate the value of the best possible weight's matrices. Now, when you attempt to train another network on a similar kind of task, it turns out that you can use the weights from the previous task. The definition "similarity" is broad here and can be avoided for the time being. But you may wonder what the advantage here is. Well, the advantages are manifold, but here are a couple of examples:

- You don't need to train your neural network from scratch, which saves you a lot of time.
- It leverages the opportunity to use state-of-the-art results from a problem domain that is similar to yours.

In literature, the task that you use the network weights from is called a source task and the task that you apply the weights to is called the target task. The network model that you use the weights from is referred to as the pre-trained model. Goodfellow et al. gave a very subtle definition of transfer learning in their book *Deep Learning*:

> "[A] situation where what has been learned in one setting is exploited to improve generalization in another setting."

The use of transfer learning has shown exceptional results in a wide range of deep learning applications in areas such as **Natural Language Processing** (**NLP**), computer vision, and more. But transfer learning has its limitations as well:

- Transfer learning can result in a performance drop when the source task is not sufficiently related to the task where transfer learning is being used.
- It gets difficult sometimes to determine how much transfer is required from the source task to the target task.

For an in-depth study of transfer learning, you are encouraged to go through the book *Hands-On Transfer Learning with Python* by Dipanjan et al. We will now learn—with the help of an example—how to use the Cloud Vision API using Python.

Setting up the Vision Client libraries

The Cloud Vision API is available through a set of libraries for different languages, called the Vision Client libraries.

One such library offered in this set is the Python Cloud Vision Client library, which we will be using in our example:

1. To install the Python Cloud Vision Client library, we use the following command in the terminal:

```
pip install --upgrade google-cloud-vision
```

It is highly recommended that you use a Python virtual environment to install the Vision Client library.

2. After the installation is complete, we will need to set up a service account to use the API.

3. As discussed previously, the steps to be followed for setting up a service account are as follows:

    1. Open the Google Cloud console.
    2. Go to **APIs | Services | Credentials.**
    3. Click on **Create credentials.**
    4. Choose **New Service Account** in the drop-down menu for selecting the service account.
    5. Fill in any name for the service account.
    6. Leave **Role** unchecked. This is not needed when using the Cloud Vision API.
    7. Click on **Create**. Confirm any warning boxes that appear.
    8. The `service account credentials` JSON file gets downloaded to your computer.

4. Now, as we did previously, export this downloaded file to the system environment. To do this, use the following command:

    - In Linux (Terminal):

```
export
GOOGLE_APPLICATION_CREDENTIALS="/home/user/Downloads/service-
account-file.json"
```

    - In Windows (Command Prompt):

```
set GOOGLE_APPLICATION_CREDENTIALS=/home/user/Downloads/service-
account-file.json
```

5. As a final step before using the Cloud Vision API, we need to enable the API within the project that we created the service account for. To do so, do the following:

    1. In the Google Cloud console's left-hand side navigation panel, click on **APIs and Services.**
    2. Click on **Enable APIs & Services.**
    3. Find the Cloud Vision API in the list that appears.
    4. Click on **Enable.**

After this, we are ready to use the Cloud Vision API using Python in our script.

The Cloud Vision API calling using Python

Let's create a new Python script (or Jupyter notebook). In order to use the Cloud Vision API, we first need to import the Cloud Vision Client library.

1. To do this, we use the following code:

```
from google.cloud import vision
```

2. With this, we're ready to move on and use the client library. In our example, we will annotate an image. The image annotation service is provided by the imageAnnotatorClient() function in the Vision library. We will create an object of the method:

```
client = vision.ImageAnnotatorClient()
```

3. Now, let's load the file to be tested for annotation into the program:

```
with open("test.jpg", 'rb') as image_file:
    content = image_file.read()
```

 Note that you should have the test.jpg file in the same working directory in order for this to work.

4. The file is currently a raw binary data file for the program. For the Cloud Vision API to work, we need to convert this into a type of image that the Vision Client will accept:

```
image = vision.types.Image(content=content)
```

5. Finally, we make the call for GCP to annotate the image via the Cloud Vision API:

```
response = client.label_detection(image=image)
labels = response.label_annotations
```

After printing the labels set by the vision API, we will be able to see all the possible objects and features that the Cloud Vision API is able to detect in the picture provided, as shown:

If you print `labels`, the result should look like this:

```
{
    "labelAnnotations": [
        {
            "description": "Horizon",
            "mid": "/m/0d1n2",
            "score": 0.98734426,
            "topicality": 0.98734426
        },
        {
            "description": "Sky",
            "mid": "/m/01bqvp",
            "score": 0.981505,
            "topicality": 0.981505
        },
        ...
    ]
}
```

The predicted labels are `Sky`, `Horizon`, `Atmosphere`, `Sunrise`, `Sunset`, `Morning`, `Ocean`, `Calm`, `Wing`, and `Evening`.

The preceding predictions are very close to the real scene that is captured in the preceding photo. It was sunrise and taken from the window of an airplane.

Using the Cloud Translation API in Python

The Cloud Translation API helps developers to easily integrate language translation functionalities into their applications. It is powered by state-of-the-art neural machine translation, which can be thought of as an amalgamation of deep learning and machine translation. The Cloud Translation API provides programmatic interfaces for using pre-trained models and building production-ready custom models.

Many developers use the Cloud Translation API's pre-trained models to dynamically translate a given set of text into a target language. The Cloud Translate API supports more than 100 languages. But this language library is evolving to empower the developer community. The following screenshot shows a translation of some text written in English to Bengali:

You can always try this on `https://cloud.google.com/translate/`. But sometimes, the language of a given text might be unknown itself. The Cloud Translation API provides a service called **label detection** to handle situations like this.

The AutoML variant of the Cloud Translation API lets us build custom models with respect to language pairs (the source language and target language) according to our needs.

Setting up the Cloud Translate API for Python

To use the Cloud Translation API with Python, we must first install the Google Cloud Translate Python library.

1. To do so, use the following `pip` command in the terminal:

```
pip install google-cloud-translate
```

2. Now, as done previously, create a service account and download the credentials file. Export this file to the path for the GOOGLE_APPLICATION_CREDENTIALS environment variable.

3. Next, find Cloud Translate API in the list of APIs to enable. Once done, we're ready to make translations directly from Python using GCP.

Using the Google Cloud Translation Python library

Create a new Jupyter notebook or a new Python script. We will now import the Google Cloud Translate API to our project.

1. To do so, use the following code:

    ```
    from google.cloud import translate_v2 as translate
    ```

2. We would need to create a Cloud Translate API object to make the service calls. We can do so as follows:

    ```
    translate_client = translate.Client()
    ```

3. Let's now begin with the translation process. First, we need a message to translate:

    ```
    original = u'नमस्ते'
    ```

    This creates a Unicode string containing the word *Namaste* in Hindi. Let's see what it converts to in English!

    We call the API to translate the text into English using the following code:

    ```
    translation = translate_client.translate(original,
    target_language="en")
    ```

    If you observe the `translation` variable, you will find that it contains the following details:

    ```
    {
        'translatedText': 'Hello',
        'detectedSourceLanguage': 'hi',
        'input': 'नमस्ते'
    }
    ```

It is simple to infer from this dictionary that the detected language was Hindi (represented by `hi`). The input is shown in the format the input was fed in. `translatedText` holds `Hello`, which is the exact translation of *Namaste*.

Summary

In this chapter, we explored some of the famous and groundbreaking deep learning-based services provided by GCP. We learned how to use Dialogflow using Python to build conversational chatbots that can learn over time. We used the Cloud Vision API to predict the objects recognized in any image. We could easily extrapolate this to a video and achieve similar results. We finally covered the Cloud Translate API for performing deep NLP-based translation using the service. All the major services provided by GCP are accessible over APIs, which makes them easily replaceable in any project. The accuracy of models created by highly trained professionals is commendable and makes the life of a web developer easier when trying to build AI-powered web solutions.

In the next chapter, we will introduce the features offered by **Amazon Web Services (AWS)** to integrate AI with web applications using Python.

7

DL on AWS Using Python: Object Detection and Home Automation

We familiarized ourselves with a few deep-learning-based offerings from Google Cloud Platform and learned how they can be used in `Chapter 6`, *Deep Learning on Google Cloud Platform Using Python*. Now that we have a fairly good overview of cloud computing, in this chapter, we will introduce another cloud computing platform, **Amazon Web Services (AWS)**, which also offers some high-performing and highly reliable deep-learning-based solutions to make life easier. In this chapter, we are going to introduce two of them in the form of APIs and learn how they can be consumed from a Python program.

We will start by setting up our AWS account and configuring boto3 in Python. We will then learn how to use the Rekognition API and the Alexa API in Python.

In this chapter, we will cover the following topics:

- Setting up your AWS account
- AWS offerings in brief
- Configuring boto3 in Python
- Using the Rekognition API in Python
- Using the Alexa API in Python

Technical requirements

You can access the code for this chapter at `https://github.com/PacktPublishing/Hands-On-Python-Deep-Learning-for-Web/tree/master/Chapter7`.

To run the code in this chapter, you'll need the following software:

- Python 3.6+
- The Python PIL library

All other installations will be described during the course of the chapter.

Getting started in AWS

Before using any AWS services or APIs, you will have to create your AWS account. In this section, we will quickly go through the steps to create an account in AWS:

1. The first step is to go to `https://aws.amazon.com/`. You should land on a page that resembles the following:

2. Then click on the **Create an AWS Account** button, which should take you to the following page:

Create an AWS account

**AWS Accounts Include
12 Months of Free Tier Access**

Including use of Amazon EC2, Amazon S3, and Amazon DynamoDB
Visit **aws.amazon.com/free** for full offer terms

Email address

Password

Confirm password

AWS account name ❶

Continue

Sign in to an existing AWS account

© 2019 Amazon Web Services, Inc. or its affiliates.
All rights reserved.
Privacy Policy   Terms of Use

3. Fill in the fields and click on **Continue**.

4. The portal will ask for some more mandatory information from you. It will also ask you to register a payment method in order to verify your details.

> If you do not provide this, you will not be entitled to use the free tier of AWS facilities.

5. Towards the very last step of your registration, you will be asked to choose between three plans—**Free**, **Developer**, and **Business**. Choose whichever is relevant to your needs and proceed.

Like Google Cloud Platform, AWS also offers free tier access. When you sign up for AWS for the first time, you get to use a wide range of AWS services and products for free, but only up to a certain quota. You can go to `https://aws.amazon.com/free/` to learn more about this.

You should get a page like the following once you follow the preceding steps:

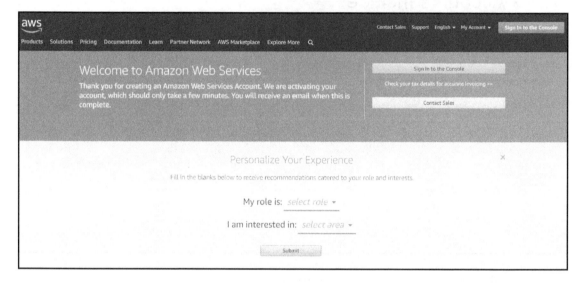

AWS has this beautiful feature of recommending solutions and services for its users. In order to make the most of this feature, you need to enter two things—your role and your subject of interest. You can see this in the preceding screenshot. Enter these two details and hit **Submit** for some targeted product recommendations.

6. The next step is to click on the **Sign In to the Console** button.

When you are successfully logged in to your AWS console, you should see the following window:

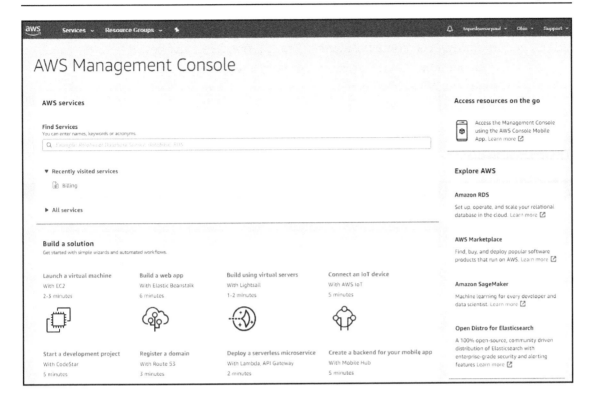

The AWS console is the place where you can find all the services and solutions that AWS has to offer. Feel free to explore the complete set of services by clicking on the **Services** tab. You can also search for a particular service from the search bar.

By now, our AWS accounts should be ready enough for us to get our hands dirty. In the next section, we'll review the offerings of AWS briefly to get a better sense of the platform.

A short tour of the AWS offerings

AWS offers its services and solutions in a variety of domains. The following are the different types of module that AWS offers (the ones in brackets are the names of the different services offered by AWS):

- Compute (EC2, Lambda, and so on)
- Storage (S3, Storage Gateway, and so on)
- Machine learning (Amazon SageMaker, AWS DeepLens, and so on)
- Database (RDS, DynamoDB, and so on)

- Migration and transfer (Snowball, DataSync, and so on)
- Networking and content delivery (CloudFront, VPC, and so on)
- Developer tools (CodeStar, CodeCommit, and so on)
- Robotics (AWS RoboMaker)
- Blockchain (Amazon Managed Blockchain)
- Analytics (Athena, CloudSearch, and so on)

There are also many others, as shown in the following screenshot:

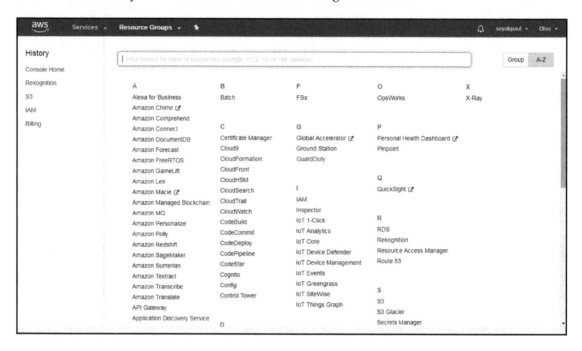

The list is actually pretty extensive, but let's restrict our focus to machine learning (also known as deep learning) services for the time being.

The search bar in the AWS console also lets you search for the AWS APIs that you may already have heard of. Let's type `Rekognition` in there and hit *Enter*. You should be provided with the home page of Rekognition, as shown in the following screenshot:

We will explore the Rekognition API in more detail later in the chapter. In the next section, we will learn how to use boto3 (an AWS SDK that provides a programming interface in Python) to interact with different AWS resources.

Getting started with boto3

boto3 is the official library for communicating with AWS APIs, provided by the AWS team. You can find the library at `https://aws.amazon.com/sdk-for-python/`, and it can be installed using the following command:

```
pip install boto3
```

After installation, you need to configure boto3 for use with your project. To configure boto3 (`https://bit.ly/2OvXAvb`), the first step is to get your AWS access keys from the **Identity and Access Management** (**IAM**) console. Go through the following steps to perform the configuration:

1. Go to your AWS IAM console at `https://console.aws.amazon.com/iam`. It will look like the following:

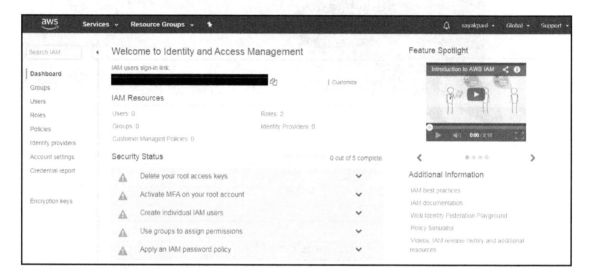

On the preceding dashboard, you will be able to see the access keys.

2. Click on **Delete your root access keys** and then **Manage Security Credentials**. You will be presented with the following window:

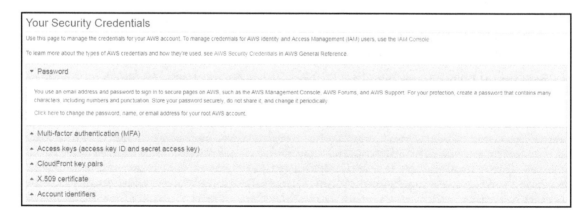

3. Expand the **Access keys (access key ID and secret access key)** tab and get the access keys from there. You should get the following message once the keys are generated successfully:

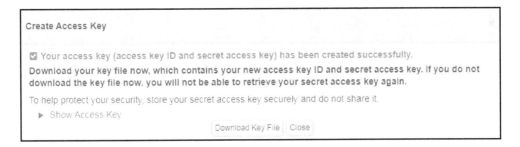

4. Download the key file and keep it in a secure place, as you will need this in order to configure boto3.

Configuring environment variables and installing boto3

Once you have the access keys, create two environmental variables, `aws_access_key_id` and `aws_secret_access_key`. Now, assign their values accordingly with the help of the keys you have. The keys will have information that will help you distinguish between the key ID and the secret access key. Now that you have configured the necessary environment variables, we can start off by loading the environment variables in Python.

Loading up the environment variables in Python

Once the library is successfully installed, you can load up the environment variables you just created with the following lines of code:

```
import os
aws_access_key_id= os.environ['aws_access_key_id']
aws_secret_access_key = os.environ['aws_secret_access_key']
```

Once the environment variables are loaded up properly, we can call boto3 to interact with an AWS resource. Let's say you want to enlist the S3 buckets that you have in your AWS account and want to upload an image to a particular bucket. S3 is the AWS resource that you want to access. If you do not have any S3 buckets in your AWS account, no worries; you can quickly create one.

Creating an S3 bucket

You can quickly create an S3 bucket by going through the following steps:

1. Go to the home page of the S3 console at `https://s3.console.aws.amazon.com/ s3`. It should look like the following:

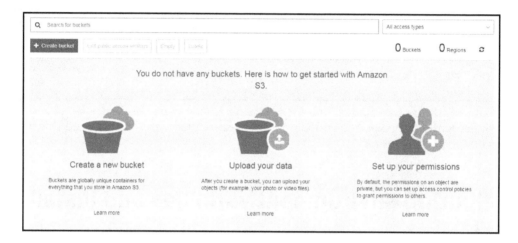

2. Click on **Create bucket**. You will be asked to enter the following details:

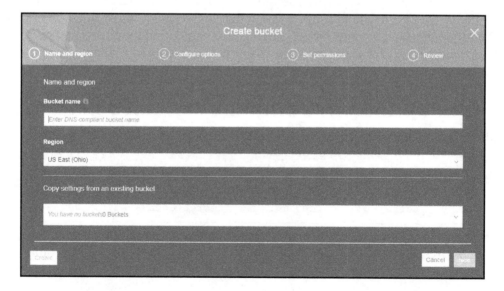

3. Give a name for your bucket, leave everything as it is, and click on **Create**. Once the bucket is successfully created, you will be able to see it from the S3 console:

Next, we will learn how to access S3 from Python code with boto3.

Accessing S3 from Python code with boto3

Now, you can access your S3 bucket from Python code. The following lines of code will show you the available buckets:

```
import boto3
s3 = boto3.resource(
    's3',
    aws_access_key_id=aws_access_key_id,
    aws_secret_access_key=aws_secret_access_key
)
```

You specified that you are interested in accessing S3 in the first argument of the `resource()`. You can read the documentation at https://bit.ly/2VHsvnP. You can now find the available buckets with the following lines of code:

```
for bucket in s3.buckets.all():
 print(bucket.name)
```

You should get the list as the output. Now, say you want to upload an image to one of the buckets. Provided that the image you want to upload is in your current working directory, the following lines of code should upload an image to a particular S3 bucket:

```
data = open('my_image.jpeg', 'rb')
s3.Bucket('demo-bucket-sayak').put_object(Key='my_image.jpeg', Body=data)
```

The preceding lines of code contain the following features:

- `my_image.jpeg` is the path of the image you want to upload.
- Within the `Bucket()` method is the name of the S3 bucket that the image will be uploaded to.

If the code is successfully executed, you should receive the following output:

```
s3.Object(bucket_name='demo-bucket-sayak', key='my_image.jpeg')
```

You can verify whether the image was uploaded by going to your AWS S3 console and then entering the bucket that you uploaded the image to. You should see something like the following in there:

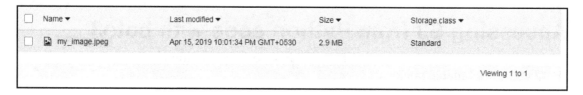

Name ▾	Last modified ▾	Size ▾	Storage class ▾
🖼 my_image.jpeg	Apr 15, 2019 10:01:34 PM GMT+0530	2.9 MB	Standard
			Viewing 1 to 1

Now that you have configured boto3 successfully in Python, we can now move on to learn how to use the Rekognition and Alexa API in Python using boto3.

Using the Rekognition API in Python

Amazon Rekognition is a deep-learning-enabled visual-analysis service that can help you search, verify, and analyze billions of images seamlessly. Let's first review the Recognition API briefly and then we will jump straight into using it in Python. Let's first go to the home page of the Rekognition API at `https://console.aws.amazon.com/rekognition/home`. We have already seen Rekognition's home page in one of the earlier sections of this chapter.

As you might have already noticed from the navigation bar, the Rekognition API has several things to offer:

- **Object and scene detection**: This lets you automatically label objects, labels, and scenes from a given image (along with confidence scores).
- **Image moderation**: This allows you to detect explicit or suggestive adult content in images, along with confidence scores.

- **Celebrity recognition**: Using this, you can automatically recognize celebrities in images (along with confidence scores).
- **Face comparison**: This can be used to see how closely faces match based on a similarity percentage.

In addition to these features, it has many more.

The solutions offered by the Rekognition API have proven to be extremely useful for a wide variety of organizations because they genuinely solve some real-world and challenging problems. You can try a quick demo of any of the solutions mentioned in the preceding list by clicking on their respective solutions on the API home page. Let's try the celebrity recognition solution.

First, go to `https://console.aws.amazon.com/rekognition/home?region=us-east-1#/celebrity-detection` (note that the region may vary). It should look like the following image:

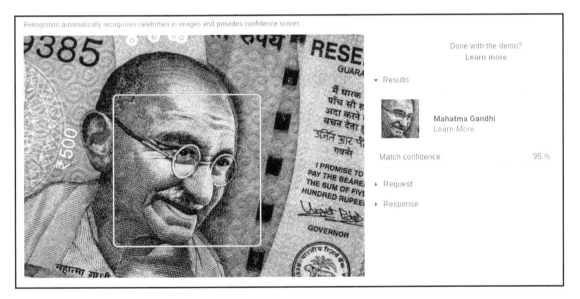

The portal will let you upload your own image and test it. Let's test my image (we could have taken images of media celebrities, but those images are copyright protected). You can see the result as expected:

Feel free to try the other solutions as well. Let's now see how the Rekognition API can be used from Python code:

1. Create a new Jupyter Notebook. First off, you will want to create a new Jupyter notebook with the name of, say, `Sample.ipynb`. You will have to provide an image that you want to test for celebrity recognition using the AWS Rekognition API, as shown in the following directory structure screenshot of Jupyter:

2. Import the environment variables for the credentials in your AWS account. You will need to import your account credentials into your script as you previously did in the boto3 configuration section. To do this, use the following code:

```
import os
aws_access_key_id= os.environ['aws_access_key_id']
aws_secret_access_key = os.environ['aws_secret_access_key']
```

3. Create an AWS Rekognition API client using boto3. We are now ready to instantiate a boto3 Rekognition API client object. To do this, we need to pass the API that we wish to use to the `boto3` object, along with the AWS region name in which you wish to use the API. You will also have to pass in the credentials that you retrieved in the previous step, as shown in the following code:

```
import boto3
client=boto3.client('rekognition', region_name='us-east-1',
aws_access_key_id=aws_access_key_id,
aws_secret_access_key=aws_secret_access_key)
```

4. Read the image from the disk and pass it to the API. There are two methods of posting files to AWS APIs from the boto3 SDK. Firstly, you could send them directly from an S3 bucket that you have permissions for, or you could send the image as a `Bytes` array from your local disk. We have already seen how you can find images from S3 buckets in the previous section.

We shall now show you an example where we take a number of images from the local disk and pass them in an API call:

1. First, read the image into a variable using Python's native method to open a file, as shown in the following code:

```
image = open("image.jpg", "rb")
```

2. Now, to pass it to the API through the client we instantiated earlier, use the following line of code:

```
response =
client.recognize_celebrities(Image={'Bytes':image.read()})
```

3. Observe the response. Once the API call has succeeded, your `response` variable will hold the information returned by the API. To see it, print the variable:

```
{'CelebrityFaces': [{'Urls': ['www.imdb.com/name/nm1682433'],
 'Name': 'Barack Obama',
 'Id': '3R3sg9u',
 'Face': {'BoundingBox': {'Width': 0.3392857015132904,
```

```
 'Height': 0.27056020498275757,
 'Left': 0.324404776096344,
 'Top': 0.06436233967542648},
 'Confidence': 99.97088623046875,
 'Landmarks': [{'Type': 'eyeLeft',
'X': 0.44199424982070923,
'Y': 0.17130307853221893},
  {'Type': 'eyeRight', 'X': 0.5501364469528198, 'Y':
0.1697501391172409},
  {'Type': 'nose', 'X': 0.4932120144367218, 'Y':
0.2165488302707672},
  {'Type': 'mouthLeft', 'X': 0.43547138571739197, 'Y':
0.25405779480934143},
  {'Type': 'mouthRight', 'X': 0.552975058555603, 'Y':
0.2527817189693451}],
 'Pose': {'Roll': -1.301725149154663,
 'Yaw': -1.5216708183288574,
 'Pitch': 1.9823487997055054},
 'Quality': {'Brightness': 82.28946685791016,
 'Sharpness': 96.63640594482422}},
 'MatchConfidence': 96.0}],
 'UnrecognizedFaces': [],
 'ResponseMetadata': {'RequestId':
'ba909ea2-67f1-11e9-8ac8-39b792b4a620',
 'HTTPStatusCode': 200,
 'HTTPHeaders': {'content-type': 'application/x-amz-json-1.1',
 'date': 'Fri, 26 Apr 2019 07:05:55 GMT',
 'x-amzn-requestid': 'ba909ea2-67f1-11e9-8ac8-39b792b4a620',
 'content-length': '813',
 'connection': 'keep-alive'},
 'RetryAttempts': 0}}
```

The API recognizes our image as that of Barack Obama. It gives us a lot of other useful information, such as the `BoundingBox` where the face was matched, the `Confidence` of the prediction, the location of the eyes, mouth, and nose, and so on. We can use this information to further operate on the image—say, to simply crop out the matched part.

4. Get the matched part of the image. To prepare a cropped version of the image in the places where it was recognized, we can use the following code:

```
from PIL import Image
from IPython.display import display

im=Image.open('image.jpg')
w, h = im.size
```

```
celeb = response['CelebrityFaces'][0]['Face']['BoundingBox']

x1 = (celeb["Left"])*w
y1 = (celeb["Top"])*h
x2 = (celeb["Left"] + celeb["Width"])*w
y2 = (celeb["Top"] + celeb["Height"])*h

box=(x1,y1,x2,y2)
im1=im.crop(box)

display(im1)
```

You should see the following image as the final result, which is the bounding box generated by the API for performing celebrity recognition:

On further exploration of the boto3 API for AWS, you'll realize that it is capable of handling all AWS services, and is not just limited to the Rekognition API. This means that, based on the API specification requirements, the preceding sample code can be used for nearly all the available APIs, with small modifications.

In the upcoming section, we'll take a look at Alexa, a flagship offering by Amazon for building voice interfaces that can span in their capabilities from being a chatbot to a virtual personal assistant. We'll learn how we can build a simple home automation solution using Alexa.

Using the Alexa API in Python

Amazon Alexa is a voice-based personal assistant developed by Amazon. The product first featured as an interface for Amazon Echo devices, which went on to inspire the Google Home devices by Google, which use Google Assistant. Other competitors of Alexa are Microsoft's Cortana and Apple's Siri. As a virtual assistant, Alexa can easily set up calls, schedule meetings, or play songs. The various tasks that Alexa can perform are called *skills* in the Alexa terminology, which we'll be following in this section.

Skills in Alexa are the main core of how we can bring functionality to the platform. Each skill needs to be invoked from the primary interface of Alexa, whereupon the skill takes over the entire functionality unless the program logic completes or the user explicitly asks for the skill to end. Skills apply the logic for the task to be performed, and so this logic needs to be stored somewhere, perhaps also along with a database and execution runtime. While a lot of skills are hosted over several services, such as Heroku, PythonAnywhere, GCP, and others, it is very common to host skills, logic code as AWS Lambda functions.

In this section, we shall be creating a sample Home Automation Alexa skill using the Python SDK for Alexa and will host it on AWS Lambda.

Prerequisites and a block diagram of the project

Before you can jump into building an Alexa skill, you will need the following two types of accounts on AWS and Amazon Developer respectively:

- An AWS account (the free tier works)—`aws.amazon.com`
- An Amazon Developer account (this is free)—`developer.amazon.com`

Once you have created these accounts—the process of which is beyond the scope of this book—you can proceed to create our skill for home automation. The architecture of the Home Automation skill we shall be creating is shown in the following block diagram:

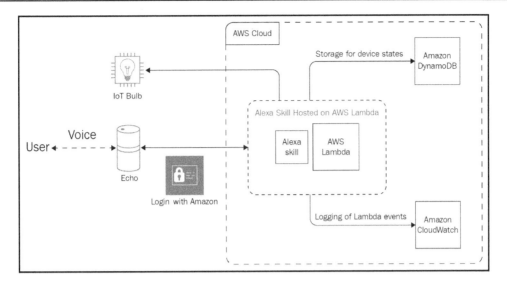

In building this skill, we shall be using the following services, which you can read more about by going to the links in the following list:

- **Amazon Alexa Skills Kit:** `https://developer.amazon.com/alexa-skills-kit`
- **Login with Amazon:** `https://developer.amazon.com/docs/login-with-amazon/minitoc-lwa-overview.html`
- **AWS CloudWatch:** `https://aws.amazon.com/cloudwatch/`
- **Amazon DynamoDB:** `https://aws.amazon.com/dynamodb/`
- **AWS Lambda:** `https://aws.amazon.com/lambda/`

Creating a configuration for the skill

Skills require a certain amount of connection between the services in order to work. In addition, the skill logic deployed on AWS Lambda needs to be configured to be used by the skill on Alexa. Create a `setup.txt` file in the root of your working folder with the following content. We shall be gradually adding to this content as we progress through the steps in this section:

```
[LWA Client ID]
amzn1.application-oa2-client.XXXXXXXXXXXXXXXXXXXXXXXXXXXXXXXX

[LWA Client Secret]
XXXXXXXXXXXXXXXXXXXXXXXXXXXXXXXXXXXXXXXXXXXXXXXXXXXXXXXXXXXXXX
[Alexa Skill ID]
amzn1.ask.skill.XXXXXXXX-XXXX-XXXX-XXXX-XXXXXXXXXXXX
```

```
[AWS Lambda ARN]
arn:aws:lambda:us-east-1:XXXXXXXXXXXX:function:skill-sample-language-
smarthome-switch

[APIs]
https://pitangui.amazon.com/api/skill/link/XXXXXXXXXXXXXX
https://layla.amazon.com/api/skill/link/XXXXXXXXXXXXXX
https://alexa.amazon.co.jp/api/skill/link/XXXXXXXXXXXXXX
```

Throughout the following sections, we will be referring to this file as `setup.txt`. This essentially only holds information about your skill. Feel free to implement this in any other text editor as well, such as Google Docs.

Setting up Login with Amazon

For the Home Automation skill, you will need the Login with Amazon service enabled. To do this, go through the following steps:

1. Go to `https://developer.amazon.com/lwa/sp/overview.html`. You will see the page shown in the following screenshot:

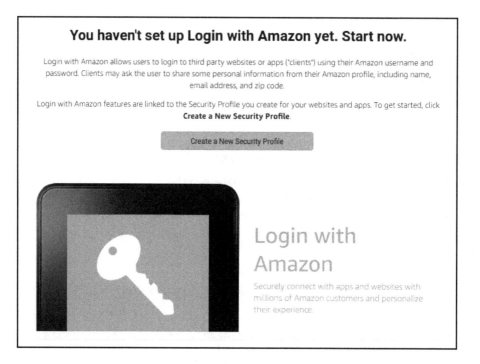

2. Click the **Create a New Security Profile** button on the page that then loads.

3. Set **Security Profile Name** as `Smart Home Automation Profile.`

4. Provide a description of the profile.

5. For **Content Privacy Notice URL**, you will need a valid privacy policy web page to push the skill to production. Create and host a privacy policy and provide the link to it in this field. A very handy tool for creating privacy policies can be found at `https://app-privacy-policy-generator.firebaseapp.com/`.

6. Click on **Save**.

7. Click on the **Security Profile** option in the gear menu that appears on the next page. You will be taken to the **Security Profile Management** page, as shown in the following image:

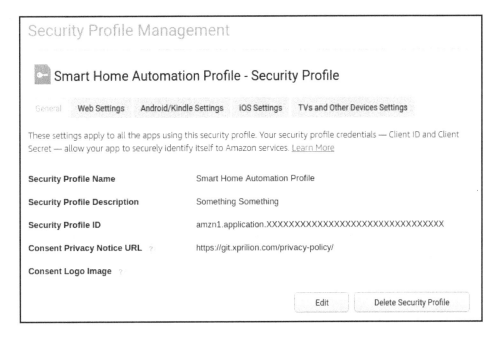

8. From the list of security profiles, click the **Web Settings** tab to the **Show Client ID and Client Secret** link for the **Home Automation Profile**.

9. Copy the displayed Client ID and Client Secret values and save them to the `setup.txt` file in the working directory, replacing the format example entries for `[LWA Client ID]` and `[LWA Client Secret]` respectively.

Keep this tab open for future steps. Go through the steps in the next section in a new browser tab.

Creating the skill

We can now proceed with creating the skill:

1. Log on to `https://developer.amazon.com/alexa/console/ask` to begin the process. You will be able to see a screen resembling the following:

2. Click on **Create Skill**.

3. Set the name to `Home Automation Skill`, or a name of your choosing.

4. Under the **Choose a model to add to your skill** section, click on the **Smart Home** model. Your selections should now resemble the following:

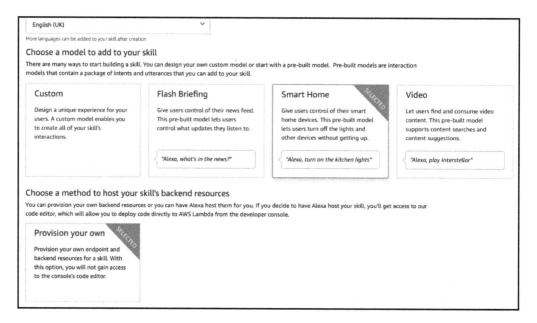

5. Click on **Create Skill** to complete the initial phase of the skill creation.

6. On the next page that appears, you'll be able to see the Skill ID. Copy this Skill ID to the `setup.txt` file in the local working directory.

Do not close this tab, as you still have fields to fill in here. Open up a new browser tab to work in in the next section.

Configuring the AWS Lambda function

Before we can add the ARN for the Lambda function to the skill endpoints configuration, we must create a configuration for the Lambda function. You can do this by going through the following steps:

1. Go to `https://console.aws.amazon.com/iam/home#/policies`. You will be presented with a screen like the one shown in the following screenshot:

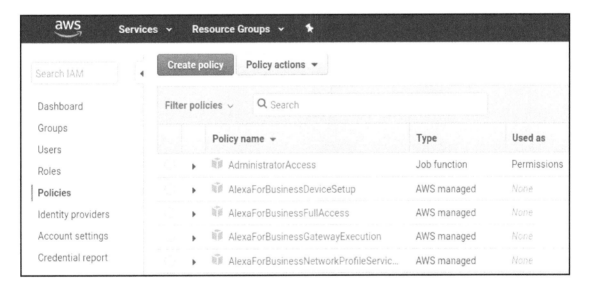

2. Click on **Create policy**.

3. Enter the following JSON in the **JSON** tab of the **Create policy** editor:

```
{
"Version": "2012-10-17",
"Statement": [
{
"Effect": "Allow",
"Action": [
```

```
        "logs:CreateLogStream",
        "dynamodb:UpdateItem",
        "logs:CreateLogGroup",
        "logs:PutLogEvents"
        ],
        "Resource": "*"
      }
    ]
  }
```

4. Click on **Review policy** and set the name of the policy to
   `HomeAutomationPolicy`.

5. Click on **Create policy**.

6. Next, on the left-hand navigation menu of the page, click on **Roles**.

7. Click on **Create role**.

8. Select **AWS service** and **Lambda**, and click on **Next: Permissions**.

9. Search for **HomeAutomationPolicy** in the filtering field. Check the policy. Your
   screen should resemble the following:

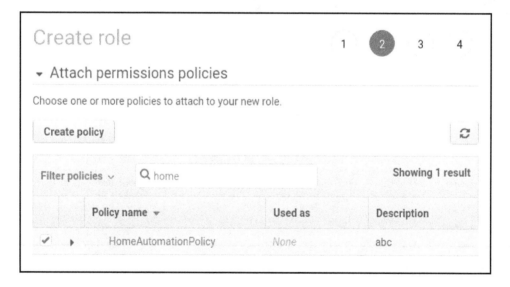

10. Click on **Next: Tags**.

11. Click on **Next: Review**.

12. Set the **Role** name to `lambda_home_automation`.

13. Click on **Create role**.

Let's now create the Lambda function.

Creating the Lambda function

With the suitable configuration for the Lambda function in place, we can now create the Lambda function itself. To do so, in the AWS console, navigate to `https://console.aws.amazon.com/lambda/home` and go through the following steps:

1. Click on **Create function**.
2. Set the function name to `homeAutomation`.
3. Select the `Python 3.6` runtime.
4. Choose the `lambda_home_automation` role from the dropdown in the existing roles in the execution roles.
5. Click on `Create function`.
6. Copy the Lambda ARN from the next page that appears, which has a message of congratulations for creating the Lambda function. Put this ARN in the `setup.txt` of our local working directory in the **[AWS Lambda ARN]** field. At this point, the screen should resemble the following screenshot:

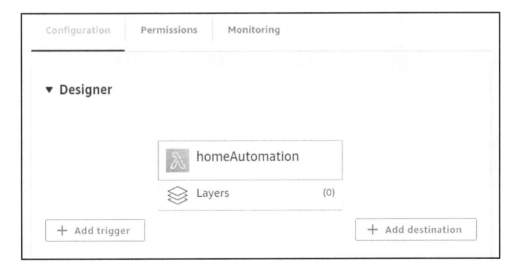

 Note that the triggers and destinations displayed on your screen might differ from the preceding screenshot.

7. On the left-hand navigation, click on **Add trigger** to bring up the drop-down list of available triggers for your Lambda function, as shown in the following screenshot:

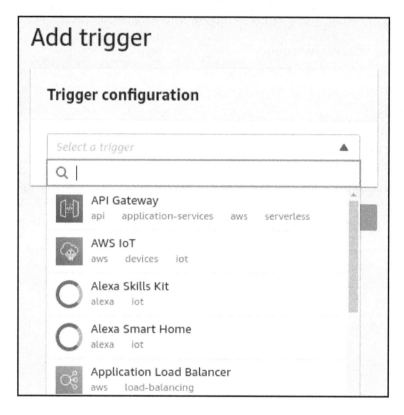

8. Click on **Alexa Skills Kit** to bring up the configuration dialogue for this trigger.
9. Paste the Alexa Skill ID in the field for **Skill ID**. We have stored this value in the `setup.txt` previously, and it will look like `amzn1.ask.skill.xxxxxxxx-xxxx-xxxx-xxxx-xxxxxxxxxxxx`.
10. Click on **Add** to add the trigger and return to the Lambda function management screen.
11. Click on **Save** at the top right of the page.

After the final step, the trigger section will display details of the connected Alexa skill. If it does not, you should check that you have correctly followed the preceding steps.

Configuring the Alexa skill

Now, we need to configure the skill that we left open in another tab of the browser. We will do this by going through the following steps:

1. Return to that tab and fill in the ARN of the Lambda function in the **Default endpoint** field.
2. Click on **SAVE**.
3. Click on **Setup Account Linking** at the bottom of the page.
4. For the **Authorization URL**, enter `https://www.amazon.com/ap/oa`.
5. For the **Access Token URL**, enter `https://api.amazon.com/auth/o2/token`.
6. For the **Client ID** field, copy `[LWA Client ID]` from the `setup.txt` file.
7. For the **Client Secret** field, copy `[LWA Client Secret]` from the `setup.txt` file.
8. Click on **Add scope** and enter `profile:user_id`.
9. Copy the **Redirect URLs** from the bottom of the page and paste them in the `setup.txt` file under the **[APIs]** section. The URLs resemble the following:

Redirect URLs (?)	https://pitangui.amazon.com/api/skill/link/XXXXXXXXXXXXX
	https://layla.amazon.com/api/skill/link/XXXXXXXXXXXXX
	https://alexa.amazon.co.jp/api/skill/link/XXXXXXXXXXXXX

10. Click on **Save**.
11. In the **Security Profile Management** browser tab, click on the **Web Settings** tab.
12. Click on **Edit**, and add the three redirect URLs to the **Allowed Return URLs** field. You will have to click on **Add another** to enter multiple URLs.
13. Click on **Save**.

Let's now set up Amazon DynamoDB for the skill.

Setting up Amazon DynamoDB for the skill

For the skill to be able to save data from users, it needs a database. We will be using the Amazon DynamoDB service for this. The steps to set up the service are as follows:

1. Go to `https://console.aws.amazon.com/dynamodb/home?region=us-east-1`.
2. Click on the **Create table** button.
3. Enter the **Table name** as `SmartHome`.
4. For the **Primary key**, enter `ItemId`.
5. Leave all defaults as they are and click on **Create**. Your screen should resemble the following screenshot in this step:

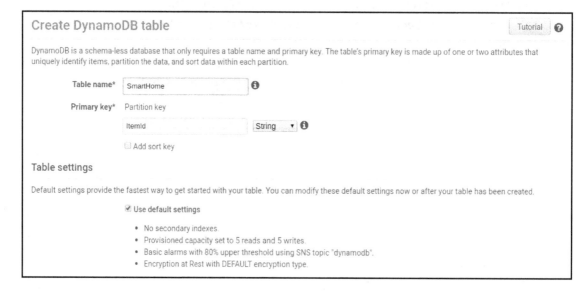

You can then go to the DynamoDB dashboard to see the table you just created; however, this can take a few moments.

Deploying the code for the AWS Lambda function

We're left with the final piece of the setup—the code that provides the logic to the AWS Lambda function. Go to your Lambda function configuration page and scroll down to the editor.

You will notice that the editor has a two-column interface: the left column displays the files in the Lambda function storage and in the right column, you can edit those files, as shown in the following screenshot:

Click on `lambda_function.py` to begin editing the file and go through the following steps:

1. Import the necessary modules. For the function to work, we will need the support of some common libraries, as shown in the following code:

```
import boto3
import json
import random
import uuid
import time
```

The boto3 API is used to connect to the Amazon DynamoDB instance we set up. The JSON module facilitates the generation of responses for the Alexa skill. The rest of the modules help to generate responses.

2. Create the `AlexaResponse` class. In order to be able to fully replicate the Alexa skill's expected format of responses, we can quickly set up a helper class that can generate the responses for the Lambda function calls. Let's name it `AlexaReponse`; the initialization of the class is shown in the following code snippet:

```
class AlexaResponse:

    def __init__(self, **kwargs):

        self.context_properties = []
        self.payload_endpoints = []
```

```
                     # Set up the response structure
                     self.context = {}
                     self.event = {
                         'header': {
                             'namespace': kwargs.get('namespace', 'Alexa'),
                             'name': kwargs.get('name', 'Response'),
                             'messageId': str(uuid.uuid4()),
                             'payloadVersion': kwargs.get('payload_version',
'3')
                         },
                         'endpoint': {
                             "scope": {
                                 "type": "BearerToken",
                                 "token": kwargs.get('token', 'INVALID')
                             },
                             "endpointId": kwargs.get('endpoint_id', 'INVALID')
                         },
                         'payload': kwargs.get('payload', {})
                     }

                     if 'correlation_token' in kwargs:
                         self.event['header']['correlation_token'] =
kwargs.get('correlation_token', 'INVALID')

                     if 'cookie' in kwargs:
                         self.event['endpoint']['cookie'] = kwargs.get('cookie',
'{}')

                     if self.event['header']['name'] == 'AcceptGrant.Response'
or self.event['header']['name'] == 'Discover.Response':
                         self.event.pop('endpoint')
```

The preceding initialization method for the AlexaResponse class sets the
expected output format and the various constant settings, such as the version
number for the payload, and some basic validation for the output object. Next, we
create the method for adding content properties and another method for setting
cookies in the responses. Finally, another method is added to set up the payload
endpoints:

```
    def add_context_property(self, **kwargs):
    self.context_properties.append(self.create_context_property(**kwarg
s))

    def add_cookie(self, key, value):

        if "cookies" in self is None:
            self.cookies = {}
```

```
        self.cookies[key] = value

    def add_payload_endpoint(self, **kwargs):
        self.payload_endpoints.append(self.create_payload_endpoint(**kwargs
        ))
```

3. Now to define the three handler methods that we created in the previous step. The methods declared in the previous step depend upon inner methods of their own. These are mostly helper functions, which have little to do with the major focus of this chapter, and so we will leave these up to your implementation of the function, which you can create by studying the response body documentation of AWS Lambda functions and Alexa skills. A sample implementation can be found in our code repository for this chapter, between lines 65 and 102 of the `lambda_function.py` file at http://tiny.cc/HOPDLW_CH7_lfpy.

4. Next, we will set up methods to generate the final response from the `AlexaResponse` class. Finally, we create methods that assimilate all the different parts—the context, event, payload, endpoints, and cookies—into a single object that is ready for interaction with the Alexa skill:

```
def get(self, remove_empty=True):

    response = {
        'context': self.context,
        'event': self.event
    }

    if len(self.context_properties) > 0:
        response['context']['properties'] = self.context_properties

    if len(self.payload_endpoints) > 0:
        response['event']['payload']['endpoints'] =
self.payload_endpoints

    if remove_empty:
        if len(response['context']) < 1:
            response.pop('context')

    return response

def set_payload(self, payload):
    self.event['payload'] = payload

def set_payload_endpoint(self, payload_endpoints):
    self.payload_endpoints = payload_endpoints

def set_payload_endpoints(self, payload_endpoints):
```

```
if 'endpoints' not in self.event['payload']:
    self.event['payload']['endpoints'] = []

self.event['payload']['endpoints'] = payload_endpoints
```

5. The `AlexaResponse` class is now complete. We will now move on to connect with the DynamoDB service using the following line:

```
aws_dynamodb = boto3.client('dynamodb')
```

6. Next, we define the primary method and entry point for the file—the `lambda_handler` method:

```
def lambda_handler(request, context):

    # JSON dump for the request
    print('Request: ')
    print(json.dumps(request))

    if context is not None:
        print('Context: ')
        print(context)
```

We will continue adding to the preceding method for the rest of this step. In the preceding lines, we declare the `lambda_handler` method, which accepts the `request` and `context` objects from the Alexa skill. It then makes a JSON dump of the request so that we can later observe it from the Amazon CloudWatch dashboard. Next, it makes of a dump of the context if any was attached to the request:

```
# Validate we have an Alexa directive
if 'directive' not in request:
    aer = AlexaResponse(
        name='ErrorResponse',
        payload={'type': 'INVALID_DIRECTIVE',
                 'message': 'Missing key: directive, Is the request a
valid Alexa Directive?'})
    return send_response(aer.get())
```

We then validate whether we have a valid Alexa directive in the request, and if none is found, an error message is generated and sent back as the response. Note the usage of the `AlexaResponse` class object here. We will be using it in the future to generate responses from this script:

```
# Check the payload version
payload_version = request['directive']['header']['payloadVersion']
if payload_version != '3':
```

```
       aer = AlexaResponse(
           name='ErrorResponse',
           payload={'type': 'INTERNAL_ERROR',
                    'message': 'This skill only supports Smart Home API
version 3'})
       return send_response(aer.get())
```

Similarly, another check is made to ensure that the payload version being requested is 3. This is because we have only developed it for the Smart Home API version 3 of Alexa:

1. First, we open the request and see what is being requested:

```
name = request['directive']['header']['name']
namespace = request['directive']['header']['namespace']
```

2. Then, we handle the incoming request from Alexa based on the `namespace`. Note that this sample accepts any `grant` request, but in your implementation, you will use the code and token to get and store access tokens:

```
if namespace == 'Alexa.Authorization':
    if name == 'AcceptGrant':
        grant_code = request['directive']['payload']['grant']['code']
        grantee_token =
request['directive']['payload']['grantee']['token']
        aar = AlexaResponse(namespace='Alexa.Authorization',
name='AcceptGrant.Response')
        return send_response(aar.get())
```

The preceding condition acts on the Alexa authorization request.

3. For the discovery and the action to turn off the switch, we use the following code:

```
if namespace == 'Alexa.Discovery':
    if name == 'Discover':
        adr = AlexaResponse(namespace='Alexa.Discovery',
name='Discover.Response')
        capability_alexa = adr.create_payload_endpoint_capability()
        capability_alexa_powercontroller =
adr.create_payload_endpoint_capability(
            interface='Alexa.PowerController',
            supported=[{'name': 'powerState'}])
        adr.add_payload_endpoint(
            friendly_name='Sample Switch',
            endpoint_id='sample-switch-01',
            capabilities=[capability_alexa,
capability_alexa_powercontroller])
        return send_response(adr.get())
    if namespace == 'Alexa.PowerController':
```

```
                    endpoint_id = request['directive']['endpoint']['endpointId']
                    power_state_value = 'OFF' if name == 'TurnOff' else 'ON'
                    correlation_token =
request['directive']['header']['correlationToken']
```

This sample always returns a `success` response for either a request to `TurnOff` or `TurnOn`.

4. Now, we check for an error when setting the state:

```
                    state_set = set_device_state(endpoint_id=endpoint_id,
            state='powerState', value=power_state_value)
                    if not state_set:
                        return AlexaResponse(
                            name='ErrorResponse',
                            payload={'type': 'ENDPOINT_UNREACHABLE', 'message':
            'Unable to reach endpoint database.'}).get()

                    apcr = AlexaResponse(correlation_token=correlation_token)
            apcr.add_context_property(namespace='Alexa.PowerController',
            name='powerState', value=power_state_value)
                    return send_response(apcr.get())
```

5. Finally, we extract the directive name and the namespace of the directive to determine the type of response to be sent back. Depending upon the directives being sent, a different response is generated and finally sent using the `AlexaResponse` class object.

6. Note the usage of the `send_response` method in the code in the previous step. We need to define that method. Its task is to send the `AlexaResponse` object in JSON format and to log it for observation in Amazon CloudWatch:

```
def send_response(response):
    print('Response: ')
    print(json.dumps(response))
    return response
```

7. Update the `device state` method. Since we're building automation for a simple switch device using Alexa, we'll need to maintain the state information of the switch. We do this by storing its state in DynamoDB. We will add an update method for this, as shown in the following code:

```
def set_device_state(endpoint_id, state, value):
    attribute_key = state + 'Value'
    response = aws_dynamodb.update_item(
        TableName='SmartHome',
        Key={'ItemId': {'S': endpoint_id}},
```

```
        AttributeUpdates={attribute_key: {'Action': 'PUT', 'Value':
{'S': value}}})
    print(response)
    if response['ResponseMetadata']['HTTPStatusCode'] == 200:
        return True
    else:
        return False
```

Next, we will test the Lambda function.

Testing the Lambda function

We can now check whether our function responds properly. To do this, we must create a test in the Lambda function's dashboard by going through these steps:

1. On the Lambda function page for the function that we created in the previous sections, at the top right, click on **Test**.
2. A dialog box will appear with the options to write a new test or use an existing one. Choose the option to **Create new test event**.
3. In the **Event template**, make that sure **Hello World** is selected.
4. Next, provide the **Event name** of `directiveDiscovery`.
5. Enter the following JSON into the editor:

```json
{
  "directive": {
    "header": {
      "namespace": "Alexa.Discovery",
      "name": "Discover",
      "payloadVersion": "3",
      "messageId": "1bd5d003-31b9-476f-ad03-71d471922820"
    },
    "payload": {
      "scope": {
        "type": "BearerToken",
        "token": "access-token-from-skill"
      }
    }
  }
}
```

At this point, your screen should resemble the following:

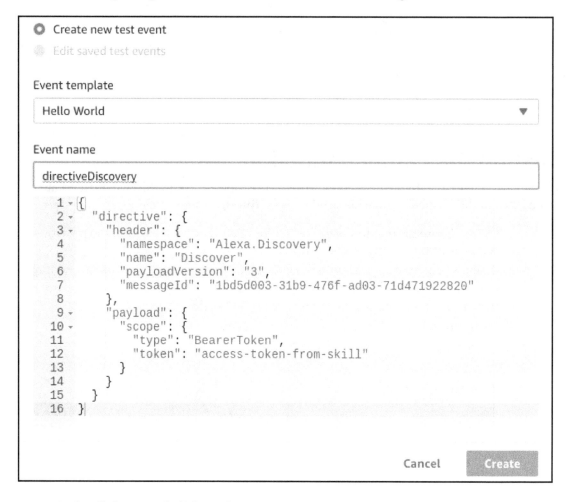

6. Scroll down and click on **Create**.
7. Once you return to the Lambda function dashboard, at the top right, select the `directoryDiscover` test from the dropdown.
8. Click on **Test**.

On completion, the test will display the response status and the response of the Lambda function. You can see the results on the page at the top of the Lambda function dashboard, which will resemble the following screenshot:

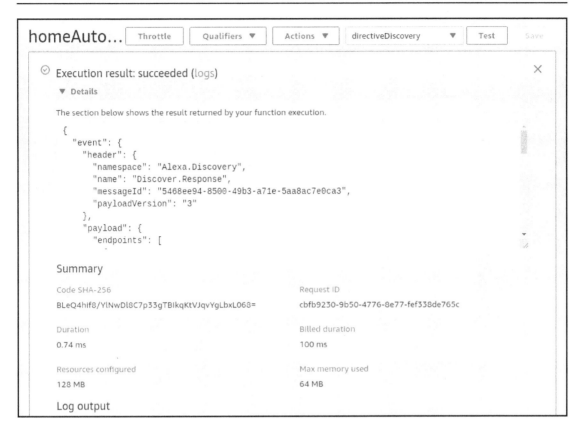

If the test fails, make sure you have followed the preceding steps carefully, making sure that the regions in which the different services exist are the same.

Testing the AWS Home Automation skill

As the last phase of this project, we will be testing our skill in the Alexa Test simulator. To do this, go through the following steps:

1. Go to `https://alexa.amazon.com` and log in.
2. Click on **Skills** in the left-hand menu.
3. Click on **Your Skills** at the top right of the page.

4. Select the **DEV SKILL** tab.

5. Click on **HomeAutomationSkill**. You should see the following screen:

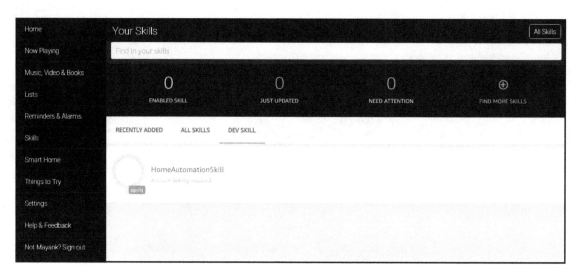

6. Click on the **Enable** button. You will be asked to allow access permissions to your Developer account.

7. Come back to the Alexa Developer console and click on **Discover devices**. A new device called **Sample Switch** will be shown as available, as shown in the following screenshot:

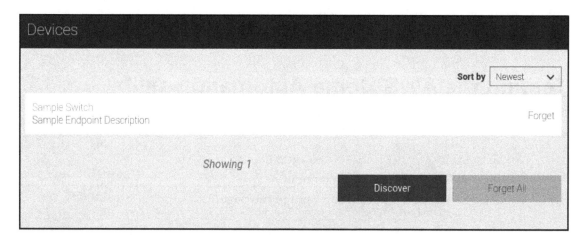

8. Now, go to the **Test** tab on the Alexa Skills Kit development page for the **HomeAutomation** skill.

9. In the simulator, type `alexa, turn on the sample switch`. If the request is accepted, then you will receive an `OK` from Alexa, as shown in the following screenshot:

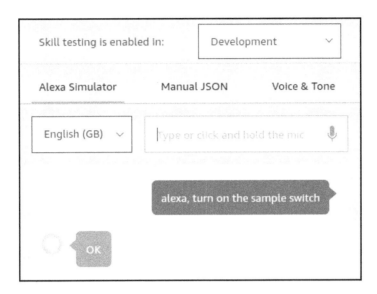

To check whether the skill is actually working, you can go to your DynamoDB table **SmartHome** and switch to the **Items** tab of the table. You should be able to see the following record:

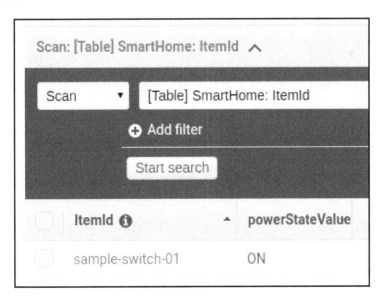

Congratulations on successfully building a simple Home Automation skill in Alexa! You can play around with this skill and build your own home automation skills for Alexa. Once you are ready to publish them for a wider audience, you can follow the advice in the documentation available at `https://developer.amazon.com/docs/alexa-for-business/create-and-publish-private-skills.html`.

Summary

In this chapter, we covered how we can use AWS using its Python API—boto3. We explored the various options and configurational requirements for using the API and looked at an example of how to use it with the Rekognition API for recognizing celebrities. We then dove deep into how to create an Alexa skill for home automation, setting up the simple task of turning a switch on/off. This can be very easily extrapolated to other smart home devices. We looked at how Alexa skill logic can be hosted over AWS Lambda and observed from AWS CloudWatch. We also explored the storage of dynamic device data in Amazon DynamoDB.

In the upcoming chapter, we will see how we can use deep learning on Microsoft's Azure platform using Python.

8
Deep Learning on Microsoft Azure Using Python

We are going to end our cloud API exploration journey with this chapter. So far, we have gently introduced ourselves to the wonderful world of APIs, specifically the APIs that let us carry out deep learning with ease. We have seen how to consume REST APIs and use them programmatically. Like **Google Cloud Platform** (**GCP**) and **Amazon Web Services** (**AWS**), Microsoft also offers its own cloud service platform, which is called Azure. As in previous chapters, we will only be focusing on the deep learning-based solutions that Azure has to offer. We will be shifting gears a bit and will also take a look at Microsoft's **Cognitive Toolkit** (**CNTK**), which is a deep learning framework like Keras.

In this chapter, we will cover the following topics:

- Setting up your account in Azure
- A quick walk-through of the deep learning solutions offered by Azure
- Using the Face API in Python
- Using the Text Analytics API in Python
- An introduction to CNTK

Technical requirements

You can access the code for this chapter from `https://github.com/PacktPublishing/Hands-On-Python-Deep-Learning-for-Web/tree/master/Chapter8`.

To run the code used in this chapter, you'll need the following software:

- Python 3.6+
- The Python PIL library
- The Matplotlib library

All other installations, such as CNTK and Django, will be described during the course of this chapter.

Setting up your account in Azure

From your previous cloud platform usage experience, you may have realized that it all starts with setting up your account and billing in a cloud provider. This is a pretty standard workflow and Azure is no exception. So, let's head over to `https://azure.microsoft.com` and follow these steps:

1. Click on the **Start free** button, as shown:

 Note that you will need a Microsoft account to proceed with the following steps. So, if you do not have one, create one at `https://account.microsoft.com/account`.

2. You will be redirected to another page, where you will again see another **Start free** button. Click on it.

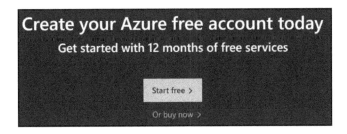

3. You will be asked to log in to your Microsoft account to proceed. Give the credentials accordingly and you should land on a page as in the following screenshot:

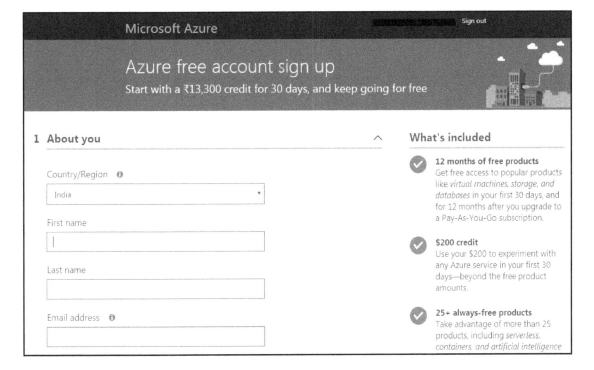

If you are a first-time user, you will get $200 of credit (depending on your currency) for free for 30 days to explore different services offered by Azure.

4. Fill in your details, which will also include verification of your identity by card.

   You might be charged a very nominal fee for this. Be sure to review the terms and conditions of the Azure free tier, which you will find at `https://azure.microsoft.com/en-in/offers/ms-azr-0003p/`.

Once this process is complete, you are all set up and ready to move to your Azure portal (`https://portal.azure.com`), which acts in the same way as the GCP and AWS consoles that you have seen in previous chapters.

The Azure portal looks like this:

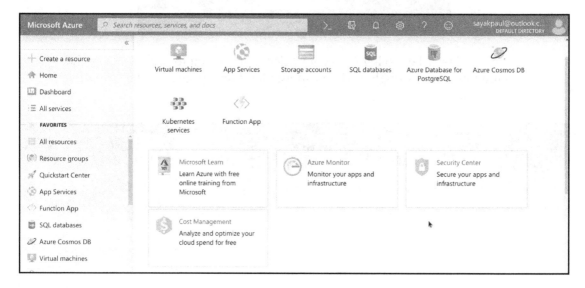

Now that you have set up your Azure account, let's explore the deep learning-based offerings of Azure in the next section.

A walk-through of the deep learning services provided by Azure

Azure's deep learning- (and general machine learning-) based offerings are broadly divided into three parts:

- **The Azure Machine Learning service** (`https://azure.microsoft.com/en-in/services/machine-learning-service/`), which provides an end-to-end machine learning life cycle, including model building, training, and deployment:

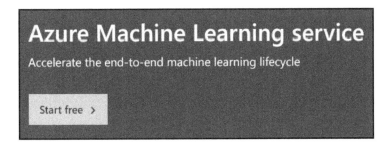

- **Machine Learning APIs** (`https://gallery.azure.ai/machineLearningAPIs`),
  which provide APIs for a wide range of learning tasks, such as content
  moderation, translation, anomaly detection, and so on:

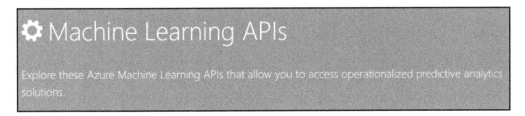

- **Azure AI** (`https://azure.microsoft.com/en-in/overview/ai-platform/`),
  which focuses on topics such as **knowledge mining**, **decision mining**, and many
  other similar machine learning capabilities in the domains of computer vision
  and language modeling:

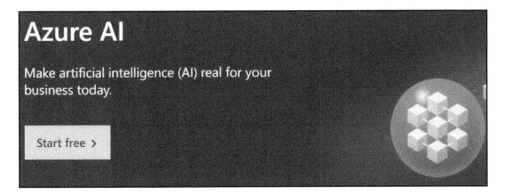

We will now study two APIs for a computer vision task and a natural language
understanding task, respectively. We will also look at how to use these APIs from Python.
Let's dive in.

Object detection using the Face API and Python

Object detection is a classic use case of computer vision and is widely applied to a number of real-world problems, such as video surveillance systems. In this section, we will be using the Face API to detect faces from a given image. This has direct use when designing video surveillance systems. You can learn more about the Face API from its official page at `https://azure.microsoft.com/en-us/services/cognitive-services/face/`.

The initial setup

Azure lets you try this API for free for a duration of 7 days, as well. But since you already have an Azure account (with free credit, I am assuming), we can do it another way, as shown:

1. Sign in to your Azure account.
2. Go to `https://azure.microsoft.com/en-us/services/cognitive-services/face/`.
3. Click on **Already using Azure? Try this service for free now.**

   You should now have a window as in the following screenshot:

4. Fill in the details accordingly and hit **Create** once you are done. You will get a popup that reads **Submitting deployment**

   Once the deployment is completed, you should land on a page as in the following screenshot:

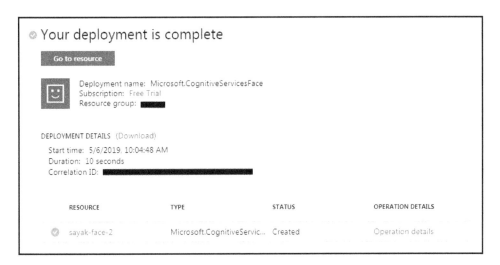

5. Click on **Go to resource** and you should be redirected to the resources page, which contains a bunch of details on it:

Just scroll down a bit and you will be able to see the endpoint of the Face API. Note that it will vary depending on the configuration details you entered while creating the deployment. The endpoint looks like `https://eastus.api.cognitive.microsoft.com/face/v1.0`. Note this down.

Now, to be able to use the Face API programmatically, you need to create the respective API keys. On that same page, there is a section at the top that says **Grab your keys**:

1   Grab your keys

Every web API call and every Docker container activation of Face requires a subscription key. For the web API this key needs to be either passed through a query string parameter or specified in the request header. For the Docker container the key needs to be passed through the Docker command.

Keys

6. Under that section, click **Keys** and you will see something as in the following screenshot:

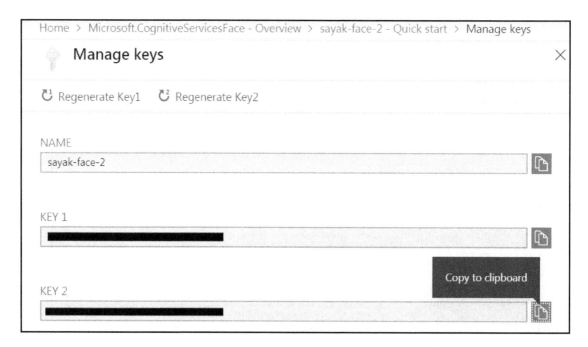

Now that you have the API keys for the Face API, you are ready to use it.

Consuming the Face API from Python code

When your program includes security credentials such as API keys, it is often a good practice to define those keys as environmental variables and then call them in your program. So, go ahead and create an environment variable to store one of the API keys of the Face API.

 To add an environment variable to your computer, you can follow this article at `https://www.twilio.com/blog/2017/01/how-to-set-environment-variables.html`.

In my case, I have named the environment variable `face_api_key`. You can put any image that contains faces in it. For this example, I will be using this image:

Create a new Jupyter notebook and follow these steps:

1. Let's now load up the environment variable using Python, as shown:

```
import os
face_api_key = os.environ['face_api_key']
```

2. Now, assign your Face API endpoint (for object detection) to a variable.
3. Also, upload the image you want to test to an online file server, such as Imgur, and retrieve the URL that allows fetching the raw image from Imgur.

In my case, I have uploaded the image to a GitHub repository and used the respective URL:

```
face_api_url =
'https://eastus.api.cognitive.microsoft.com/face/v1.0/detect'

image_url=
'https://raw.githubusercontent.com/PacktPublishing/Hands-On-Python-
Deep-Learning-for-Web/master/Chapter8/sample_image.jpg'
```

Note that in the preceding API, only the endpoint name at the end of the URL changes. In most cases, the part before the endpoint name will remain constant throughout your use of Cognitive Services, unless a change is required by the Azure platform itself.

4. Now, import the `requests` module and set up the API payload as shown:

```
import requests
params = {
'returnFaceId': 'true',
'returnFaceLandmarks': 'false',
'returnFaceAttributes': 'age,gender',
}
```

5. Now, we are in a position to make a request to the Face API.

The following lines of code do this for you:

```
# Define the header param
headers = { 'Ocp-Apim-Subscription-Key': face_api_key }
# Define the body params
params = {
'returnFaceId': 'true',
'returnFaceLandmarks': 'false',
'returnFaceAttributes': 'age,gender',
}
```

6. We can now display the response received from the API:

```
# Make the call to the API
response = requests.post(face_api_url, params=params,
headers=headers, json={"url": image_url})
# Get the response and log
faces = response.json()
print('There are {} faces im the given
image'.format(str(len(faces))))
```

In this case, the code returned is as follows:

```
There are 2 faces in the given image
```

Pay attention to the `returnFaceAttributes` body parameter, which lets you specify several attributes of faces and the Face API will analyze the given faces with respect to those attributes. To find out more about these attributes, check out the documentation at `http://bit.ly/2J3j6nM`.

Let's embed the response we got from the API in the image in a presentable manner. We will show the probable gender and probable age of the detected faces in the image. We will do this using the `matplotlib`, `PIL`, and `io` libraries and we'll be using a Jupyter notebook to work on the following segments of code in this section. We will start by importing the libraries:

```
%matplotlib inline #Only for Jupyter Notebook
import matplotlib.pyplot as plt
from PIL import Image
from matplotlib import patches
from io import BytesIO
```

To display overlays on the image with the response received from the API, we use the following method:

1. Store the API response:

   ```
   response = requests.get(image_url)
   ```

2. Create an image from the response content:

   ```
   image = Image.open(BytesIO(response.content))
   ```

3. Create an empty figure:

   ```
   plt.figure(figsize=(8,8))
   ```

4. Show the image created with the response:

   ```
   ax = plt.imshow(image, alpha=0.6)
   ```

5. Iterate over the faces specified in the earlier section and extract the necessary information:

   ```
   for face in faces:
   # Extract the information
   fr = face["faceRectangle"]
   ```

```
fa = face["faceAttributes"]
origin = (fr["left"], fr["top"])
p = patches.Rectangle(origin, fr["width"], fr["height"],
fill=False,
 linewidth=2, color='b')
ax.axes.add_patch(p)
 plt.text(origin[0], origin[1], "%s,
%d"%(fa["gender"].capitalize(), fa["age"]),
 fontsize=20, weight="bold", va="bottom")
# Turn off the axis
_ = plt.axis("off")
plt.show()
```

You should have an image like this:

You are encouraged to play around with the different parameters that the API provides. We will now study a **Natural Language Understanding (NLU)** API.

Extracting text information using the Text Analytics API and Python

Whether knowingly or unknowingly, we must all have encountered some of the astonishing use cases of natural language processing. Be it autocorrect, the next word suggestion, or language translation, these use cases are too important to neglect. In this section, we are going to use the Text Analytics API (`https://azure.microsoft.com/en-us/services/cognitive-services/text-analytics/`) to extract meaningful information from a given piece of text.

You can try the API for free using the previously mentioned link and see its power. In the following example, I entered the phrase `I want to attend NeurIPS someday and present a paper there` and the Text Analytics API extracted four meaningful pieces of information from it:

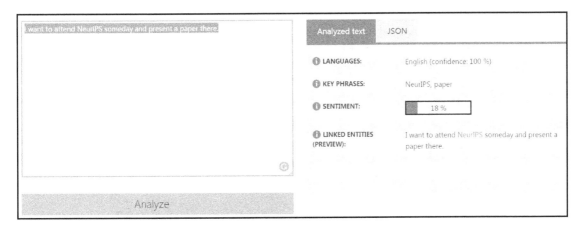

Observe how gracefully the API was able to extract all the key pieces of information from the phrase.

We will now see how to do this programmatically using Python. The setup steps are going to be exactly the same as the preceding ones. Just go to `https://portal.azure.com/#create/Microsoft.CognitiveServicesTextAnalytics` and follow the steps there. Once you have the respective API keys to consume the Text Analytics API, move on to the following subsection. Do not forget to note down the respective endpoint, as well. The endpoint should start with `https://eastus.api.cognitive.microsoft.com/text/analytics/v2.0`. This URL will not work alone; it needs to have a suffix pointing to the right method to be invoked.

Using the Text Analytics API from Python code

This section will show you how to use the Text Analytics API in your own Python code. The following are the steps for using it:

1. We will begin this section by importing the libraries we need:

```
import requests
import os
from pprint import pprint
```

2. We will then load the API key for the Text Analytics API from the environment variable:

```
api_key = os.environ['text_api_key']
```

3. Let's now specify a few URLs to store the API endpoints:

```
text_analytics_base_url = \
'https://eastus.api.cognitive.microsoft.com/text/analytics/v2.0'
language_api_url = text_analytics_base_url + "/languages"
sentiment_api_url = text_analytics_base_url + "/sentiment"
key_phrase_api_url = text_analytics_base_url + "/keyPhrases"
```

4. Let's now define the `headers` parameter by supplying the API key:

```
headers = {"Ocp-Apim-Subscription-Key": api_key}
```

5. Let's also define the body parameter. In my case, I will keep the same phrase I showed earlier in the GUI-based demo:

```
documents = { 'documents': [
{ 'id': '1', 'text': 'I want to attend NeurIPS someday and present
a paper there.' }
]}
```

6. We can now make calls to the respective APIs of Text Analytics. Let's start by detecting the language:

```
response = requests.post(language_api_url, headers=headers,
json=documents)
language = response.json()
pprint(language)
```

We get the response accordingly, as shown:

```
{'documents': [{'detectedLanguages': [{'iso6391Name': 'en',
                                        'name': 'English',
                                        'score': 1.0}],
                'id': '1'}],
 'errors': []}
```

Note that I have highlighted the language. Now, let's move on to the sentiment analysis part:

```
response = requests.post(sentiment_api_url, headers=headers,
json=documents)
sentiment = response.json()
pprint(sentiment)
```

The sentiment displayed is as shown:

```
{'documents': [{'id': '1', 'score': 0.17243406176567078}], 'errors': []}
```

Note that the phrase used here contains neither a positive sentiment nor a negative sentiment, hence the score. We will now extract the key phrases from the given text:

```
response = requests.post(key_phrase_api_url, headers=headers,
json=documents)
phrases = response.json()
print(phrases)
```

The key phrases are as shown:

```
{'documents': [{'id': '1', 'keyPhrases': ['NeurIPS', 'paper']}], 'errors': []}
```

Notice how the endpoints have changed with respect to the tasks. You can explore more about the different parameters of the endpoints we used in the preceding example at `http://bit.ly/2JjLRfi`.

An introduction to CNTK

CNTK is an offering by Microsoft. The framework is a part of the ONNX format initiative, which allows easy conversion of models between different neural toolkit frameworks. The framework is responsible for a huge portion of the deep learning production workload on Microsoft software and platforms. Launched in 2016, the framework has been a contender to popular frameworks such as TensorFlow, PyTorch, and so on. The framework is completely open source and can be found at `https://github.com/microsoft/CNTK`.

CNTK powers enterprise services, such as Cortana and Bing, and advertisements, such as Skype Translate, Microsoft Cognitive Services, and several others. It has been proven to work faster than competitors such as TensorFlow and PyTorch on several applications.

In this section, we will study some fundamentals of CNTK and then proceed to create a Django application to carry over the CNTK-based model to the web.

Getting started with CNTK

CNTK is one of the easiest frameworks to get started with, thanks to its simple syntax and ability to work without the concept of sessions, as is the case in TensorFlow, which is confusing to most learners. Let's see how we can set up CNTK on our local machines or on Google Colaboratory.

Installation on a local machine

The CNTK framework supports both 64-bit and 32-bit architecture machines. However, it only supports Python versions up to version 3.6, at the time of writing this book. You can verify the latest supported versions at `https://pypi.org/project/cntk/`. Furthermore, CNTK is not available as a built binary on macOS, currently.

To install the framework, you can either use the `pip` package manager or install it using compiled binaries on Anaconda. Assuming a Python environment is set up, you can use the following commands to install CNTK on both Windows and Linux:

- Without Anaconda, use the following for the CPU version:

    ```
    # For CPU version
    pip install cntk
    ```

- Use the following for the GPU-enabled version:

    ```
    # For the GPU enabled version
    pip install cntk-gpu
    ```

- On Anaconda-enabled machines, the CNTK framework can be installed using `pip` with the following command:

    ```
    pip install <url>
    ```

`<url>` can be obtained from the CNTK website at `http://tiny.cc/cntk`.

The command will resemble the following:

```
pip install
https://cntk.ai/PythonWheel/CPU-Only/cntk-2.6-cp35-cp35m-win_amd64.whl
```

We can now begin with its installation on Google Colaboratory.

Installation on Google Colaboratory

The CNTK framework is not available on the Google Colaboratory platform by default and so must be installed along with other requisite modules. To install CNTK on a Google Colaboratory runtime, use the following command at the top of the script:

```
!apt-get install --no-install-recommends openmpi-bin libopenmpi-dev
libopencv-dev python3-opencv python-opencv && ln -sf /usr/lib/x86_64-linux-
gnu/libmpi_cxx.so /usr/lib/x86_64-linux-gnu/libmpi_cxx.so.1 && ln -sf
/usr/lib/x86_64-linux-gnu/openmpi/lib/libmpi.so /usr/lib/x86_64-linux-
gnu/openmpi/lib/libmpi.so.12 && ln -sf /usr/lib/x86_64-linux-gnu/libmpi.so
/usr/lib/x86_64-linux-gnu/libmpi.so.12 && pip install cntk
```

 Note that the preceding command is a single-line command. If you break it up into multiple lines, you should make sure you add the required changes to the command.

Once the preceding step runs successfully, you will not need to use this command again in that runtime. So, the command can be commented out in future runs of the program.

It is conventional to import CNTK to Python projects by the `C` alias. We use the following code to import the library to the project:

```
import cntk as C
```

We can check the version of CNTK installed using the following line:

```
print(C.__version__)
```

With CNTK imported to the project, we're ready to proceed with the precursory requirements of creating a deep learning model.

Creating a CNTK neural network model

In this section, we'll complete the steps required before creating a predictive neural network and then we will create the neural network itself:

1. We begin by importing the necessary modules to the project:

```
import matplotlib.pyplot as plt
%matplotlib inline

import numpy as np
from sklearn.datasets import fetch_openml
import random

import cntk.tests.test_utils
from sklearn.preprocessing import OneHotEncoder

import cntk as C # if you have not done this before in the project
```

The `fetch_openml()` method of the `sklearn` modules helps us directly download the dataset used in this example to the project—the MNIST Handwritten Digits dataset. The `OneHotEncoder` method is used for the one-hot encoding of the labels.

2. Next, the few constants that are required during the program execution are set up:

```
num_samples = 60000
batch_size = 64
learning_rate = 0.1
```

We will perform the training on 60,000 samples with an initial learning rate of `0.1`. This rate can be dynamically updated during the training.

3. We then need to create a method for generating random mini-batches for the training:

```
class Batch_Reader(object):
    def __init__(self, data , label):
        self.data = data
        self.label = label
        self.num_sample = data.shape[0]

    def next_batch(self, batch_size):
        index = random.sample(range(self.num_sample), batch_size)
        return
self.data[index,:].astype(float),self.label[index,:].astype(float)
```

The preceding method on each call generates batches equal to the size set in the previous step—for example, 64 samples in each batch. These samples are taken randomly from the dataset.

4. The dataset now needs to be fetched; to do so, we use the following line of code:

```
mnist = fetch_openml('mnist_784')
```

Once the data has been fetched, it can be separated into training and test datasets, as shown:

```
train_data = mnist.data[:num_samples,:]
train_label = mnist.target[:num_samples]
test_data = mnist.data[num_samples:,:]
test_label = mnist.target[num_samples:]
```

5. Labels in the datasets need to be one-hot encoded before being fed into the training model. To do so, we use the following code:

```
enc = OneHotEncoder()
enc.fit(train_label[:,None])
train_encoded = enc.transform(train_label[:,None]).toarray()
```

6. We can now create a generator object for the training batches generator, as shown:

```
train_reader = Batch_Reader(train_data, train_encoded)
```

7. Let's quickly carry out the preceding steps for the `test` dataset, too:

```
enc = OneHotEncoder()
enc.fit(test_label[:,None])
test_encoded = enc.transform(test_label[:,None]).toarray()

test_reader = Batch_Reader(test_data, test_encoded)
```

8. Now, let's create a CNTK neural network model. We first begin by defining some constants:

```
dimensions = 784
classes = 10
hidden_layers = 3
hidden_layers_neurons = 400
```

We define the dimensions of the input data as 784. Recall our example from Chapter 3, *Creating Your First Deep Learning Web Application*, where we used the MNIST dataset. The images in the MNIST dataset are stored in the format of single-dimension arrays containing 28 x 28 values in the range of 0 to 255. The images belong to 10 different classes, corresponding to each digit in the Arabic numeral system. We keep a provision of 3 hidden layers, each with 400 neurons in them.

9. We then create two CNTK input variables to use while creating the model. This is one of the most important concepts of CNTK.

```
input = C.input_variable(dimensions)
label = C.input_variable(classes)
```

An input variable in CNTK is essentially a placeholder that we use to fill samples during model training and evaluation or testing. The shape of the input from the dataset must exactly match the dimensions declared in the input variables declaration in this step. It is important to mention here that a lot of people confuse the dimensions of input with the number of features a dataset has. A dataset that has *N* number of features and *M* number of samples has an (*M, N*) shape and so the dimensions of this dataset is simply 2:

```
def create_model(features):
    with C.layers.default_options(init = C.layers.glorot_uniform(),
activation = C.ops.relu):

        hidden_out = features

        for _ in range(hidden_layers):
            hidden_out =
C.layers.Dense(hidden_layers_neurons)(hidden_out)

        network_output = C.layers.Dense(classes, activation =
None)(hidden_out)
        return network_output
```

10. We create the create_model() method, which takes the input of the features as the argument.

First, the defaults are set for the model to use the uniform distribution of the initialization of weights and other values. The default activation function is set to ReLU.

The first layer contains the features themselves and the final layer contains a vector with a dimension equal to the number of classes. All the layers in between contain a completely connected network of 3 hidden layers with 400 neurons each and ReLU activation:

```
model = create_model(input/255.0)
```

Finally, we create the model using the previous function. Dividing by 255 provides normalization to the dataset, rendering the values in the image arrays between 0 and 1.

Training the CNTK model

With the model created, we can now move on to training the model and making it learn to predict. To do so, we need to use the CNTK model object and fit the samples in the dataset to it. We can, at the same time, log loss and other evaluation metrics. We need to carry out the following steps to train our model:

1. Create placeholders for loss and the classification error:

```
loss = C.cross_entropy_with_softmax(model, label)
label_error = C.classification_error(model, label)
```

2. Now, we can set up a trainer object for the CNTK framework, which is used to perform the actual training:

```
lrs = C.learning_rate_schedule(learning_rate, C.UnitType.minibatch)
learner = C.sgd(model.parameters, lrs)
trainer = C.Trainer(model, (loss, label_error), [learner])
```

3. Let's perform the training now:

```
epochs = 10
num_iters = (num_samples * epochs) / batch_size

for i in range(int(num_iters)):

    batch_data, batch_label =
train_reader.next_batch(batch_size=batch_size)

    arguments = {input: batch_data, label: batch_label}
    trainer.train_minibatch(arguments=arguments)

    if i % 1000 == 0:
        training_loss = False
        evalaluation_error = False
```

```
        training_loss = trainer.previous_minibatch_loss_average
        evalaluation_error =
trainer.previous_minibatch_evaluation_average
        print("{0}: , Loss: {1:.3f}, Error: {2:.2f}%".format(i,
training_loss, evalaluation_error * 100))
```

We set the number of epochs for training as 10 to allow quick training and evaluations. You can set it to a higher value for more accuracy in training; however, this may lead to no better training or overfitting, in some cases. At every 1,000th iteration, we display the loss and evaluation error obtained up to then. The general trend for these should be toward decline.

Testing and saving the CNTK model

Before continuing with turning this project into a web application using the Django framework, let's quickly test the accuracy obtained in this training of the model. We will carry out the following to make predictions from the model:

```
predicted_label_probs = model.eval({input: test_data})
```

This creates a NumPy array of probabilities for each label in the dataset. This has to be converted into indices and compared to the labels of the test data. We do this as shown:

```
predictions = np.argmax(predicted_label_probs, axis=1)
actual = np.argmax(test_encoded, axis=1)
correct = np.sum(predictions == actual)
print(correct / len(actual))
```

We find around 98% accuracy in the prediction. This is a very good value and we will move on to saving the model and using it through Django. To save the CNTK model, we do the following:

```
model.save("cntk.model")
```

With the model saved successfully, you will have to download the model file to your local system if you've used Colaboratory to build the model. Next, we can move on to deploying the model on a Django-based server.

A brief introduction to Django web development

Django is one of the most popular frameworks for web development using Python. The framework is lightweight, robust, and actively maintained by the community, which quickly patches security holes and adds new features. In this book, we've covered the Flask framework, which is essentially a bare-bones framework for Python web development. However, Django comes with a lot of built-in features that implement state-of-the-art methods and practices.

A Django project is initially structured in the following manner:

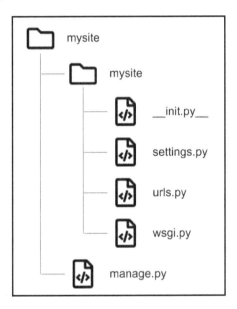

These files are auto-generated when you create a new Django project using the `django-admin` tool. The top-level directory, `mysite`, represents the name of the Django project. Each Django project contains apps. Apps are similar to the concept of modules in software development. They are usually independent pieces of the complete project and are put together by the `mysite` master app within the project directory. Each project can have several apps inside it.

Let's learn how to get started with Django and create a new project!

Getting started with Django

The foremost step before using Django is to install it. Fortunately, the framework is easily installable as a module from the Python PIP repository. It is also available on the Conda repository. To install Django, open a new terminal window and use the following command:

```
conda install django
```

Alternatively, if you prefer PIP, use the following command:

```
pip install django
```

This will install the Django module to your Python environment.

To check whether it has been successfully installed, use the following command in the terminal:

```
python -m django --version
```

This should produce an output of a version number—for example, – 2.0.8. If not, check your installation of Django.

Creating a new Django project

Django provides a handy utility named the django-admin tool, which can be used to generate the boilerplate code required for a Django project. To create a new project named, say, cntkdemo, use the following code:

```
django-admin startproject cntkdemo
```

This will create all the boilerplate folders and files. However, we must create at least one app within the project. Change your active working directory to the cntkdemo folder using the terminal. Use the following command to create an app inside this project:

```
python manage.py startapp api
```

So, we have created a folder named api with the following folders inside it; all the files are auto-generated with placeholder code and documentation:

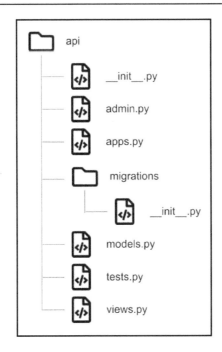

We can now proceed with the coding of the initial UI.

Setting up the home page template

Let's now create a web page that loads when the / route is accessed. Remember the api app that we created in the project? Let's make the index page a part of this app for the sake of simplicity. While it is possible to create this route in the urls.py file of the mysite app, we will provide the api app with its own route handling file.

Let's begin with the steps for setting up the home page template:

1. Create a file, urls.py, inside the api folder. The complete path of this file relative to the project directory would be mysite/api/urls.py. Inside this file, let's add the / route, using the following code:

```
from django.urls import path

from . import views

urlpatterns = [
    path('', views.indexView), # This line handles the '/' route.
]
```

2. Save this file. The preceding code essentially adds a new path, /, to the `api` app (note, not to the project!). It imports all the views available in the `views.py` file of the `api` app. Note that `indexView` still does not exist. We will create this view after the next step.

3. The `api` app is not linked to the main project app. We need to add the following lines to the `mysite/mysite/urls.py` file to enable the route handling by the `api` app's route handler:

```python
from django.contrib import admin
from django.urls import path
from django.urls import include # -- Add this line!

urlpatterns = [
  path('', include('api.urls')), # -- Add this line!
  path('admin/', admin.site.urls),
]
```

The first line imports a utility for including app-specific routing settings to the project app. We use this to include the `urls.py` file inside the `api` app using the `api.urls` string. This automatically converts the strings to lines of code that try to find and include the correct file.

4. In the `views.py` file inside the `api` app directory, add the following lines:

```python
from django.http import HttpResponse
from django.template import loader
```

The `HttpResponse` method allows the `view` method to return an HTML response. The `loader` class provides us with methods to load HTML templates from the disk.

5. Let's now create the `indexView` method:

```python
def indexView(request):
  template = loader.get_template('api/index.html')
  context = {}
  return HttpResponse(template.render(context, request))
```

The `indexView` method loads the `api/index.html` template file and renders it with the variables provided in the `context` dictionary, along with the `request` parameters available to the template. Currently, we pass a blank context because we do not have any values to send to the template. But again, the `api/index.html` file defined previously does not exist.

6. Let's create the folder for holding templates and link it to the project settings. To do so, go to the root directory of the project and create a folder named `templates`. We need the project to be able to recognize this folder as the directory for the templates. To do so, we need to modify the `TEMPLATES` settings in the `mysite/mysite/settings.py` file:

```
TEMPLATES = [
  {
  'BACKEND': 'django.template.backends.django.DjangoTemplates',
  'DIRS': [os.path.join(BASE_DIR, 'templates')], # -- Add this line!
  'APP_DIRS': True,
  'OPTIONS': {
  'context_processors': [
```

Upon adding the preceding line, the project will look for the templates inside the `mysite/templates/` folder.

7. Create the `index.html` template file.

   Notice that our template file route in step 4 exists within an `api` directory. Create a folder named `api` inside the `templates` directory. Inside this, create the `index.html` file with the following code:

```
{% load static %}
. . .
        <div class="jumbotron">
            <h3 class="jumbotronHeading">Draw here!</h3>
            . . .
        </div>
        <div class="jumbotron">
            <h3>Prediction Results</h3>
            <p id="result"></p>
        </div>
        <div id="csrf">{% csrf_token %}</div>
    </div>
    <script
src='https://cdnjs.cloudflare.com/ajax/libs/jquery/2.1.3/jquery.min
.js'></script>
    <script src="{% static "/index.js" %}"></script>
. . .
```

We've included some required scripts at the end of the preceding code block, including a script to fetch the CSRF token from the backend.

8. Now, let's add a `canvas` element to `div` with the `jumbotron` class in the
   previous code block, where we will draw the digits. We'll also add a slider for
   selecting the width of the drawing pen, as shown:

```html
<div class="jumbotron">
    <h3 class="jumbotronHeading">Draw here!</h3>
    <div class="slidecontainer">
        <input type="range" min="10" max="50" value="15"
id="myRange">
        <p>Value: <span id="sliderValue"></span></p>
    </div>
    <div class="canvasDiv">
        <canvas id="canvas" width="350" height="350"></canvas>
        <p style="text-align:center;">
            <button class="btn btn-success" id="predict-btn"
role="button">Predict</button>
            <button class="btn btn-primary" id="clearButton"
role="button">Clear</button>
        </p>
    </div>
</div>
```

The `template` file also includes two static files—`style.css` and `script.js`. We
will be creating these files in the upcoming section. We have not yet created the
script for sending the data to the server and rendering the response received.

9. Now, we will begin adding the JavaScript code required to communicate with
   the backend APIs. First, we create a method to check whether we need a CSRF
   token to communicate with the backend. This is only a utility function and is not
   related to calling the backend APIs, which may, at times, be designed to accept
   requests without CSRF tokens. We create this function as shown:

```javascript
<script type="text/javascript">
    function csrfSafeMethod(method) {
        return (/^(GET|HEAD|OPTIONS|TRACE)$/.test(method));
    }
```

10. Then, we create a `click` handler for the `Predict` button. This handler function
    first sets up the proper headers required to make the call to the backend APIs
    and then converts the drawing present on the canvas into a data URL string:

```javascript
$("#predict-btn").click(function() {

    var csrftoken = $('input[name=csrfmiddlewaretoken]').val();

    $.ajaxSetup({
```

```
        beforeSend: function(xhr, settings) {
            if (!csrfSafeMethod(settings.type) && !this.crossDomain) {
                xhr.setRequestHeader("X-CSRFToken", csrftoken);
            }
        }
    });

    $('#predict-btn').prop('disabled', true);

    var canvasObj = document.getElementById("canvas");
    var img = canvasObj.toDataURL();
    // MORE CODE TO BE ADDED BELOW THIS LINE

    // MORE CODE TO BE ADDED ABOVE THIS LINE
});
</script>
```

11. Finally, we add the code to the `click` handler function of the `Predict` button to make the Ajax call to the backend with the data from the canvas, as shown:

```
$("#predict-btn").click(function() {
...
        // MORE CODE TO BE ADDED BELOW THIS LINE
        $.ajax({
            type: "POST",
            url: "/predict",
            data: img,
            success: function(data) {
                console.log(data);
                var tb = "<table class='table table-
hover'><thead><tr><th>Item</th><th>Confidence</th></thead><tbody>";
                var res = JSON.parse(data);
                console.log(res);
                $('#result').empty.append(res.data);
                $('#predict-btn').prop('disabled', false);
            }
        });
        // MORE CODE TO BE ADDED ABOVE THIS LINE
...
});
    </script>
```

12. Before we can create the static files, we need to create a folder for them and link it to the project. This is similar to how we created the `templates` folder. First, create a folder, `static`, in the project directory with a `mysite/static/` path. Then, modify the `STATIC` configuration in the `mysite/mysite/settings.py` file, as shown:

```
STATIC_URL = '/static/'

STATICFILES_DIRS = [
    os.path.join(BASE_DIR, "static"), # -- Add this line!
]
```

We can now create and load static files into the project templates using the `{% load static %}` directive at the top of the template files, as we did in the `index.html` file.

13. Create `style.css` and `script.js`—since these files are not explicitly relevant to the context of this book, you can download them directly from `http://tiny.cc/cntk-demo`.

 Please note here that without the `script.js` file, the project will not run.

We have created the setup for the prediction of the images drawn on a canvas present in the `index.html` template file. However, the `/predict` route is yet to be created. Let's see how CNTK models can be loaded and used in Django in the next section.

Making predictions using CNTK from the Django project

In this section, we'll first set the required route, the view, and the imports for the CNTK model to work with Django. We will then load the CNTK model from the saved file and make predictions using it.

Setting up the predict route and view

Recall how we created the / route and its corresponding view in the api app:

1. First, add the following line to mysite/api/urls.py:

```
urlpatterns = [
    path('', views.indexView),
    path('predict', views.predictView), # -- Add this line!
]
```

This creates the /predict route. However, the view, predictView, is not yet created.

2. Add the following lines to the views.py file in the api app:

```
from django.http import JsonResponse

def predictView(request):
    # We will add more code below this line

    # We will add more code above this line
    return JsonResponse({"data": -1})
```

Notice the placeholders in the preceding lines. We'll add more here in the next steps.

Making the necessary module imports

Now, let's load all the modules required to make predictions with the CNTK model, as in the following steps:

1. Add the following lines of imports to the views.py file of the api app:

```
import os
from django.conf import settings
```

2. We'll need the preceding imports to load the model from the disk:

```
import cntk as C
from cntk.ops.functions import load_model
```

The preceding lines import the CNTK module to the Django project. The load_model method will help us load the saved CNTK model file.

The following modules are used to manipulate the images that the predictions will be made on:

```
from PIL import Image
import numpy as np
```

The following modules provide utility for handling Base64-encoded strings, which is the format that the `index.html` page sends the canvas data in the request:

```
import re
import base64
import random
import string
```

The other libraries will be explained when they are used in the upcoming sections.

Loading and predicting using the CNTK model

We will now further edit the `predictView` view by following these steps:

1. First, read the Base64-encoded image string data to a variable using the following code:

```
def predictView(request):
    # We will add more code below this line

    post_data = request.POST.items()
    pd = [p for p in post_data]
    imgData = pd[1][0].replace(" ", "+")
    imgData += "=" * ((4 - len(imgData) % 4) % 4)
```

The Base64-decoded string does not have proper padding and contains spaces that need to be converted into +. The last two lines in the previous code block perform the same manipulations on the string.

2. Next, we will convert this Base64-encoded string into a PNG image and save it to disk with the following lines:

```
filename = ''.join([random.choice(string.ascii_letters +
string.digits) for n in range(32)])

convertImage(imgData, filename)
```

The first line creates a 32-character-long random string for the filename. The next line calls the `convertImage` method, which stored the `base64` string as the filename provided.

3. However, the `convertImage` method has not yet been defined. Outside of the `predictView` method, add the definition for the function, as shown:

```
def convertImage(imgData, filename):
    imgstr = re.search(r'base64,(.*)', str(imgData)).group(1)
    img = base64.b64decode(imgstr)
    with open(filename+'.png', 'wb') as output:
        output.write(img)
```

The method strips out the extra metadata from the string. It then decodes the string and saves it as a PNG file.

4. Let's return back to the `predictView` method. We will first load the saved `image` file:

```
image = Image.open(filename+'.png').convert('1')
```

We will also convert the image into a black and white channel only. This reduces the number of channels in the image from 3 to 1.

5. Recall that all images in the MNIST dataset have dimensions of 28 x 28. We must resize our current image to the same dimensions. We do so with the following line:

```
image.thumbnail((28,28), Image.ANTIALIAS)
```

6. Now, we convert the image into a NumPy array with the following lines:

```
image_np = np.array(image.getdata()).astype(int)
image_np_expanded = np.expand_dims(image_np, axis = 0)
```

`np.expanded_dims` is a simple utility in NumPy used to add an extra dimension to the array for proper compatibility with most machine learning libraries.

7. Load the CNTK model. First, create a folder named `data` in the root directory of the project and copy the saved `model` file there in `mysite/data/cntk.model`.

We now load the CNTK model in the `predictView` method, as shown:

```
model = load_model(os.path.join(settings.BASE_DIR,
"data/cntk.model"))
```

8. Finally, we can predict the label of the image, as shown:

```
predicted_label_probs = model.eval({model.arguments[0]:
image_np_expanded})
data = np.argmax(predicted_label_probs, axis=1)
```

The `eval` method, in its first argument, expects the NumPy array of the image and returns a list of probabilities of each output class. The `np.argmax` method is used to find the index of the class with the highest probability.

9. To return the output, modify the `return` part of the `predictView` method, as shown:

```
# We will add more code above this line
return JsonResponse({"data": str(data[0])})
```

The predicted label for the image is sent as a digit contained in the `data` variable of the JSON response, which is displayed on the page.

Testing the web app

Finally, we can test the CNTK + Django app we have developed. To do so, open the terminal and direct it to the root directory of the project.

Use the following command to start the Django server:

```
python manage.py runserver
```

The server starts at `http://localhost:8000` if the port is free. Open the page in a web browser. Draw your digit on the canvas provided and click on the **Predict** button. You will be able to see the result from the model at the bottom of the page, as shown:

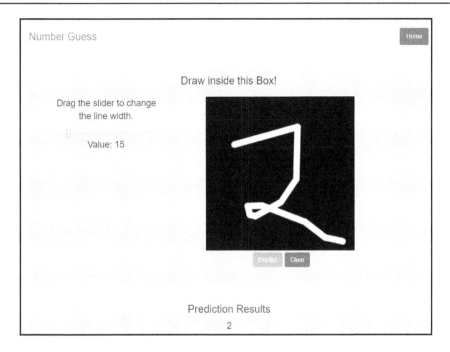

Notice that the model returns the correct output in the preceding screenshot, which is **2**. Hence, we conclude the deployment of CNTK models using Django.

Summary

In this chapter, we covered the offerings from Microsoft AI and the Azure cloud for performing deep learning on websites. We saw how the Face API can be used to predict the gender and age of people in images, as well as how the Text Analytics API can be used to predict the language of a given text and the key phrases in the provided text or the sentiment of any sentence. Finally, we created a deep learning model using CNTK on the MNIST dataset. We saw how the model can be saved and then deployed via a Django-based web application in the form of an API. This deployment of the saved model via Django can be easily adapted for other deep learning frameworks, such as TensorFlow or PyTorch.

In the next chapter, we will discuss a generalized framework for building production-grade deep learning applications using Python.

4
Deep Learning in Production (Intelligent Web Apps)

This section provides different case studies showing how to develop and deploy deep learning-web applications (using deep learning APIs) along with showing measures to secure web applications using deep learning.

This section comprises the following chapters:

9
A General Production Framework for Deep Learning-Enabled Websites

We have covered decent ground on using industry-grade cloud **Deep Learning** (DL) APIs in our applications in previous chapters and we have learned about their use through practical examples. In this chapter, we will cover a general outline for developing DL-enabled websites. This will require us to bring together all the things that we have learned so far so that we can put them to use in real-life use cases. In this chapter, we will learn how to structure a DL web application for production by first preparing the dataset. We will then train a DL model in Python and then wrap the DL models in APIs using Flask.

The following is a high-level summary of this chapter:

- Defining our problem statement
- Breaking the problem into several components
- Building a mental model to bind the project components
- How we should be collecting the data
- Following a directory structure for our project
- Building the project from scratch

Technical requirements

You can access the code used in this chapter at `https://github.com/PacktPublishing/` `Hands-On-Python-Deep-Learning-for-Web/tree/master/Chapter9`.

To run the code used in this chapter, you'll need the following software:

- Python 3.6+
- The Python PIL library
- NumPy
- Pandas
- The **Natural Language Toolkit (NLTK)**
- Flask 1.1.0+ and compatible versions of the following:
    - FlaskForm
    - wtforms
    - flask_restful
    - flask_jsonpify

All other installations will be described during the course of this chapter.

Defining the problem statement

Any project should start with a well-defined problem statement or the project development is bound to suffer. The problem statement governs all the major steps involved in an overall project development pipeline, starting from project planning to project cost.

In a DL-based web project, for example, the problem statement will direct us to the following:

- Determine what kind of data we would need.
- How much complexity there would be in terms of code, planning, and other resources.
- What kind of user interface we would develop.
- How much human involvement there would be so that an estimate can be prepared on the project's manpower and so on.

Hence, a well-defined problem statement is really required in order for us to get started with further project development.

Imagine being a DL engineer at a company that is planning to build a recommendation system to suggest products from a product listing based on some user-provided criteria. Your boss has asked you to develop a **Proof of Concept** (**PoC**) based on this. So, how should we go about it? As mentioned previously, let's start by defining the problem statement first.

The main entity that provides inputs to the final recommendation system is a user. Based on the user's preferences (let's call the input features preferences for now), the system would provide a list of products that best match their preference. So, long story short, the problem statement can be written as follows:

Given a set of input features (user preferences), our task is to suggest a list of products.

Now that we have a well-defined problem statement to proceed, let's go ahead and build up the next steps in the following section.

Building a mental model of the project

Looking at the problem statement, you might feel tempted to open a browser and start searching for some datasets. But when it comes to properly develop a project, definite planning is required to structure it piece by piece. A project without a structure is nothing more than a rudderless ship. So, we will be cautious about this from the start. We will discuss the modules that are going to play a very essential role in our project. This includes several mental considerations as well. I like to call this phase building a mental model of the project.

Let's take some time to discuss the problem statement further, so as to figure out the essential modules we would need to develop.

Our project concerns recommending products to users based on their preferences. So, in order to perform this recommendation, we would need a system that knows how to understand the set of preferences a user is providing to it. To be able to make sense of these preferences, the system would need some kind of training that we would be implementing DL. But what about preferences? How would they look like? You will often encounter these questions in real-world project situations that need humans in the loop.

Now, think for a second and try to think of the aspects you typically look for while choosing a product to buy. Let's list them here:

- What are the specifications of the product? If I want a large size T-shirt, I should not be recommended a small size T-shirt.
- What is the cost of the product? Users have a limited amount of money is this recommendation good for their wallet?
- What brand is this product? Users often have brand preferences for similar products manufactured by several companies.

Note that the preceding pointers are not in any particular order.

So, from the preceding section, we are starting to get a sense of what we would need, which is an interface (which will essentially be a web page, in our case) for a user to provide their preferences. Taking these preferences into account, our system would predict a set of products that it found to be the most appropriate ones. This is where the DL part comes into play. As we will recollect from earlier chapters, for a DL model to work on a given problem, it needs to be trained on some data that represents the problem as closely as possible. Let's now discuss the data part of our system.

We have a readily available dataset for our project—the Amazon Fine Food Reviews dataset provided by Amazon and created by the Stanford Network Analysis Project team. While the dataset is large in size, we will not be using the full dataset when creating the demonstration in this chapter. An immediate question that might get triggered here is how would the dataset look? We need to formulate a rough plan to decide the following:

- What features we would be choosing to construct the dataset
- Where we would be looking to collect the data

Let's add a bit of enhancement to the original problem statement before proceeding further from here. Here's the original problem statement:

Given a set of input features (user preferences), our task is to suggest a list of products.

Users will not like our system if it recommends them substandard products. So, we would modify the problem statement a bit, as follows:

Given a set of input features (user preferences), our task is to suggest a list of the best possible products to buy.

For our system to recommend a list of the best possible products with respect to a given criterion, it first needs to know the average ratings of the products. Along with the average ratings, it would be useful to have the following information about a particular product, apart from its name:

- Specifications
- Category of product
- Seller name
- Average price
- Expected delivery time

While preparing the data, we would look for the previous pointers about a particular product. Now comes the question of where we would be collecting the data from. The answer is Amazon! Amazon is known for its services in the e-commerce industry in providing us with various products and information about them, such as their ratings, product specifications, the price of the items, and so on. But say Amazon does not allow you to download this data directly as a zipped file. In order to get the data from Amazon in the desired form, we would have to resort to web scraping.

Up to this point in the discussion, we are certain on two broad areas of the project:

- An interface to receive preferences from the user
- Data that would represent the problem statement we are dealing with

For DL modeling, we will be starting with simple, fully-connected, neural network-based architecture. It's often useful to start with a simple model and gradually increase the complexity because it makes the code base easier to debug.

So, from this, it is safe enough to say that the following three modules are going to play an essential role in this project:

- An interface
- Data
- A DL model

Hopefully, you now have a fair idea about approaching the development of a project in the first place. What questions you should be asking at this stage and what considerations you may have to make can be worked out from the involved framework you now have.

We would not want our recommendation system to be biased toward anything. There can be many types of biases hidden in the data and naturally enough, it can cause the DL system that uses it to inherit that bias.

To find out more about different types of biases in machine learning systems, you are encouraged to refer to this article at `https://developers.google.com/machine-learning/crash-course/fairness/types-of-bias`. In our case, a staggering example of bias would be a situation where a male visitor gets product recommendations that are averaged out. The recommendations might only come on the basis of his gender but not based on any other visitor-browsing pattern. This can be erroneous and may have been done mistakenly. But instances like this can make our model very inappropriate. In the next section, we will be discussing a few points to learn how can we avoid bias on the data.

Avoiding the chances of getting erroneous data in the first place

What is erroneous data? Are we only talking about data with wrong values? The answer is no. Besides data having wrong or missing values, erroneous data can have subtle but grave errors that may lead to poor training of the model or even bias. So, it is important to identify such erroneous data and remove it before training our model. There are five main ways of identifying these errors:

- Look for missing values.
- Look for values that seem out of scale or possibility—in other words, outliers.
- Do not include any features in the dataset that might cause data leakage.
- Ensure that all categories of evaluation have a similar number of samples in the dataset.
- Ensure that your design of the solution to the problem itself does not introduce a bias.

Once we are clear on these points, we are ready to move on to the more specific areas that we need to be careful about during the collection of data. It is important that during data collection a proper plan is prepared to keep in mind all the properties of the data source and the requirements of the problem statement.

Suppose you are scraping data for products from US-based outlets on Amazon and end up searching for products on the Indian version of Amazon instead. The scraper might give you data from India-based outlets, which may not be suitable for recommendation to US-based residents.

Further, since Amazon—and similar services, such as Flipkart—takes the help of recommender systems to target the *most suitable* products for their customers, during data collection, the scraper should not become prey to such recommendations. It is important that the scraper clears its context every now and then and avoids getting biased results due to the AI put in place by Amazon.

Let's take an example from the Amazon Fine Food Reviews dataset. Though on the first look the dataset looks pretty balanced, we can uncover a lot of bias in the dataset. Consider the length of the text that the customers write for their reviews of products. Let's plot them in a graph against the score they were rated. The following graphs show the plot for products rated 1 and 2 stars:

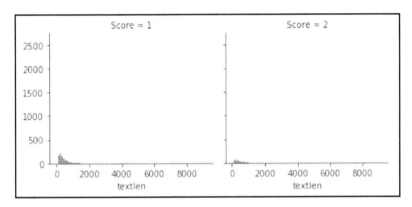

The following graphs show the plot for products rated 3 and 4 stars:

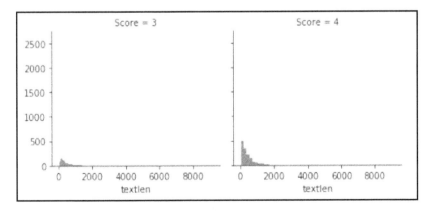

The following graph shows the plot for products rated 5 stars:

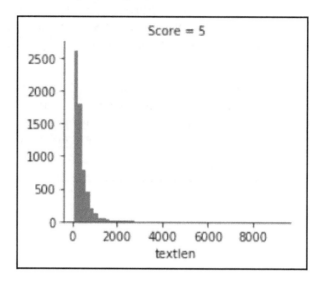

Notice how more positive reviews have more written text in them. This would directly convert into most of the words in the dataset, leading to a higher rating from the user. Now, consider a scenario where a user writes a lengthy review with a low rating and a generally negative opinion about the product. Since our model is trained to associate larger lengths of reviews to positive ratings, it would mark the negative review as positive.

The bottom line here is that real-world data can contain many edge cases, as shown, and if they are not handled in a proper manner, you will most likely get an erroneous model.

How not to build an AI backend

Considering the vastness that web applications can grow to and the strong dependence of nearly every other platform on a backend that runs as a web-based service, it is important for the backend to be well thought of and properly executed. AI-based applications, even in a PoC stage, are often not blazingly fast in responding or take a lot of time to train on the new samples.

While we will be discussing tips and tricks to make a backend that does not choke under pressure due to bottlenecks, we need to lay down a few pointers that need to be avoided in the best possible way when developing an AI-integrated backend for a website.

Expecting the AI part of the website to be real time

AI is computationally expensive and needless to say, this is undesirable for a website that aims to serve its clients in the quickest time possible. While smaller models or using browser AI (such as TensorFlow.js or other libraries) can provide the experience of real-time AI responses, even they suffer issues where the client is in a slow network area or using a low-end device. So, both the methods of in-browser AI models or lightweight AI models replying near instantaneously are subject to device configuration and network bandwidth. Hence, the backend of the website, which is supposed to make quick responses to the client, should ideally be separated from the part that handles the AI model responses. Both, working in parallel, should maintain a common data storage and a proper method of interaction between the two, such that the backend code responsible for responding to the clients has less dependence on the AI model part.

Assuming the incoming data from a website is ideal

Even though the website or app corresponding to the project might resemble an ideal method of data collection, the data coming from it must not be assumed to be free of errors. Bad network requests, malicious connections, or simply garbage input provided by users can lead to data that is unfit for training. A non-malicious user may have network issues and refresh the same page 10 to 20 times in a short time frame, which should not add to the viewing-based importance of that page. All data collected from the website must be subject to cleanup and filtering based on the requirements of the model. It must be kept in mind that the challenges faced by websites will almost certainly affect the quality of data collected.

A sample end-to-end AI-integrated web application

Now that we have discussed an overview and the pitfalls to avoid when creating an AI-powered website backend, let's move on to creating one—albeit a rather simple one—that demonstrates the general overview of the solution.

We will cover the following steps, as stated previously:

- The collection of data as per the problem statement
- Cleaning and preprocessing the data
- Building the AI model
- Creating an interface
- Using the AI model on the interface

While we have previously discussed the pitfalls of collecting the data, we will briefly discuss here the tools and methods that can be employed to complete the task.

Data collection and cleanup

For the purpose of collecting data, from a general perspective, there could be several data sources. You could scrape data off websites or simply download some prepared dataset. Other methods could also be employed, such as the following:

- Generating data on the fly within the runtime of applications/websites
- Logging from applications or smart devices
- Collecting data directly from users via systematic forms (such as quizzes or surveys)
- Collecting data from survey agencies
- Observational data measured by specific methods (scientific data) and other ways

`beautifulsoup` is a library commonly used to perform web scraping. `Scrapy` is yet another popular tool and can be used very rapidly.

The data cleaning would entirely depend on the form of data collected by you and has been discussed in previous chapters of the book. We will assume that you are able to convert your data into a format that is suitable for how you wish to proceed with the model-building part. For the further topics in this section, we will use a prepared dataset titled Amazon Fine Food Reviews, which can be downloaded from `https://www.kaggle.com/snap/amazon-fine-food-reviews`. Once you extract the downloaded ZIP file, you'll get the dataset as a file called `Reviews.csv`.

A good starting point to observe how to perform web scraping and prepare a clean dataset is `https://github.com/Nilabhra/kolkata_nlp_workshop_2019`.

Building the AI model

Now, we will prepare the AI model, which will recommend products based on the user's query. To do so, let's create a new Jupyter notebook.

Making the necessary imports

We begin by importing the required Python modules to the project:

```
import numpy as np
import pandas as pd
import nltk
from nltk.corpus import stopwords
from nltk.tokenize import WordPunctTokenizer
from sklearn.model_selection import train_test_split
from sklearn.feature_extraction.text import TfidfVectorizer

# Comment below line if you already have stopwords installed
nltk.download('stopwords')
```

We import `TfidfVectorizer` to help us create **Term Frequency-Inverse Document Frequency** (**TF-IDF**) vectors for performing natural language processing. TF-IDF is a numerical measure of how important a word in a single document is, given a number of documents that may or may not contain the words. Numerically, it increases the importance value when a single word occurs frequently in a single document but not in other documents. TF-IDF is so popular that over 80% of the world's natural language-based recommender systems currently use it.

We are also importing `WordPunctTokenizer`. A tokenizer performs the function of breaking down a text into elemental tokens. For example, a large paragraph may be broken down into sentences and further into words.

Reading the dataset and preparing cleaning functions

We will read the Amazon Fine Food Reviews dataset with the `ISO-8859-1` encoding. This is only to ensure that we do not lose out on any special symbols used in the text of the review:

```
df = pd.read_csv('Reviews.csv', encoding = "ISO-8859-1")
df = df.head(10000)
```

Since the dataset is very large, we've restricted our work in this chapter to the first 10,000 rows in the dataset.

We would need to remove stop words from the text and filter out symbols such as brackets and other symbols not natural to written text. We will create a function named `cleanText()`, which will perform the filtering and removal of stop words:

```
import string
import re

stopwordSet = set(stopwords.words("english"))

def cleanText(line):
    global stopwordSet
    line = line.translate(string.punctuation)
    line = line.lower().split()
    line = [word for word in line if not word in stopwordSet and len(word)
>= 3]
    line = " ".join(line)
    return re.sub(r"[^A-Za-z0-9^,!.\/'+-=]", " ", line)
```

Using the preceding function, we have removed the stop words and any words shorter than three characters from the text. We have filtered out punctuation and are only keeping the relevant characters from the text.

Slicing out the required data

The dataset contains more data than is useful to us for the demo at hand. We will extract the ProductId, UserId, Score, and Text columns to prepare our demo. The names of the products are encrypted for privacy reasons, just as the names of the users are encrypted:

```
data = df[['ProductId', 'UserId', 'Score', 'Text']]
```

Keeping data encrypted and free of personal information is a challenge in data science. It is important to remove parts from the dataset that would make it possible to identify the private entities that are a part of the dataset. For example, you would need to remove people and organization names from the text of the review to stop the products and users from being identified, despite them having encrypted product and user IDs.

Applying text cleaning

We will now apply the text filtering and stop word removal function to clean the text in the dataset:

```
%%time
data['Text'] = data['Text'].apply(cleanText)
```

The time taken for the task is displayed.

 Note that the preceding code block will only work in Jupyter Notebook and not in normal Python scripts. To run it on normal Python scripts, remove the `%%time` command.

Splitting the dataset into train and test parts

Since we have a single dataset, we will break it into two parts, with the feature and label parts separated:

```
X_train, X_valid, y_train, y_valid = train_test_split(data['Text'],
df['ProductId'], test_size = 0.2)
```

We will use the `train_test_split()` method from the `sklearn` module to split the dataset into 80% for training and 20% for testing.

Aggregating text about products and users

We will now aggregate the dataset's reviews by users and product IDs. We'll need the reviews for each product to determine what that product would be a good choice for:

```
user_df = data[['UserId','Text']]
product_df = data[['ProductId', 'Text']]
user_df = user_df.groupby('UserId').agg({'Text': ' '.join})
product_df = product_df.groupby('ProductId').agg({'Text': ' '.join})
```

Similarly, reviews aggregated by users will help us determine what a user likes.

Creating TF-IDF vectorizers of users and products

We will now create two different vectorizers one is for users and the other for products. We will need these vectorizers in place to determine the similarity between the requirements of the users and what the reviews tell us about any given product. First, we will create the vectorizer for users and display its shape:

```
user_vectorizer = TfidfVectorizer(tokenizer =
WordPunctTokenizer().tokenize, max_features=1000)
user_vectors = user_vectorizer.fit_transform(user_df['Text'])
user_vectors.shape
```

Then, we will create the vectorizer for products:

```
product_vectorizer = TfidfVectorizer(tokenizer =
WordPunctTokenizer().tokenize, max_features=1000)
product_vectors = product_vectorizer.fit_transform(product_df['Text'])
product_vectors.shape
```

We use `WordPunctTokenizer` to break down the text and use the `fit_transform` method of the `TfidfVectorizer` object to prepare the vectors, which map the word dictionary to their importance in documents.

Creating an index of users and products by the ratings provided

We use the `pivot_table` method of the `pandas` module to create a matrix of user ratings against products. We will use this matrix to perform matrix factorization to determine the products that a user likes:

```
userRatings = pd.pivot_table(data, values='Score', index=['UserId'],
columns=['ProductId'])
userRatings.shape
```

We will also convert the `TfidfVectorizer` vectors for users and products into matrices suitable for matrix factorization:

```
P = pd.DataFrame(user_vectors.toarray(), index=user_df.index,
columns=user_vectorizer.get_feature_names())
Q = pd.DataFrame(product_vectors.toarray(), index=product_df.index,
columns=product_vectorizer.get_feature_names())
```

We can now create the matrix factorization function.

Creating the matrix factorization function

We will now create a function to perform matrix factorization. Matrix factorization became a popular family of algorithms used for recommender systems during the Netflix Prize challenge in 2006. It is a family of algorithms that decomposes a user-item matrix into a set of two lower-dimension rectangular matrices that can be multiplied to restore the original higher-order matrix:

```
def matrix_factorization(R, P, Q, steps=1, gamma=0.001,lamda=0.02):
    for step in range(steps):
        for i in R.index:
```

```
            for j in R.columns:
                if R.loc[i,j]>0:
                    eij=R.loc[i,j]-np.dot(P.loc[i],Q.loc[j])
                    P.loc[i]=P.loc[i]+gamma*(eij*Q.loc[j]-lamda*P.loc[i])
                    Q.loc[j]=Q.loc[j]+gamma*(eij*P.loc[i]-lamda*Q.loc[j])
        e=0
        for i in R.index:
            for j in R.columns:
                if R.loc[i,j]>0:
                    e= e + pow(R.loc[i,j]-
np.dot(P.loc[i],Q.loc[j]),2)+lamda*(pow(np.linalg.norm(P.loc[i]),2)+pow(np.
linalg.norm(Q.loc[j]),2))
        if e<0.001:
            break
    return P,Q
```

We then perform the matrix factorization and log the time taken:

```
%%time
P, Q = matrix_factorization(userRatings, P, Q, steps=1,
gamma=0.001,lamda=0.02)
```

After this, we need to save the model.

Saving the model as pickle

Now, create a folder called `api` in the `root` directory of your project. Then, save the trained model, which is the lower-order matrices obtained after factorization of the user-products rating matrix:

```
import pickle
output = open('api/model.pkl', 'wb')
pickle.dump(P,output)
pickle.dump(Q,output)
pickle.dump(user_vectorizer,output)
output.close()
```

Saving the models as binary pickle files allows us to quickly load them back into the memory during deployment of the model on the backend of the website.

Now that we are done developing the predictive model, we will move on to building an interface for the application to work on.

Building an interface

To build an interface for the web application, we need to think about how we would want our users to interact with the system. In our case, we are expecting the user to be presented with suggestions based on what they search for in a search bar the moment they submit the search query. This means we need the system to respond in real time and generate suggestions on the fly. To build this system, we will create an API that will respond to the search query.

Creating an API to answer search queries

We will create an API that accepts queries in the form of HTTP requests and replies with suggestions of products based on the search query entered by the user. To do so, follow these steps:

1. We will begin by importing the required modules for the API. We discussed these imported modules in the previous section:

```
import numpy as np
import pandas as pd
from nltk.corpus import stopwords
from nltk.tokenize import WordPunctTokenizer
from sklearn.feature_extraction.text import TfidfVectorizer
from sklearn.feature_extraction.text import CountVectorizer
from flask import Flask, request, render_template, make_response
from flask_wtf import FlaskForm
from wtforms import StringField, validators
import io
from flask_restful import Resource, Api
import string
import re
import pickle
from flask_jsonify import jsonify
```

2. We will also import the `Flask` module to create a quick HTTP server that can serve on a defined route in the form of an API. We will instantiate the `Flask` app object as shown:

```
DEBUG = True
app = Flask(__name__)
app.config['SECRET_KEY'] = 'abcdefgh'
api = Api(app)
```

The value of `SECRET_KEY` in the app configuration is up to you.

3. We will then create a `class` function to handle the text input that we receive in the form of a search query from the user:

```
class TextFieldForm(FlaskForm):
    text = StringField('Document Content',
validators=[validators.data_required()])
```

4. To encapsulate the API methods, we wrap them in a `Flask_Work` class:

```
class Flask_Work(Resource):
    def __init__(self):
        self.stopwordSet = set(stopwords.words("english"))
        pass
```

5. The `cleanText()` method we used during model creation is again required. It will be used to clean and filter out the search query entered by the user:

```
def cleanText(self, line):
    line = line.translate(string.punctuation)
    line = line.lower().split()
    line = [word for word in line if not word in self.stopwordSet and
len(word) >= 3]
    line = " ".join(line)
    return re.sub(r"[^A-Za-z0-9^,!.\/'+-=]", " ", line)
```

6. We define a home page for the application, which will be loaded from the `index.html` file that we create in the templates later:

```
def get(self):
    headers = {'Content-Type': 'text/html'}
    return make_response(render_template('index.html'), 200, headers)
```

7. We create the `post` method-based prediction route, which will respond with the product suggestions upon receiving the user's search query:

```
def post(self):
    f = open('model.pkl', 'rb')
    P, Q, userid_vectorizer = pickle.load(f), pickle.load(f),
pickle.load(f)
    sentence = request.form['search']
    test_data = pd.DataFrame([sentence], columns=['Text'])
    test_data['Text'] = test_data['Text'].apply(self.cleanText)
    test_vectors = userid_vectorizer.transform(test_data['Text'])
    test_v_df = pd.DataFrame(test_vectors.toarray(),
index=test_data.index,
columns=userid_vectorizer.get_feature_names())
```

```
        predicted_ratings = pd.DataFrame(np.dot(test_v_df.loc[0], Q.T),
index=Q.index, columns=['Rating'])
        predictions = pd.DataFrame.sort_values(predicted_ratings,
['Rating'], ascending=[0])[:10]

        JSONP_data = jsonpify(predictions.to_json())
        return JSONP_data
```

8. We attach the `Flask_Work` class to the `Flask` server. This completes the script on running. We have put an API in place that suggests products based on the user's search query:

```
api.add_resource(Flask_Work, '/')


if __name__ == '__main__':
    app.run(host='127.0.0.1', port=4000, debug=True)
```

Save this file as `main.py`. With the API script created, we need to host the server.

9. To do so on a local machine, run the following command in the terminal:

```
python main.py
```

This will start the server on the computer on port 4000, as shown:

```
* Serving Flask app "main" (lazy loading)
* Environment: production
  WARNING: Do not use the development server in a production environment.
  Use a production WSGI server instead.
* Debug mode: on
* Running on http://127.0.0.1:4000/ (Press CTRL+C to quit)
* Restarting with stat
* Debugger is active!
* Debugger PIN: 218-648-473
```

However, we still need to prepare a user interface to use this API. We will do so in the following section.

Creating an interface to use the API

We will now create a simple, minimal UI to use the API we created. In essence, we will create a single search bar where the user enters the product or product specification that they want and the API returns recommendations based on the user's query. We will not be discussing the code for building the UI, but we have included it in the GitHub repository, which can be found at http://tiny.cc/DL4WebCh9.

This UI will be visible at `http://127.0.0.1:4000` once you start the server, as shown in step 9 of the *Creating an API to answer search queries* section.

The interface we created looks like this:

The user enters a search query and gets recommendations, as shown:

Our application does not have the benefit of saving user sessions. Also, it does not have parameters for the expected budget of the user, which is often a deciding factor in whether the product is a good fit for the user. It is easy to add these features to web applications and leverage their benefits.

Summary

As a general overview, web applications that hone the power of DL have a few set methods to do so via APIs, in-browser JavaScript, or by silently embedding DL models in the backend of the application. In this chapter, we saw how to use the most common of these methods—an API-based DL web application—while at the same time, we saw a rough overview of how to design similar solutions. We covered the thought process that goes into the identification of the problem statement and a subsequent solution, along with the pitfalls and pain points to avoid during the design of a web application that integrates DL models.

In the next chapter, we will cover an end to end project that integrates DL on web applications for security purposes. We will see how DL can help us recognize suspicious activity and block spam users.

Securing Web Apps with Deep Learning

10

Security is of the utmost importance to any website—and all software, in general. These days, security threats are evolving with the rise of available computing power and developments in the field of technology. So, it is important that websites employ the best possible measures of security to keep their data and user information secure. Websites with online commercial activities are always at high risk and it is very common for them to face security attacks that have not been seen before. New attacks are particularly difficult for rule-based security systems to identify and stop; so, you can look at the options offered by deep learning-powered security systems, which can effectively replace rule-based systems and are also capable of correctly identifying and blocking new threats.

This chapter discusses several tricks and techniques that you can use to secure websites using deep learning with Python. We will present reCAPTCHA and Cloudflare and discuss how they are used to enhance the security of websites. We will also show you how to implement security mechanisms to detect malicious users on websites using deep learning-based techniques and a Python backend. The following topics will be covered in this chapter:

- The story of reCAPTCHA
- DIY – malicious user detection on Django
- Using reCAPTCHA in web applications with Python
- Website security with Cloudflare

We will begin this chapter's discussion with the story of reCAPTCHA—an ingenious tool, created by Google, that changed the internet.

Technical requirements

You can access the code for this chapter at `https://github.com/PacktPublishing/Hands-On-Python-Deep-Learning-for-Web/tree/master/Chapter10`.

You'll need the following software to run the code in this chapter:

- Python 3.6+
- TensorFlow 1.14
- Keras compatible with TensorFlow 1.14
- Django 2.x

The story of reCAPTCHA

Easy on Humans, Hard on Bots—that is the tagline of reCAPTCHA, which states the simple idea that reCAPTCHA is a system that establishes whether a user on an application or website is a genuine human user or an automated script. reCAPTCHA is a specific implementation of the CAPTCHA technology—a method that uses visuals with distorted, squiggly letters and numbers and challenges the user to decipher the contents of the visual image and write it out in a plain format.

If you were a regular internet user in the early 2000s, you would have seen images resembling the following CAPTCHA on a number of websites:

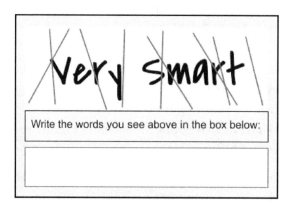

CAPTCHA is an acronym for **Completely Automated Public Turing Test To Tell Computers and Humans Apart**.

Popularized by Yahoo, the CAPTCHA system was rapidly adopted for use on millions of websites. However, despite the boost to security this system provided to websites, it was time-consuming and was often being beaten by rogue programmers. Every so often, people would create new CAPTCHA systems with varied designs and combinations of elements in the visuals.

At the same time, developers were tackling a very different problem—one of digitizing printed books and other texts. A quick solution was to scan books; that is, using an **Optical Character Reader** (**OCR**) to convert books into preliminary digital text form. The conversions were fine for printed content that was made with standard fonts and whose scans were obtainable in good quality. However, the conversion accuracy suffered for malformed prints and manuscripts. People were increasingly uploading images to online platforms in the quest to extract text from those images and to use them for several purposes, such as determination of content in images, locations, or brands mentioned.

The origin of CAPTCHA is disputed with claims of invention from multiple groups, but it was in 2003 that Luis von Ahn coined the term CAPTCHA, and he later became the founder of reCAPTCHA, which was acquired by Google.

A pioneer of crowdsourcing, Luis von Ahn used the reCAPTCHA program to display very small chunks of text cropped from scans of printed books. Only humans would be able to solve these challenges easily, and automated programs would fail. At the same time, these books were being slowly digitized by contributions from a large number of human users, through unknown crowdsourcing activity. reCAPTCHA still remained a nuisance for users but the issue of digitizing books was solved.

Over time, reCAPTCHA evolved to use AI-based systems to identify real and fake users. At the time of writing this book, reCAPTCHA is being actively developed by Google and is currently on its third version, where it allows the invisible verification of users in the background of the web page and only displays a challenge when the user cannot be successfully verified. This saves a lot of time for genuine users and poses a challenge to machines.

We will now build a website to use deep learning-based models and reCAPTCHA to provide security elements to a website.

Malicious user detection

A malicious user on a website is any user who attempts to perform tasks that they are not authorized to do. In today's world, the threats posed by malicious users are increasing exponentially, with huge databases of personal information from several global tech giants, government agencies, and other private firms being exposed to the public by hackers. It is important to have systems in place that can automatically mitigate these malicious attacks.

In order to recognize the malicious users in our sample web app, we have created a model that is able to learn the usual behavior of a user and raises the alarm if the user behavior at any instance changes significantly from their past usage.

Anomaly detection is a popular branch of machine learning. It is a collection of algorithms that are used to detect data samples in a given dataset that do not fall along with the majority of the data sample properties. To detect a cat in a dog shelter would be anomaly detection. Anomaly detection is performed in several ways:

- By using minimum-maximum ranges of columns
- By finding out sudden spikes in the plots of the data
- By marking points lying on the extreme ends as outliers (anomalies) when data is plotted under a Gaussian curve

Support vector machines, k-nearest neighbors, and Bayesian networks are some of the most popular algorithms used for anomaly detection.

How can we define usual behavior for users on a website?

Assume that you use a website where you normally log in using your laptop. Mostly, it takes you a maximum of two attempts to successfully log in to the website. If one day you suddenly start using a new laptop, the login would be suspicious and would probably be a malicious attempt to hack your account. It would be more so if the location of the new device was somewhere you have not been to recently or ever before. It would also be highly suspicious if you took 10 attempts to log in to your account. The state of not being in any suspicious state of usage is the usual behavior of the user on a website.

Sometimes, the anomaly may not be due to the irregular behavior of any specific user. Due to changes in the server, the regular traffic of the users and so their behavior might change. We have to be careful to not mark all users as malicious in such circumstances. Also, the irregular behavior of a user may be caused due to reasons other than hacking attempts on their account. If a genuine user suddenly starts accessing parts of the website that they should not have access to, it is an anomaly and needs to be prevented.

In our sample website, we will integrate a system like this. To do so, we will be putting a check on the login page of the website where we will try to determine whether a user's login is normal or anomalous. We will be taking into consideration the page that the user logs in from, as a website may have multiple login pages, and try to determine whether it is a usual page for the user to login from. If the user attempts to log in from a page that they generally do not log in from, we will mark it as an anomaly. This is just one simple criterion for checking anomalous users, with a scope of several hundreds of other parameters.

An LSTM-based model for authenticating users

We will break down this section into two major sub-sections:

1. Building the security check model
2. Hosting the model as an API

Let's begin with the first section.

Building a model for an authentication validity check

To authenticate the user based on their login activity, we will need an API that checks the requests. We can build this model using the following steps:

1. Let's begin by developing the authentication model that determines whether a user is not acting in a regular manner. We begin by importing the necessary modules in a Jupyter notebook running Python 3.6+, as shown:

```
import sys
import os
import json
import pandas
import numpy
from keras.models import Sequential
from keras.layers import LSTM, Dense, Dropout
from keras.layers.embeddings import Embedding
from keras.preprocessing import sequence
from keras.preprocessing.text import Tokenizer
from collections import OrderedDict
```

2. We can now import the data into the project. We will be using the dataset at `https://github.com/PacktPublishing/Hands-On-Python-Deep-Learning-for-Web/blob/master/Chapter10/model/data/data-full.csv`. We load the dataset into the project, as shown:

```
file = 'data-full.csv'

df = pandas.read_csv(file, quotechar='|', header=None)
df_count = df.groupby([1]).count()
total_req = df_count[0][0] + df_count[0][1]
num_malicious = df_count[0][1]

print("Malicious request logs in dataset:
{:0.2f}%".format(float(num_malicious) / total_req * 100))
```

You will see some general statistics about the data, as shown:

```
            0
1
0   13413
1   13360
Malicious request logs in dataset: 49.90%
```

You will observe that the data contains text, as shown:

```
In [8]: json.loads(X[0])

Out[8]: {'timestamp': 1502738643671,
         'method': 'post',
         'query': {},
         'path': '/login',
         'statusCode': 401,
         'source': {'remoteAddress': '12.93.106.47'},
         'route': '/login',
         'headers': {'host': 'localhost:8002',
         'connection': 'keep-alive',
         'cache-control': 'no-cache',
         'accept': '*/*',
         'accept-encoding': 'gzip, deflate, br',
         'accept-language': 'en-US,en;q=0.8,es;q=0.6',
         'content-type': 'application/json',
         'content-length': '36'},
         'requestPayload': {'username': 'KenM2', 'password': 'ic'},
         'responsePayload': {'statusCode': 401,
         'error': 'Unauthorized',
         'message': 'Invalid Login'}}
```

This observation is important and we'll be referring to this screenshot in future steps.

3. However, all the data is in string format. We need to convert it into appropriate types of values. Also, the dataset currently consists of just one DataFrame; we will break it into two parts—the training columns and the labels column—with the following code:

```
df_values = df.sample(frac=1).values

X = df_values[:,0]
Y = df_values[:,1]
```

4. Also, we need to lose some of the columns as we only want to use features in the dataset that are relevant to our task:

```
for index, item in enumerate(X):
    req = json.loads(item, object_pairs_hook=OrderedDict)
    del req['timestamp']
    del req['headers']
    del req['source']
    del req['route']
    del req['responsePayload']
    X[index] = json.dumps(req, separators=(',', ':'))
```

5. With this done, we are now ready to proceed with tokenizing the request body. Tokenizing is a method where we break large paragraphs down into sentences and sentences into words. We can perform tokenization with the following code:

```
tokenizer = Tokenizer(filters='\t\n', char_level=True)
tokenizer.fit_on_texts(X)
```

6. With the tokenization done, we convert each request body entry into vectors. We do so because we need a numerical representation of the data for the computer to be able to perform calculations on it. After that, we further split the dataset into two more parts—75% of the dataset is for training and the rest is for testing purposes. Similarly, the labels column is split using the following code:

```
num_words = len(tokenizer.word_index)+1
X = tokenizer.texts_to_sequences(X)

max_log_length = 1024
split = int(len(df_values) * .75)

X_processed = sequence.pad_sequences(X, maxlen=max_log_length)
X_train, X_test = X_processed[0:split],
X_processed[split:len(X_processed)]
Y_train, Y_test = Y[0:split], Y[split:len(Y)]
```

Remember from step 2 that this data mainly contained text. When it comes to text data, there is most likely a context and a specific order associated with it.

For example, consider the words of this sentence—*Sachin Tendulkar is a great cricketer*. The order of the words must not be changed in order to convey the expected meaning. This is where the importance of maintaining order and context comes into the picture when you deal with text data in machine learning.

In our case, we will use a special type of recurrent neural network—**Long Short-Term Memory (LSTM)**—which will learn to recognize the regular user behavior.

A detailed discussion on LSTM is beyond the scope of this book but if you are interested, you can refer to `http://bit.ly/2m0RWnx` to learn about it in detail.

7. We now add the layers, along with the word embeddings, which helps maintain the relationship between the numerically encoded text and the actual words, using the following code:

```
clf = Sequential()
clf.add(Embedding(num_words, 32, input_length=max_log_length))
clf.add(Dropout(0.5))
clf.add(LSTM(64, recurrent_dropout=0.5))
clf.add(Dropout(0.5))
clf.add(Dense(1, activation='sigmoid'))
```

Our output is a single neuron that either holds 0 or 1 in the case of a non-anomalous or an anomalous login attempt, respectively.

8. We then compile the model and print a summary using the following code:

```
clf.compile(loss='binary_crossentropy', optimizer='adam',
metrics=['accuracy'])
print(clf.summary())
```

The summary of the model is produced, as shown:

```
Layer (type)                   Output Shape                Param #
=================================================================
embedding_1 (Embedding)        (None, 1024, 32)            2016

dropout_1 (Dropout)            (None, 1024, 32)            0

lstm_1 (LSTM)                  (None, 64)                  24832

dropout_2 (Dropout)            (None, 64)                  0

dense_1 (Dense)                (None, 1)                   65
=================================================================
Total params: 26,913
Trainable params: 26,913
Non-trainable params: 0
_____
None
```

Now, we are ready to move on to training the model:

1. We use the `fit()` method of the model as shown:

   ```
   clf.fit(X_train, Y_train, validation_split=0.25, epochs=3,
   batch_size=128)
   ```

2. We will quickly check the accuracy achieved by the model. We can see that the model is more than 96% accurate on the validation data. This score is quite impressive given that this is our first model. We can check the accuracy of the model using the following code:

   ```
   score, acc = clf.evaluate(X_test, Y_test, verbose=1,
   batch_size=128)
   print("Model Accuracy: {:0.2f}%".format(acc * 100))
   ```

   You should see an output as in this screenshot:

   ```
   In [15]: print("Model Accuracy: {:0.2f}%".format(acc * 100))
            Model Accuracy: 96.47%
   ```

3. Let's save these weights. We will use them to create an API that is used for authenticating the users. We can save the model using the following code:

   ```
   clf.save_weights('weights.h5')
   clf.save('model.h5')
   ```

With the model ready, we can now move on to hosting it as a Flask API.

Hosting the custom authentication validation model

Let's now create the API that will accept the login attempt from the user and return its confidence in the validity of the login:

1. We begin by importing the required modules for creating a Flask server, as shown:

```
from sklearn.externals import joblib
from flask import Flask, request, jsonify
from string import digits

import sys
import os
import json
import pandas
import numpy
import optparse
from keras.models import Sequential, load_model
from keras.preprocessing import sequence
from keras.preprocessing.text import Tokenizer
from collections import OrderedDict
```

2. We now need to import the saved model and weights from the model training step. Once we do so, we need to recompile the model and make its predict function using the make_predict_function() method:

```
app = Flask(__name__)

model = load_model('lstm-model.h5')
model.load_weights('lstm-weights.h5')
model.compile(loss = 'binary_crossentropy', optimizer = 'adam',
metrics = ['accuracy'])
model._make_predict_function()
```

3. We will be using a data cleaning function to strip out numbers and other non-useful text in the incoming queries from the client app:

```
def remove_digits(s: str) -> str:
    remove_digits = str.maketrans('', '', digits)
    res = s.translate(remove_digits)
    return res
```

4. Next, we create the /login route in the app, which will accept the login credentials and other request header details from the client app when the user attempts to log in. Notice that we still drop out some extra request headers as we did during the training.

5. Once we clean the data, we tokenize and vectorize it. These steps are the same as the preprocessing we did during training. This is to ensure that the incoming request is processed exactly as it was during the training phase:

```
@app.route('/login', methods=['GET, POST'])
def login():
    req = dict(request.headers)
    item = {}
    item["method"] = str(request.method)
    item["query"] = str(request.query_string)
    item["path"] = str(request.path)
    item["statusCode"] = 200
    item["requestPayload"] = []

    X = numpy.array([json.dumps(item)])
    log_entry = "store"

    tokenizer = Tokenizer(filters='\t\n', char_level=True)
    tokenizer.fit_on_texts(X)
    seq = tokenizer.texts_to_sequences([log_entry])
    max_log_length = 1024
    log_entry_processed = sequence.pad_sequences(seq,
maxlen=max_log_length)

    prediction = model.predict(log_entry_processed)
    print(prediction)
    response = {'result': float(prediction[0][0])}
    return jsonify(response)
```

Finally, the app returns its confidence in the user being authenticated in the form of a JSON.

6. To run the server on the desired port, we need to add the following lines at the end of the script:

```
if __name__ == '__main__':
    app.run(port=9000, debug=True)
```

7. Lastly, we save the server script file as main.py. We will get the server running by using the following command on the system:

```
python main.py
```

This will start the Flask server, which listens in on the loopback IP `127.0.0.1`, and at port `9000`. You can easily host this script on a virtual machine in the cloud and make it available to all your apps and websites as a common security checkpoint API.

We can now move on to creating our web app that runs on the Django framework.

A Django-based app for using an API

The website that we are creating to consume the user-authentication check API will be a simple billboard demo. The website will have provisions for users to log in and then post bills to a billboard. While the app is simple, it contains two major features of deep learning-based security integrations—anomaly detection during user authentication and the implementation of reCAPTCHA during posting bills—to avoid spam.

The steps to create the application are discussed in the following sections.

The Django project setup

In this section, we'll be working with Django. Make sure that you have a working Django installation on your system before proceeding with this section. You can find installation instructions for Django in the *A brief introduction to Django web development* section in Chapter 8, *Deep Learning on Microsoft Azure Using Python*.

Now, we will create a Django project. To do so, we use the following command:

```
django-admin startproject webapp
```

This will create the `webapp` directory in the current folder. We will be adding all of our future code in this directory. The current directory structure looks as follows:

```
webapp/
    manage.py
    webapp/
        __init__.py
        settings.py
        urls.py
        wsgi.py
    db.sqlite3
```

With this done, we are now ready to create an app inside the project, which is shown in the next section.

Creating an app in the project

As discussed in Chapter 8, *Deep Learning on Microsoft Azure Using Python*, we must now add apps to the website project. To do so, we use the following command:

```
cd webapp
python manage.py startapp billboard
```

The preceding command will create an app called billboard in the project. However, we still have to link this app to the project.

Linking the app to the project

To add the app to the project, we need to add the app name to the list of apps in settings.py in the project settings file, as in the following code. In settings.py, add the following change:

```
# Application definition

INSTALLED_APPS = [
    'billboard',  # <---- ADD THIS LINE
    'django.contrib.admin',
    'django.contrib.auth',
    'django.contrib.contenttypes',
    'django.contrib.sessions',
    'django.contrib.messages',
    'django.contrib.staticfiles',
]
```

With this, we are ready to create the routes on the website.

Adding routes to the website

To add routes to the project, we edit the urls.py file of webapp:

```
from django.contrib import admin
from django.urls import path, include # <--- ADD 'include' module

urlpatterns = [
    path('', include('billboard.urls')), # <--- ADD billboard.urls path
    path('admin/', admin.site.urls),
]
```

However, the billboard.urls path does not exist. We'll create the path to proceed.

Creating the route handling file in the billboard app

Create a new file, called `urls.py`, in the `billboard` folder, as shown:

```
from django.urls import path
from django.contrib.auth.decorators import login_required

from . import views

urlpatterns = [
    path('', login_required(views.board), name='View Board'),
    path('add', login_required(views.addbill), name='Add Bill'),
    path('login', views.loginView, name='Login'),
    path('logout', views.logoutView, name='Logout'),
]
```

Save this as `webapp/billboard/urls.py`. Notice that we have imported some `views` items to this route handling file. Also, we have used the `login_required` method. This indicates that we can start working on the authentication of the website.

Adding authentication routes and configurations

To add the routes for authentication, add the following at the end of the `webapp/settings.py` file:

```
LOGIN_URL = "/login"
LOGIN_REDIRECT_URL = '/'
LOGOUT_REDIRECT_URL = '/logout'
```

These lines indicate that we will need a `/login` and a `/logout` route.

Creating the login page

To create the login page, we'll need to add the `/login` route to `urls.py` in the billboard app. However, we've already done that. Next, we need to add the `loginView` view to the `views.py` file of the billboard app:

```
def loginView(request):
    if request.user.is_authenticated:
        return redirect('/')
    else:
```

```
            if request.POST:
                username = request.POST['username']
                password = request.POST['password']
                user = authenticate(request, username=username,
    password=password)
                ## MORE CODE BELOW THIS LINE
                ## MORE CODE ABOVE THIS LINE
                else:
                    return redirect('/logout')
            else:
                template = loader.get_template('login.html')
                context = {}
                return HttpResponse(template.render(context, request))
```

The preceding function first checks whether the username and password being passed to it exist in the user database. So, we'll need a user model, in the future, to store users in the database file, db.sqlite3, which was created during the project creation step.

The function will then make a call to the authentication check model API to validate whether the user login is of normal behavior. The validation is carried out as in the following code:

```
def loginView(request):
    ...
                ## MORE CODE BELOW THIS LINE
                if user is not None:
                    url = 'http://127.0.0.1:9000/login'
                    values = { 'username': username, 'password': password }
                    data = urllib.parse.urlencode(values).encode()
                    req = urllib.request.Request(url, data=data)
                    response = urllib.request.urlopen(req)
                    result = json.loads(response.read().decode())
                    if result['result'] > 0.20:
                        login(request, user)
                        return redirect('/')
                    else:
                        return redirect('/logout')
                ## MORE CODE ABOVE THIS LINE
    ...
```

The preceding code block validates the user login and, if it's found to be invalid, performs a logout action and redirects the user back to log in again.

We'll need to add some necessary imports to the view.py file for this, as shown:

```
from django.shortcuts import redirect
from django.contrib.auth import authenticate, login, logout
```

```
from django.http import HttpResponse
from django.template import loader

from django.conf import settings
from django.urls import reverse_lazy
from django.views import generic

from django.contrib.auth.models import User

import urllib
import ssl
import json
```

Notice that we also imported the `logout` method from `django.contrib.auth`. This will be used to create a `logout` view.

Creating a logout view

Now, let's create the `logout` view. This is very simple to do, as shown:

```
def logoutView(request):
    logout(request)
    return redirect('/')
```

Now, let's create a template of the login page.

Creating a login page template

To create a template, we first need to create the folders required.

Create a folder called `templates` in the `billboard` directory. The directory structure will now look as in the following code:

```
webapp/
    manage.py
    webapp/
        __init__.py
        settings.py
        urls.py
        wsgi.py
    billboard/
        templates/
        __init_.py
        admin.py
```

```
apps.py
models.py
tests.py
urls.py
views.py
```

Inside the `templates` folder, we'll place our template files. Let's first create `base.html`, which we will extend in all other templates. This will contain the CSS and JS includes, along with the general block structure of the page.

 We have provided a sample of this file at `https://github.com/PacktPublishing/Hands-On-Python-Deep-Learning-for-Web/blob/master/Chapter10/webapp/billboard/templates/base.html`.

Once this is done, we're ready to create the `login.html` file, which will carry out the process of sending the login values to the server:

```
{% extends 'base.html' %}
{% block content %}
<div class="container">
    <div class="row">
        <div class="form_bg">
            <form method="post">
                {% csrf_token %}
                <h2 class="text-center">Login Page</h2>
                # WE'LL ADD MORE CODE BELOW THIS LINE
                ...
                # WE'LL ADD MORE CODE ABOVE THIS LINE
            </form>
        </div>
    </div>
</div>
{% endblock %}
```

Notice that we have extended the `base.html` template in the preceding view template.

 You can read more about extending Django templates at `https://tutorial.djangogirls.org/en/template_extending/`.

The form in this login page makes a POST request and so requires the passing of the CSRF token. We can now create the page that renders after the login is done.

The billboard page template

Since we've already set up the base.html file, we can simply extend it in the board.html template file to create the billboard display page:

```
{% extends 'base.html' %}
{% block content %}
<div class="container">
    <div class="row">
        {% for bill in bills %}
        <div class="col-sm-4 py-2">
            <div class="card card-body h-100">
                <h2>{{ bill.billName }}</h2>
                <hr>
                <p>
                    {{ bill.billDesc }}
                </p>
                <a href="#" class="btn btn-outline-secondary">{{
bill.user.username }}</a>
            </div>
        </div>
        {% endfor %}
    </div>
</div>
{% endblock %}
```

In the preceding block of code, we have iterated over all the available bills items in the billboard's database and displayed them using a for loop in the template. The use of the base.html template allows us to reduce the amount of repeated code in the view templates.

After this, we will create the page that will have the code to add a new bill to the billboard.

Adding to Billboard page template

To create the page template that adds a bill to the billboard, we use the following code to create the add.html template file:

```
{% extends 'base.html' %}
{% block content %}
<div class="container">
    <div class="row">
        <div class="form_bg">
            <form method="post" id="form">
                {% csrf_token %}
```

```
                <h2 class="text-center">Add Bill</h2>
                <br />
                <div class="form-group">
                    <input type="text" class="form-control" id="billname"
name="billname" placeholder="Bill Name">
                </div>
                <div class="form-group">
                    <input type="text" class="form-control" id="billdesc"
name="billdesc" placcholdcr-"Dcscription">
                </div>
                <br />
                <div class="align-center">
                    <button type="submit" class="btn btn-success"
id="save">Submit</button>
                </div>
            </form>
        </div>
    </div>
</div>
{% endblock %}
```

In the preceding block of code, we have extended the `base.html` template to add a form that allows us to add bills. Notice the use of the CSRF token in the `form` element. In Django, we always need to pass valid CSRF tokens while making POST requests.

 You can read more about CSRF tokens in Django at `https://docs.djangoproject.com/en/3.0/ref/csrf/`.

But wait, we've not yet added the views to handle the billboard page and the addition of the bills page. Let's add them now!

The billboard model

We need to add the views to see all the bills on the billboard page. However, for this, we first need to create the model to hold all the bills.

In the `models.py` file, add the following code:

```
from django.utils.timezone import now
from django.contrib.auth.models import User

class Bills(models.Model):
    billName = models.CharField("Bill Name", blank=False, max_length=100,
```

```
default="New Bill")
    user = models.ForeignKey(User, on_delete=models.CASCADE)
    billDesc = models.TextField("Bill Description")
    billTime = models.DateTimeField(default=now, editable=False)

    class Meta:
        db_table = "bills"
```

In the preceding code, we created a new model called `Bills`. This will store the details for all of the bills added by users on the billboard. The `user` model is linked with this model as a foreign key. Save this file as `webapp/billboard/models.py`.

 You can read more about foreign keys and other keys at `https://www.sqlite.org/foreignkeys.html`.

With this done, we can now use the `Bills` model in the views.

Creating the billboard view

To start using the `Bills` model in the app, we first need to import it to the `views.py` file.

Add the following line at the top of the `view.py` file:

```
from .models import Bills
```

Then, we can add the view for the billboard, as shown:

```
def board(request):
    template = loader.get_template('board.html')
    context = {}
    context["isLogged"] = 1

    Bill = Bills.objects.all()

    context["bills"] = Bill

    return HttpResponse(template.render(context, request))
```

Next, we need to create the view for adding the bills.

Creating bills and adding views

In this view, we will create the bills. If a valid POST request is made to the route served by the addbill method, we create a new Bill object and save it to the database. Otherwise, we display the form for adding bills to the user. Let's see how we can do this in the following code:

```
def addbill(request):
    if request.POST:
            billName = request.POST['billname']
            billDesc = request.POST['billdesc']
            Bill = Bills.objects.create(billName=billName,
user=request.user, billDesc=billDesc)
            Bill.save()
            return redirect('/')
    else:
        template = loader.get_template('add.html')
        context = {}
        context["isLogged"] = 1

        return HttpResponse(template.render(context, request))
```

However, we still need to create the admin user before using the app.

Creating the admin user and testing it

To create the admin user, we use the following command:

```
python manage.py createsuperuser
```

We can now migrate the database change by using the following commands:

```
python manage.py makemigrations
python manage.py migrate
```

An output similar to the following is produced:

```
^C(base) xprilion@x1:~/html/Hands-On-Python-Deep-Learning-for-Web/Chapter10/webapp$ python manage.py migrate
Operations to perform:
  Apply all migrations: admin, auth, contenttypes, sessions
Running migrations:
  Applying contenttypes.0001_initial... OK
  Applying auth.0001_initial... OK
  Applying admin.0001_initial... OK
  Applying admin.0002_logentry_remove_auto_add... OK
  Applying contenttypes.0002_remove_content_type_name... OK
  Applying auth.0002_alter_permission_name_max_length... OK
  Applying auth.0003_alter_user_email_max_length... OK
  Applying auth.0004_alter_user_username_opts... OK
  Applying auth.0005_alter_user_last_login_null... OK
  Applying auth.0006_require_contenttypes_0002... OK
  Applying auth.0007_alter_validators_add_error_messages... OK
  Applying auth.0008_alter_user_username_max_length... OK
  Applying auth.0009_alter_user_last_name_max_length... OK
  Applying sessions.0001_initial... OK
```

Now, let's secure the billboard postings using the reCAPTCHA tool.

Using reCAPTCHA in web applications with Python

To add the reCAPTCHA to the website, we first need to obtain the API keys from the Google reCAPTCHA console:

1. First, log in to your Google account and go to `https://www.google.com/recaptcha`.

2. Next, click on **Admin Console** at the top-right.

3. Add your site to the console by following the steps shown on your screen. If you're testing on your local system, you'll have to specify `127.0.0.1` as one of the URLs.

4. Obtain the API keys for your domain.

   The screen that you get your domain's API keys on should look similar to the following screenshot:

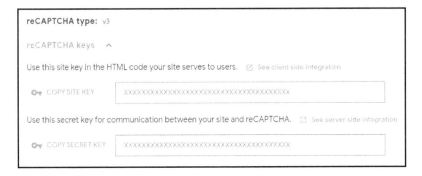

5. Now, add the secret key to the `settings.py` file of the web app, as shown:

```
GOOGLE_RECAPTCHA_SECRET_KEY =
'6Lfi6ncUAAAAANJYkMC66skocDgA1REblmx0-3B2'
```

6. Next, we need to add the scripts to be loaded to the `add.html` template. We'll add it to the billboard app page template, as shown:

```
<script
src="https://www.google.com/recaptcha/api.js?render=6Lfi6ncUAAAAIa
JgQCDaR3s-FGGczzo7Mefp0TQ"></script>
<script>
    grecaptcha.ready(function() {
        grecaptcha.execute('6Lfi6ncUAAAAIaJgQCDaR3s-
FGGczzo7Mefp0TQ')
        .then(function(token) {
            $("#form").append('<input type="hidden" name="g-
recaptcha-response" value="'+token+'" >');
        });
    });
</script>

{% endblock %}
```

Note that the key used in this step is the client/site key.

7. Finally, we need to validate the reCAPTCHA in the add billboard view, as shown:

```
def addbill(request):
    if request.POST:
        recaptcha_response = request.POST.get('g-recaptcha-
response')
        url = 'https://www.google.com/recaptcha/api/siteverify'
        values = {  'secret': settings.GOOGLE_RECAPTCHA_SECRET_KEY,
```

```
                        'response': recaptcha_response}
            context = ssl._create_unverified_context()
            data = urllib.parse.urlencode(values).encode()
            req = urllib.request.Request(url, data=data)
            response = urllib.request.urlopen(req, context=context)
            result = json.loads(response.read().decode())
            if result['success']:
                # Do stuff if valid
        else:
            # Do actions when no request is made
```

You can grab the full working version of the addbill method in the previous code block from https://github.com/PacktPublishing/Hands-On-Python-Deep-Learning-for-Web/blob/master/Chapter10/webapp/billboard/views.py.

With the previous changes made, we're finally ready to test run the website with all its security measures in place. Run the following command to start the website server:

```
python manage.py runserver
```

You should be able to see the website's login page, as shown:

 Note that at this point, you'll need to have the Flask server, which performs the login validation, running at the same time.

Upon login, you'll see the billboard page with bills posted on it. Head over to the **Add Bill** button to add a new bill, as shown:

Notice the reCAPTCHA logo at the bottom-right corner of the screen. This indicates that the page is protected against spamming by using reCAPTCHA. If you are able to post successfully, the billboard is displayed again with the submitted bill. If not, you'll be presented with a reCAPTCHA verify challenge.

Website security with Cloudflare

Cloudflare is the industry's leading web infrastructure and website security provider. It creates a layer of security and fast content delivery between a website and its users, hence routing all the traffic through its servers, which enables security and other features on websites. In 2017, Cloudflare provided DNS services to over 12 million websites. These services include content delivery networks, **Distributed Denial of Service** (**DDoS**) attack protection, hacking attempt protection, and other internet security services, such as leeching protection.

In 2014, Cloudflare reported mitigating a 400 Gib/s DDoS attack on a customer, which was soon followed by a 500 Gib/s attack the next year. The largest attack on any website recorded has been on GitHub, where it faced a DDoS of 1.4Tb/s flooding. GitHub was using Akamai Prolexic (an alternative to Cloudflare) and was able to withstand the attack, going down only for 10 minutes before coming back up entirely. Cloudflare offers DDoS protection to all its users free of charge.

To get started with deploying the services of Cloudflare on your website, you need to set up Cloudflare as an intermediate layer between your users and the hosting server. The following diagram depicts how Cloudflare sits on the network:

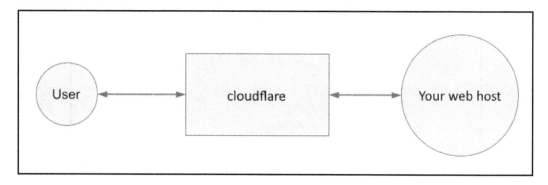

So, the detection of spam and malicious users that we created the previous custom solutions for, with the help of Google's reCAPTCHA, is automatically taken care of by Cloudflare to a basic extent (in the free tier, with more powerful solutions in the higher tiers as you upgrade). It is, therefore, very intuitive and simple for a small team of developers to push off their security needs to Cloudflare's systems and to rest assured that they are protected against a number of security breaches.

Summary

In this chapter, we saw how we can provide security to websites using Cloudflare's services. We also saw how to create security APIs that can be used in integration with web applications and other security services such as reCAPTCHA. It is crucial for any website—small or large—to have these security measures in place in order for their website services to function properly. There have been major breaches in recent times, and countless others that have been attempted by AI-powered systems that do not make it onto the news because they were not an issue. Security using deep learning is a burning topic of research and it is believed that in the near future, security systems will all rely strongly on deep learning to recognize and eliminate threats.

In the next chapter, we will discuss how to set up a production-grade deep learning environment. We will discuss the architecture designs you could follow, depending on their size requirements, and the state-of-the-art service providers and tools.

11
DIY - A Web DL Production Environment

In previous chapters, we saw how to use some notable **Deep Learning** (**DL**) platforms, such as **Amazon Web Services** (**AWS**), **Google Cloud Platform** (**GCP**), and Microsoft Azure, to enable DL in our web applications. We then saw how to make websites secure using DL. However, in production, the challenge is often not just building the predictive model—the real problems arise when you want to update a model that is already sending responses to users. How much time and business can you lose in the 30 seconds or 1 minute that it may take to replace the model file? What if there are models customized for each user? That might even mean billions of models for a platform such as Facebook.

You need to have definite solutions for updating models in production. Also, since the ingested data may not be in the format that the training is performed in, you need to define flows of data, such that they are morphed in a seamless manner for usage.

In this chapter, we will discuss the methods by which we update models in production and the thought that goes into choosing each method. We will begin with a brief overview and then demonstrate some famous tools for creating DL data flows. Finally, we will implement our own demonstration of online learning or incremental learning to establish a method for updating a model in production.

We will be covering the following topics in this chapter:

- An overview of DL in production methods
- Popular tools for deploying ML in production
- Implementing a demonstration DL web production environment
- Deploying the project to Heroku
- Security, monitoring, and performance optimizations

Technical requirements

You can access the code for this chapter at `https://github.com/PacktPublishing/Hands-On-Python-Deep-Learning-for-Web/tree/master/Chapter11`.

You'll need the following software to run the code used in this chapter:

- Python 3.6+
- Flask 1.1.12+

All other installations will be made during the course of this chapter.

An overview of DL in production methods

Be it DL or classic **Machine Learning (ML)**, when it comes to using models in production, things can get challenging. The main reason is that data fuels ML and data can change over time. When an ML model is deployed in production, it is re-trained at certain intervals as the data keeps changing over time. Therefore, re-training ML is not a luxury but a necessity when you are thinking of production-based purposes. DL is only a sub-field of ML and it is no exception to the previous statements. There are two popular methods that ML models are trained on—batch learning and online learning, especially when they are in production.

We will be discussing online learning in the next section. For this section, let's introduce ourselves to the concept of batch learning. In batch learning, we start by training an ML model on a specific chunk of data and when the model is done training on that chunk, it is supplied with the next chunk of data and this process continues until all the chunks are exhausted. These chunks are referred to as batches.

In real-life projects, you will be dealing with large volumes of data all the time. It would not be ideal to fit those datasets in memory at once. Batch learning comes to our aid in situations such as this one. There are disadvantages to using batch learning and we will get to them in the next section. You may wonder (or may not, as well), but yes, we perform batch learning whenever we train a neural network in this book.

Just like training, the concepts of batches can be applied to serving ML models, as well. Serving ML models here means using machine models to make predictions on unseen data points. This is also known as inference. Now, model serving can be of two types—online serving, where the prediction needs to be made as soon as the model is met with the data point(s) (we cannot afford latency here), and offline serving, where a batch of data points is first gathered and the batch is run through the model to get predictions. Note that in the second case, we can opt in for a bit of latency.

Note that there are several engineering aspects as well that are directly attached to production ML systems. Discussing them is beyond the scope of this book, but you are encouraged to check online for courses by the GCP team.

Let's try to summarize and further understand the preceding discussion with the following diagram:

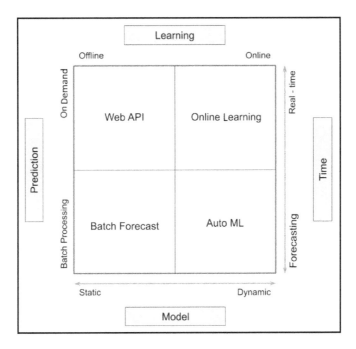

This diagram depicts the requirements of your AI backend and the various parameters that can affect the choice of the solution that you make. We will discuss all of the aspects and choices available, as in this diagram, in the following section.

So, we have four major types of solutions that you may usually find in implementations of DL in production:

- A web API service
- Online learning
- Batch forecasting
- Auto ML

Let's look at each of them in detail.

A web API service

We have a model that is trained by a separate script on the backend and is stored as a model and then deployed as an API-based service. Here, we're looking at a solution that produces results *on-demand* but the training occurs offline (not in the execution span of the portion of code responsible for responding to the client queries). Web APIs respond to a single query at a time and yield singular results.

This is by far the most commonly used method for deploying DL in production since it allows accurate training performed offline by data scientists and a short deployment script to create an API. In this book, we have mostly carried out deployments of this kind.

Online learning

Another form of on-demand predictions via the backend is online learning. However, in this methodology, the learning happens during the execution of the server script and so the model keeps changing with every relevant query. While such a method is dynamic and unlikely to become stale, it is often less accurate than its static counterpart—web APIs. Online learning, too, yields a single result at a time.

In this chapter, we have demonstrated an example of online learning. We will discuss the tools that are helpful for online learning in the coming sections.

Batch forecasting

In this method, a number of predictions are made at once and stored on the server, ready to be fetched and used when the user needs them. However, as a static training method, this method allows training the model offline and so offers greater accuracy to the training, similar to web APIs.

In other words, batch forecasting can be understood as a batch version of web APIs; however, the predictions are not served by an API. Rather, the predictions are stored and fetched from a database.

Auto ML

Making predictions is only one part of the entire process of having DL in production. A data scientist is also responsible for cleaning and organizing the data, creating a pipeline, and optimizations. Auto ML is a way of eliminating the need for such repetitive tasks.

Auto ML is a batch forecasting method where the need for human intervention is removed. So, the data, as it comes, goes through a pipeline and the forecasts are regularly updated. So, this method provides more up-to-date predictions than the batch forecasting method.

Let's now discuss some tools for rapidly realizing some of the methods we have presented.

Popular tools for deploying ML in production

In this section, we will be discussing some popular tools used for putting ML in production systems. The core utility provided by these tools is automating the learning-prediction-feedback pipeline and facilitating the monitoring of the model's quality and performance. While it is very much possible to create your own tools for this, it is highly recommended that you use any of the following tools, as per the requirements of your software.

Let's begin by discussing `creme`.

creme

`creme` is a Python library that allows us to perform online learning efficiently. Before we look at `creme` in action, let's have a brief discussion about online learning itself:

In online learning, ML models are trained on one instance at a time, instead of being trained on a batch of data (which is also known as batch learning). To be able to appreciate the use of online learning, it's important to understand the cons of batch learning:

- In production, we need to re-train ML models on new data over time. Batch learning forces us to do this but this comes at a cost. The cost not only lies in computational resources but also the fact that the models are re-trained from scratch. Training models from scratch is not always useful in production environments.
- The features and labels of data can change over time. Batch learning does not allow us to train ML models that can support dynamic features and labels.

This is exactly where we need to use online learning, which enables us to do the following:

- Train ML models using only one instance at a time. So, we won't require a batch of data to train an ML model; it can be trained instantaneously using data as it becomes available.
- Train ML models with dynamic features and labels.

Online learning has got several other names, but they all do the same thing:

- Incremental learning
- Sequential learning
- Iterative learning
- Out-of-core learning

`creme`, as mentioned earlier, is a Python library for performing online learning. It is an extremely useful thing to keep in your ML toolbox, especially when you are dealing with a production environment. `creme` is heavily inspired by scikit-learn (which is a very popular ML library in Python), which makes it very easy to use. To get a comprehensive introduction to `creme`, you are encouraged to check out the official GitHub repository for `creme` at `https://github.com/creme-ml/creme`.

Enough talking! Let's go ahead and first install `creme`. It can be done by using the following command:

```
pip install creme
```

To get the latest version of `creme`, you can use the following commands:

```
pip install git+https://github.com/creme-ml/creme
# Or through SSH:
pip install git+ssh://git@github.com/creme-ml/creme.git
```

Let's take a look at a quick example by following these steps:

1. We first make a few necessary imports from the `creme` module:

```
from creme import compose
from creme import datasets
from creme import feature_extraction
from creme import metrics
from creme import model_selection
from creme import preprocessing
from creme import stats
from creme import neighbors

import datetime as dt
```

   Notice that the naming convention of `creme` is similar to that of the `sklearn` library for an easier migration experience.

2. We then fetch a dataset provided by the `creme` module itself to the data variable:

```
data = datasets.Bikes()
```

   We will be working on this dataset, which contains information about bike-ride sharing.

 While the dataset is included in the `creme` library, you can read more about it at `https://archive.ics.uci.edu/ml/datasets/bike+sharing+dataset`.

3. Next, we build a pipeline using `creme`, as shown:

```
model = compose.Select("humidity", "pressure", "temperature")
model += feature_extraction.TargetAgg(by="station",
how=stats.Mean())
model |= preprocessing.StandardScaler()
model |= neighbors.KNeighborsRegressor()
```

   Notice the use of the `|=` and `+=` operators. `creme` makes it possible to use these operators, which makes understanding the data pipeline very intuitive. We can obtain a detailed representation of the pipeline built in the previous code block by using the following command:

model

The output of the previous command is as shown:

```
Pipeline([('TransformerUnion', TransformerUnion (
          Select (
            humidity
            pressure
            temperature
          ),
          TargetAgg (
            by=['station']
            how=Mean ()
            target_name="target"
          )
        )), ('StandardScaler', StandardScaler (
          with_mean=True
          with_std=True
        )), ('KNeighborsRegressor', KNeighborsRegressor([])) ])
```

We can also get a visual representation of this pipeline by using the following command:

```
model.draw()
```

This produces the following graph:

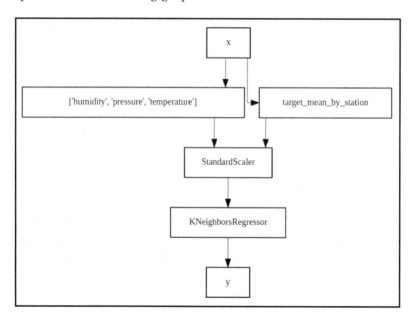

4. Finally, we run the training and obtain the scoring metric at an interval of every 30,000 row of the dataset. On the production server, this code will result in batch forecasting at every 1 minute:

```
model_selection.progressive_val_score(
  X_y=data,
  model=model,
  metric=metrics.RMSE(),
  moment='moment',
  delay=dt.timedelta(minutes=1),
  print_every=30_000
)
```

So, `creme` makes it very simple to create batch forecasting and online learning deployments in production with its lucid syntax and debugging facilities.

We'll now discuss another popular tool—Airflow.

Airflow

As an effective ML practitioner, you will need to programmatically handle workflows such as the previous one and be able to automate them, as well. Airflow provides you with a platform to efficiently do this. This link—`https://airflow.apache.org`—is an excerpt taken from Airflow's official website. Airflow is a platform used to programmatically author, schedule, and monitor workflows.

The main advantage of this is that tasks represented on **Directed Acyclic Graphs** (**DAGs**) can easily be distributed across available resources (often known as workers). It also makes it easier to visualize your entire workflow and this turns out to be very helpful, especially when a workflow is very complicated. If you need a refresher on DAGs, the article at `https://cran.r-project.org/web/packages/ggdag/vignettes/intro-to-dags.html` can help. This will become much clearer when you see this implemented in a little while.

When you are designing an ML workflow, you need to think of many different things, such as the following:

- The data collection pipeline
- The data preprocessing pipeline
- Making the data available to the ML model
- Training and evaluation pipelines for the ML model
- The deployment of the model
- Monitoring the model, along with other things

For now, let's go ahead and install Airflow by executing the following line:

```
pip install apache-airflow
```

Although Airflow is Python-based, it is absolutely possible to use Airflow to define workflows that incorporate different languages for different tasks.

Once installed, you can invoke the admin panel of Airflow and view the list of DAGs on it, as well as manage them and trigger a lot of other useful functions, as shown:

1. To do so, you must first initialize the database:

   ```
   airflow initdb
   ```

2. You should see a number of tables being created on a SQLite3 database. If successful, you will be able to start the web server by using the following command:

   ```
   airflow webserver
   ```

   Open http://localhost:8080 on your browser. You will be presented with a screen as in the following screenshot:

A number of example DAGs are presented. You can try running them for a brief play!

Let's now discuss a very popular tool called AutoML.

AutoML

DL or AI solutions are not limited to building cutting-edge accurate models in Jupyter Notebook when it comes to industrial usage. There are several steps in the formation of AI solutions, beginning with collecting raw data, converting the data into a format that can be used with predictive models, creating predictions, building an application around the model, and monitoring and updating the model in production. AutoML aims to automate this process by automating the pre-deployment tasks. Often, AutoML is mostly about orchestrating the data and Bayesian hyperparameter optimization. AutoML only sometimes means a fully automated learning pipeline.

One famous library available for AutoML is provided by `H2O.ai` and it is called `H2O.AutoML`. To use it, we can install it using the following commands:

```
# Using Conda installer
conda install -c h2oai h2o

# Using PIP installer
pip install -f
http://h2o-release.s3.amazonaws.com/h2o/latest_stable_Py.html h2o
```

`H2O.AutoML` is very simple to understand due to the similarity of its syntax with other popular ML libraries.

Implementing a demonstration DL web environment

We will now take a deep dive into building a sample production application that uses online learning on the backend. We will be creating an application that can predict heart diseases, based on the Cleveland dataset. We will then deploy this model to Heroku, which is a cloud container-based service. Finally, we will demonstrate the online learning feature of the application.

 You can find out more about Heroku by going to `https://heroku.com`.

Let's list the steps that we will be covering:

1. Build a predictive model on Jupyter Notebook.
2. Build a backend for the web application that predicts on the saved model.
3. Build a frontend for the web application that invokes incremental learning on the model.
4. Update the model on the server side incrementally.
5. Deploy the application to Heroku.

We will begin with the zeroth step; that is, observing the dataset.

The UCI Heart Disease dataset contains 303 samples, with 76 attributes in each. However, most of the research work on the dataset has been centered around a simplified version of the Cleveland dataset with 13 attributes, as defined here:

- Age
- Sex
- Chest pain type:
    - Typical angina
    - Atypical angina
    - Non-anginal pain
    - Asymptomatic
- Resting blood pressure
- Serum cholesterol in mg/dl
- Fasting blood sugar > 120 mg/dl
- Resting electrocardiographic results:
    - Normal
    - Having ST-T wave abnormality (T wave inversions and/or ST elevation or depression of > 0.05 mV)
    - Showing probable or definite left ventricular hypertrophy by Estes' criteria
- Maximum heart rate achieved
- Exercise-induced angina
- Oldpeak = ST depression induced by exercise relative to rest
- The slope of the peak exercise ST segment
- Number of major vessels (0-3) colored by fluoroscopy
- Thal: 3 = normal; 6 = fixed defect; 7 = reversible defect

There will be a final column, which is the target we will be predicting. This will make the problem at hand a classification between normal and affected patients.

 You can read more about the Cleveland dataset at `https://archive.ics.uci.edu/ml/datasets/Heart+Disease`.

Let's now begin building the heart disease detection model.

Building a predictive model

In this subsection, we will begin by building a simple neural network using Keras, which will classify, from a given input, the probability that a patient has heart disease.

Step 1 – Importing the necessary modules

We begin by importing the required libraries:

```
import pandas as pd
import numpy as np
from sklearn.model_selection import train_test_split
np.random.seed(5)
```

We have imported the `pandas` and `numpy` modules. Along with these, we have imported the `train_test_split` method from the scikit-learn library to help us quickly split the dataset into training and testing parts.

Step 2 – Loading the dataset and observing

Let's load the dataset, assuming it to be stored in a folder named `data` that is on the same directory level as that of the directory containing our Jupyter notebook:

```
df = pd.read_csv("data/heart.csv")
```

We'll quickly observe the DataFrame to see whether all the columns have been imported correctly:

```
df.head(5)
```

This produces the following output in the Jupyter notebook:

	age	sex	cp	trestbps	chol	fbs	restecg	thalach	exang	oldpeak	slope	ca	thal	target
0	63	1	3	145	233	1	0	150	0	2.3	0	0	1	1
1	37	1	2	130	250	0	1	187	0	3.5	0	0	2	1
2	41	0	1	130	204	0	0	172	0	1.4	2	0	2	1
3	56	1	1	120	236	0	1	178	0	0.8	2	0	2	1
4	57	0	0	120	354	0	1	163	1	0.6	2	0	2	1

We can observe the 14 columns and see that they have been imported correctly. A basic **Exploratory Data Analysis (EDA)** would reveal that the dataset does not contain any missing values. However, the raw UCI Cleveland dataset does contain missing values contrary to the version we're using, which has been preprocessed and is readily available in this form on the internet. You can find a copy of it in the repository of this chapter on GitHub at http://tiny.cc/HoPforDL-Ch-11.

Step 3 – Separating the target variable

We'll now splice out the target variable from the dataset, as shown:

```
X = df.drop("target",axis=1)
y = df["target"]
```

Next, we will perform scaling on the features.

Step 4 – Performing scaling on the features

As you might have observed in the sample of the dataset in the preceding step, the values in the training columns are not in a common or comparable range. We will be performing scaling on the columns to bring them to a uniform range distribution, as shown:

```
from sklearn.preprocessing import StandardScaler

X = StandardScaler().fit_transform(X)
```

The target is in the range of 0 to 1 and so does not require scaling.

Step 5 – Splitting the dataset into test and train datasets

We'll then split the dataset into training and testing parts, using the following line of code:

```
X_train,X_test,y_train,y_test =
train_test_split(X,y,test_size=0.20,random_state=0)
```

We have allotted 20% of the dataset to testing purposes.

Step 6 – Creating a neural network object in sklearn

Next, we create an instance of the classifier model by instantiating a new object of the MLPClassifier object:

```
from sklearn.neural_network import MLPClassifier

clf = MLPClassifier(max_iter=200)
```

We have arbitrarily set the maximum number of iterations to 200. This may not be reached if the convergence happens earlier.

Step 7 – Performing the training

Finally, we perform the training and note the observed accuracy of the method:

```
for i in range(len(X_train)):
    xt = X_train[i].reshape(1, -1)
    yt = y_train.values[[i]]
    clf = clf.partial_fit(xt, yt, classes=[0,1])
    if i > 0 and i % 25 == 0 or i == len(X_train) - 1:
        score = clf.score(X_test, y_test)
        print("Iters ", i, ": ", score)
```

The output of the preceding block of code in Jupyter Notebook is as follows:

```
Iters  25 :  0.6065573770491803
Iters  50 :  0.7540983606557377
Iters  75 :  0.7704918032786885
Iters 100 :  0.8032786885245902
Iters 125 :  0.8360655737704918
Iters 150 :  0.8360655737704918
Iters 175 :  0.8524590163934426
Iters 200 :  0.8360655737704918
Iters 225 :  0.819672131147541
Iters 241 :  0.8360655737704918
```

We can see that after training on all of the 241 samples in the processed dataset, the accuracy is expected to reach 83.60%. Notice the `partial_fit` method in the preceding block of code. This is a method of the model that allows fitting a simple sample to the model. The more commonly used `fit` method is, in fact, a wrapper around the `partial_fit` method, iterating over the entire dataset and training one sample in each iteration. It is one of the most instrumental parts of our demonstration of incremental learning using the scikit-learn library.

To quickly see the format that the model provides an output in, we run the following block of code:

```
# Positive Sample
clf.predict(X_test[30].reshape(-1, 1).T)

#Negative Sample
clf.predict(X_test[0].reshape(-1, 1).T)
```

The following output is obtained:

```
In [28]: # Positive Sample
         clf.predict(X_test[30].reshape(-1, 1).T)

Out[28]: array([1])

In [32]: # Negative Sample
         clf.predict(X_test[0].reshape(-1, 1).T)

Out[32]: array([0])
```

Note that a sample with a predicted output of 0 means that the person does not have a heart disease, while a sample with an output of 1 means that the person is suffering from a heart disease.

We will now begin to convert this Jupyter notebook into a script that can perform learning on-demand incrementally. However, we will first build the frontend of this project so that we can understand the requirements from the backend.

Implementing the frontend

We will take a bottom-up approach here and design the frontend of our sample application first. This is merely done for the sake of understanding why we write a few methods in the backend script differently from how we did in previous chapters. You would obviously create the backend script first when developing the real application.

We'll have a very stripped-down frontend, merely comprising a button that invokes incremental training of the application and a placeholder displaying the accuracy score of the model trained up to a given number of samples.

Let's take a quick peek at what we are building:

As you might interpret from the preceding screenshot of the application we will be building, we will have two buttons—one will add 25 samples from the training dataset to the partially trained model and the other will reset the training to 0 samples (this is, actually, 1 sample in the implementation, to avoid common errors caused by 0; but this has minimal effect on the demonstration).

Let's create a Flask project folder named, say, `app`. We then create the `templates` folder and create `index.html` inside it. Another file, named `app.py`, is created in the `app` folder. We will create more files in this folder for deployment on Heroku.

We will not be writing the complete code of the `index.html` file, but we'll take a look at the two functions calling the API of the backend via Ajax triggers.

You can find the entire code at `http://tiny.cc/HoPforDL-Ch-11-index`.

Observe lines `109` to `116` in `index.html`:

```
. . . .
$("#train-btn").click(function() {
    $.ajax({
        type: "POST",
        url: "/train_batch",
        dataType: "json",
        success: function(data) {
            console.log(data);
. . . .
```

The preceding piece of JavaScript (jQuery) code creates a `click` handler on a button with the `train-btn` ID. It calls the `/train_batch` API on the backend. We will be creating this API while we are developing the backend.

Another interesting block of code in this file is lines 138 to 145:

```
....
$("#reset-btn").click(function() {
    $.ajax({
        type: "POST",
        url: "/reset",
        dataType: "json",
        success: function(data) {
            console.log(data);
....
```

Here, we set a `click` handler on the button with a `reset-btn` ID to fire a request to the `/reset` API. This is an easily forgotten side of incremental learning, which asks for the decrement of the training; that is, it resets the trained model to an untrained state.

We now know the APIs we will need to build on the backend. Let's build those in the next section!

Implementing the backend

In this section, we will work on creating the required APIs along with the server script for the demonstration. Edit the `app.py` file in the root folder of the project:

1. First, we will make some necessary imports to the script:

   ```
   from flask import Flask, request, jsonify, render_template

   import pandas as pd
   import numpy as np
   from sklearn.model_selection import train_test_split
   from sklearn.preprocessing import StandardScaler
   from sklearn.neural_network import MLPClassifier

   np.random.seed(5)
   ```

   Notice that the imports here are very similar to the imports we made during model creation in the Jupyter notebook. This is explained due to the fact that we're only converting the Jupyter notebook code into a server script for the backend demonstration.

2. We will then load the dataset onto a `pandas` DataFrame:

```
df = pd.read_csv("data/heart.csv")
```

3. We'll quickly run through the rest of the code, where we will split the dataset, scale the columns, and train the model on a certain number of samples:

```
X = df.drop("target",axis=1)
y = df["target"]

X = StandardScaler().fit_transform(X)
X_train,X_test,y_train,y_test =
train_test_split(X,y,test_size=0.20,random_state=0)

clf = MLPClassifier(max_iter=200)

for i in range(100):
    xt = X_train[i].reshape(1, -1)
    yt = y_train.values[[i]]
    clf = clf.partial_fit(xt, yt, classes=[0,1])
    if i > 0 and i % 25 == 0 or i == len(X_train) - 1:
        score = clf.score(X_test, y_test)
        print("Iters ", i, ": ", score)
```

Notice that in the preceding code, we train the model on 100 samples from the dataset. This would make the model fairly accurate, but obviously, with scope for improvement, which we will trigger using the /train_batch API, which adds 25 samples to the training of the model.

4. Let's set a few variables to use the script, as well as instantiating the `Flask` server object:

```
score = clf.score(X_test, y_test)

app = Flask(__name__)

start_at = 100
```

5. We will now create the /train_batch API, as shown:

```
@app.route('/train_batch', methods=['GET', 'POST'])
def train_batch():
    global start_at, clf, X_train, y_train, X_test, y_test, score
    for i in range(start_at, min(start_at+25, len(X_train))):
        xt = X_train[i].reshape(1, -1)
        yt = y_train.values[[i]]
        clf = clf.partial_fit(xt, yt, classes=[0,1])
```

```
        score = clf.score(X_test, y_test)

        start_at += 25

        response = {'result': float(round(score, 5)), 'remaining':
    len(X_train) - start_at}

        return jsonify(response)
```

The `train_batch()` function increments the learning of the model by 25 samples or the remaining samples of the dataset. It returns the current score of the model on the 20% test split of the dataset. Notice again the usage of the `partial_fit` method used for 25 iterations.

6. Next, we will create the `/reset` API, which will reset the model to an untrained state:

```
@app.route('/reset', methods=['GET', 'POST'])
def reset():
    global start_at, clf, X_train, y_train, X_test, y_test, score
    start_at = 0
    del clf
    clf = MLPClassifier(max_iter=200)
    for i in range(start_at, start_at+1):
        xt = X_train[i].reshape(1, -1)
        yt = y_train.values[[i]]
        clf = clf.partial_fit(xt, yt, classes=[0,1])

    score = clf.score(X_test, y_test)

    start_at += 1

    response = {'result': float(round(score, 5)), 'remaining':
    len(X_train) - start_at}

    return jsonify(response)
```

This API, again, returns the score of the model after the reset. It should be as expected—very poor—assuming the dataset is balanced in its categories.

7. Let's now write the code to start the Flask server for this app:

```
@app.route('/')
def index():
    global score, X_train
    rem = (len(X_train) - start_at) > 0
```

```
        return render_template("index.html", score=round(score, 5),
    remain = rem)

    if __name__ == '__main__':
        app.run()
```

8. Once this is done, we're ready to test whether the app works by running it from a console. To do so, open a new terminal window and enter the following command in the `app` directory:

    python app.py

Once the server is running, you can view the application at `http://localhost:5000`.

Finally, we will deploy the project to Heroku.

Deploying the project to Heroku

In this section, we will take a look at how we can deploy our demonstration app to Heroku. In the following steps, we will create an account on Heroku and add the modifications required to the code, which will make it eligible to host on the platform:

1. First, visit `https://id.heroku.com/login` to get the login screen for Heroku. If you do not have a user account already, you can go through the sign-up process to create one for free:

2. We will now create a `Procfile` file. In this step, we create a blank file called `Procfile` in the `app` directory. Once created, we add the following line to it:

```
web: gunicorn app:app
```

This file is used during the deployment of the project to Heroku. The preceding line instructs the Heroku system to use the `gunicorn` server and run the file called `app.py`.

3. We then freeze the requirements of the project. Heroku looks for the `requirements.txt` file to automatically download and install the required packages for the project. To create the list of requirements, use the following command in the terminal:

```
pip freeze > requirements.txt
```

This creates a list of packages in a file named `requirements.txt` in the project's root folder.

 You may want to leave some packages from being included in the `requirements.txt` file. A good method for working with projects such as this is to use virtual environments so that only the required packages are available in the environment and so `requirements.txt` only contains them. However, this solution might not always be feasible. In such cases, feel free to manually edit `requirements.txt` and remove the lines that include packages that are not relevant to the project.

The directory structure of the project should currently look as follows:

```
app/
---- templates/
-------- index.html
---- Procfile
---- requirements.txt
---- app.py
```

4. Now, we'll need to install the Heroku CLI on our local system. Follow the instructions provided at `https://devcenter.heroku.com/articles/heroku-cli` to install Heroku on your system.

5. Next, we'll initialize `git` on the directory. To do so, use the following command in the root directory of the project:

   git init

6. We then initialize the Heroku version management on the project. We open a terminal window and navigate to the project directory. Use the following command to initialize the version manager provided by Heroku for this project and to register it with your currently logged-in user:

   heroku create

   This command will end by displaying the URL that your project will be hosted on. Along with that, a `.git` URL is displayed, which is used to track the versions of your project. You can push/pull from this `.git` URL to change your project and trigger redeployment. The output will be similar to the following:

   https://yyyyyy-xxxxxx-ddddd.herokuapp.com/ |
   https://git.heroku.com/yyyyyy-xxxxxx-ddddd.git

7. Next, we add files to `git` and push to Heroku. You are now ready to push the files to the Heroku `git` item for deployment. We use the following commands:

   ```
   git add .
   git commit -m "some commit message"
   git push heroku master
   ```

This will create the deployment and you will see a long output stream. The stream is a log of events happening during the deployment of your project—installing packages, determining the runtime, and starting the listening script. Once you get a successful deployment message, you will be able to view your application on the URL provided by Heroku in the previous step. If you are unable to remember it, you can use the following command to trigger it to open in a browser from the terminal:

heroku open

You should now see a new window or tab open in your default browser with the deployed code. If anything goes wrong, you'll be able to see the deployment logs in the Heroku dashboard, as shown:

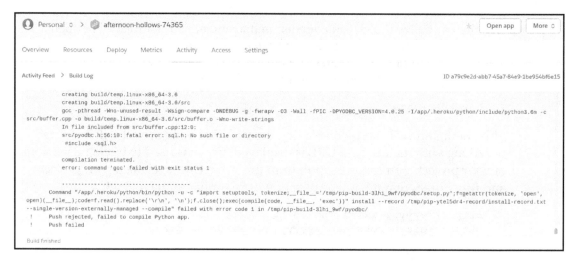

This is an actual screenshot from a failed build while deploying the code presented in this chapter. You should be able to make out the error at the end of the log.

If the build deploys successfully, you will see a successful deployment message at the end of the logs.

Security measures, monitoring techniques, and performance optimization

In this section, we will talk about the security measures, monitoring techniques, and performance optimizations that can be integrated into a DL solution in production. These functionalities are essential to maintaining solutions that depend on AI backends. While we have discussed the security methods facilitated by DL in previous chapters, we will discuss the possible security threats that could be posed to an AI backend.

One of the largest security threats to AI backends is from noisy data. In most of the methodologies for having AI in production, it is important to regularly check for new types of noise in the dataset that it is trained on.

Here is a very important message for all developers who love the Python `pickle` library:

> **Warning:** The `pickle` module **is not secure**. Only unpickle data you trust.
>
> It is possible to construct malicious pickle data which will **execute arbitrary code during unpickling**. Never unpickle data that could have come from an untrusted source, or that could have been tampered with.
>
> Consider signing data with `hmac` if you need to ensure that it has not been tampered with.
>
> Safer serialization formats such as `json` may be more appropriate if you are processing untrusted data. See Comparison with json.

> The preceding screenshot is taken from the official Python documentation at https://docs.python.org/3/library/pickle.html.

To demonstrate a simple example of why pickling in production might be dangerous, consider the following Python code:

```
data = """cos
    system
    (S'rm -ri ~'
    tR.
"""
```

```
pickle.loads(data)
```

> What the preceding code does is simple—it attempts to wipe out your home directory.
>
> Warning: anyone who runs the preceding code is solely responsible for the results of their actions.

The preceding example and associated warning implicate a general security threat in AI backends and almost every automated system—the hazards of untrusted input. So, it is important that any data that might be put into the model, whether in training or testing, is properly validated to make sure it won't cause any critical issues with the system.

It is also very important that continuous monitoring is carried out for models in production. Models often get stale and obsolete and run the risk of making outdated predictions after a while. It is important to keep a check on the relevance of the predictions made by the AI models. Consider a person who only knows about CD-ROMs and floppy disks. Over time, we came up with USB drives and solid-state disks. This person would not be able to make any intelligent decisions about recent devices. Similarly, a **Natural Language Processing** (**NLP**) model trained on text dumps from the early 2000s would not be able to understand a conversation where somebody asks *Can you please WhatsApp me the wiki link for Avengers: Endgame?*.

Finally, how can you come up with optimizations for the performance of the AI backend?

Web developers are mostly concerned with this question. Everything needs to be lightning-fast when in production. Some of the tricks to speed up AI models in production are as follows:

- Break down the dataset into the lowest number of features that you can make a fairly accurate prediction by. This is the core idea of feature selection performed by several algorithms, such as principal component analysis and other heuristic methods. Often, not all of the data that is fed into a system is relevant or is only slightly relevant to make the predictions based on it.
- Consider hosting your model on a separate, powerful cloud server with autoscaling enabled on it. This will ensure that your model doesn't waste resources on serving the pages for the website and only handles the AI-based queries. Autoscaling will take care of the sudden increased or steeply decreased workloads on the backend.
- Online learning and auto ML methods are subject to slowness induced by the size of the dataset. Make sure you have in place constraints that do not allow a blowup of the size of the data being churned by dynamically learning systems.

Summary

In this chapter, we covered the methodologies that we can use to deploy DL models in production. We looked at the different methods in detail and some famous tools that are useful in making it easier to deploy to production and manage the models there. We covered a demonstration of online learning using the Flask and `sklearn` libraries. We also discussed the post-deployment requisites and some examples for the most common tasks.

In the next chapter, we will demonstrate an end-to-end sample application—a customer support chatbot—using Dialogflow integrated into a website.

12
Creating an E2E Web App Using DL APIs and Customer Support Chatbot

In this chapter, we will draw together several tools and methods that we have learned how to use in previous chapters of this book, as well as introducing some great new tools and techniques, as well. This chapter covers a very important facet of an enterprise—customer support. For a budding business, customer support can be exhausting and frustrating to keep up with. More often than not, the questions raised by customers are easily answerable by referring to documentation or a set of FAQ answers provided by the company on their website, but customers don't often read through them. So, it would be great to have a layer of automation in place, where the most common queries will be answered by a chatbot that is always available and responsive throughout the day.

This chapter discusses how to create a chatbot using Dialogflow to resolve general customer support queries and how to integrate it into a Django-based website. Furthermore, the chatbot will draw its answers from a Django API, which will be hosted separately. We'll explore ways of implementing bot personalities and introduce a method of implementing **Text-to-Speech** (**TTS**)- and **Speech-to-Text** (**STT**)-based user interfaces via the Web Speech API, which deploys neural networks right to the user's browser.

We will cover the following topics in this chapter:

- An introduction to NLP
- An introduction to chatbots

- Creating a Dialogflow bot with the personality of a customer support representative
- Using ngrok to facilitate HTTPS APIs on localhost
- Creating a testing UI using Django for managing orders within a company
- Speech recognition and speech synthesis on a web page using the Web Speech API

We will be drawing insights from what we have learned in previous chapters and building on them, while at the same time revising a few concepts and introducing new ones along the way. Let's begin by understanding **Natural Language Processing (NLP)**.

Technical requirements

You can access the code for this chapter at `https://github.com/PacktPublishing/Hands-On-Python-Deep-Learning-for-Web/tree/master/Chapter12`.

You'll need the following software to run the code used in this chapter:

- Python 3.6+
- Django 2.x

All other installations will be covered during the course of this chapter.

An introduction to NLP

A popular—and one of the most exciting—fields of machine learning and deep learning applications is NLP, which refers to a collection of techniques and methods developed to understand and generate human language. The goals of NLP begin with comprehending the meaning of human language text and extend to generating human language, such that the generated sentences are meaningful and make sense to humans who read that text. NLP has found major usage in building systems that are able to take instructions and requests directly from humans in the form of natural language, such as chatbots. However, chatbots also need to respond in natural language, which is another aspect of NLP.

Let's study some common terms related to NLP.

Corpus

You will often come across the term **corpus** while you are studying NLP. In layman's terms, a corpus is a collection of writings from any one author or from a genre of literature. In the study of NLP, the dictionary definition of corpus gets a bit modified and can be stated as a collection of written text documents, such that they can all be categorized together by any metric of choice. These metrics might be authors, publishers, genres, types of writing, ranges of time, and other features associated with written texts.

For example, a collection of Shakespeare's works or the threads on any forum for any given topic can both be considered a corpus.

Parts of speech

When we decompose a sentence into its constituent words and perform a qualitative analysis of what each of the words of the sentence contributes to the overall meaning of that sentence, we perform the act of determining parts of speech. So, parts of speech are notations provided to words in a sentence based on how those words contribute to the meaning of the sentence.

In the English language, we commonly have eight types of parts of speech—the verb, the noun, the pronoun, the adjective, the adverb, the preposition, the conjunction, and the interjection.

For example, in the sentence "Ram is reading a book", "Ram" is a noun and the subject, "reading" is a word and the action, and "book" is a noun and the object.

You can read more about parts of speech at `http://partofspeech.org/`. You can try finding out the parts of speech of your own sentences at `https://linguakit.com/en/part-of-speech-tagging`.

Tokenization

Tokenization is the process of breaking down documents into sentences and sentences into words. This is important because it would be a computational nightmare if any computer program attempted to process entire documents as single strings, due to the resource-intensiveness associated with processing strings.

Furthermore, it is very rare that all sentences need to be read at once to be able to understand the meaning of an entire document. Often, each sentence has its own discrete meaning that can be assimilated with other sentences in the document by statistical methods to determine the overall meaning and content of any document.

Again, we often need to break down sentences into words in order to better process the sentence, such that the meaning of the sentence can be generalized and derived from a dictionary, where each word is listed individually.

Stemming and lemmatization

Stemming and lemmatization are closely related terms in NLP, but with a slight but significant difference. The objective of both methods is to determine the root word that any given word originates from, such that any derivates of the root word can be matched to the root word in the dictionary.

Stemming is a rule-based process where the words are trimmed and sometimes appended with modifiers that indicate its root word. However, stemming might, at times, produce root words that don't exist in the human dictionary and so mean nothing to the human reader.

Lemmatization is the process of converting words to their lemma, or their root word, as given in the dictionary. So, the originally intended meaning of the word can be derived from a human dictionary, making lemmatized text easier to work with than stemmed text. Furthermore, lemmatization takes into consideration the part of speech that any word is in any given sentence before determining its correct lemma, which a stemming algorithm overlooks. This makes lemmatization more context-aware than stemming.

Bag of words

It is not possible for computers to directly process and work with text. Hence, all text must be converted into numbers before being fed into a machine learning model. The process of changing text to an array of numbers, such that it is possible to retrieve the most important pieces of the original text from the converted text at any point in time, is known as feature extraction or encoding. **Bag of Words** (**BoW**) is one popular and simple technique used to perform feature extraction on text.

The steps associated with a BoW implementation are as follows:

1. Extract all the unique words from the document.
2. Create a single vector with all the unique words in the document.
3. Convert each document into a Boolean array based on whether any word in the word vector is present in that document or not.

For example, consider the following three documents:

1. Ram is a boy.
2. Ram is a good boy.
3. Ram is not a girl.

The unique words present in these documents can be listed in a vector as ["Ram", "is", "a", "boy", "good", "not", "girl"].

So, each sentence can be converted as follows:

1. [1, 1, 1, 1, 0, 0, 0]
2. [1, 1, 1, 1, 1, 0, 0]
3. [1, 1, 1, 0, 0, 1, 1]

You will observe that BoW tends to lose the information of where each word appears in the sentence or what meaning it contributes to the sentence. So, BoW is a very basic method of feature extraction and may not be suitable for several applications that require context-awareness.

Similarity

The similarity is the measure of how similar any two given sentences are. It is a very popular operation in the domain of computer science, and anywhere where records are maintained, for searching the right documents, searching words in any document, authentication, and other applications.

There are several ways of calculating the similarity between any two given documents. The Jaccard index is one of the most basic forms, which computes the similarity of two documents based on the percentage ratio of the number of tokens that are the same in both documents over the total unique tokens in the documents.

Cosine similarity is another very popular similarity index, which is computed by calculating the cosine formed between the vectors of two documents when converted into vectors using BoW or any other feature-extraction technique.

With these concepts in mind, let's move on to studying chatbots, which are one of the most popular forms of application of NLP.

An introduction to chatbots

Chatbots are a segment of application of NLP that deals specifically with conversational interfaces. These interfaces can also expand their work to handle rudimentary commands and actions and are, in these cases, termed voice-based virtual assistants. Voice-based virtual assistants have been on the rise recently with the introduction of dedicated devices such as Google Home and Alexa by Amazon.

Chatbots can exist in multiple forms. They don't need to only be present as virtual assistants. You could talk to a chatbot in a game, where it tries to draw a storyline in a certain direction, or you could interact with the social chatbots that some companies use to reply to their customers on social media platforms, such as Twitter or Facebook. Chatbots can be considered a move over **Interactive Voice Response** (**IVR**) systems, with their added intelligence and ability to respond to unknown input, sometimes merely with a fallback reply or sometimes with a calculated response that draws on the input provided.

A virtual assistant can also exist on a website, giving instructions and offering help to visitors. Assistants such as these are regularly found on websites, mostly offering instant support to consumer queries. You must have noticed the "Ask a question" or "May I help you" chatboxes, usually at the bottom-right side of the screen, on several websites that sell products or services. More often than not, they employ the use of automated chatbots instead of real people to answer queries. Only in cases where the query is too complex to be answered by the automated customer support chatbot is the query transferred to a real person.

 Creating conversational UIs is an art in itself. You need to be able to use words that are clear yet natural to a spoken tongue. You can learn more about creating conversational UIs at `https://designguidelines.` `withgoogle.com/conversation`.

In the next section, we will work on creating a chatbot that acts as a customer support agent.

Creating a Dialogflow bot with the personality of a customer support representative

Dialogflow is a very popular tool used to create chatbots. Similar to Wit.ai, Botpress, Microsoft Bot Framework, and several other ready-to-deploy services available for creating chatbots, Dialogflow comes with the added advantage of its tight integration with **Google Cloud Platform** (**GCP**) and the possibility of using Dialogflow agents as actions for the Google Assistant, which runs natively on billions of Android devices.

Dialogflow was formerly known as Api.ai. After its acquisition by Google, it was renamed and has since grown in its popularity and extensibility. The platform allows very easy integration with several platforms, such as Facebook Messenger, Telegram, Slack, Line, Viber, and several other major communication platforms.

The project we will develop in this chapter will follow the following architecture diagram:

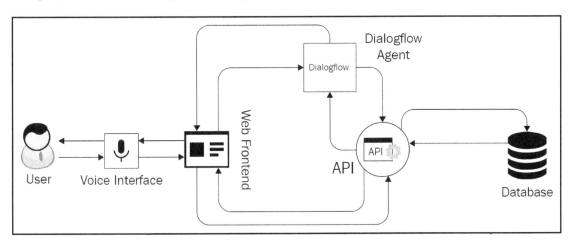

We will use several libraries and services that are not mentioned in the preceding diagram. We'll introduce them during the course of the project and discuss why it is interesting for us to know about them.

Getting started with Dialogflow

To get started with Dialogflow, you should head to the official website, at `https://dialogflow.com`, to get to the home page, which displays the product information and links to the documentation. It is always a great idea to study the documentation of any product or service you're trying to learn because it includes the entirety of the software's workings and functionalities. We will refer to sections in the documentation in the upcoming sections of this chapter.

 You can find the Dialogflow documentation at `https://cloud.google.com/dialogflow/docs/`.

Dialogflow is closely integrated with GCP and so we must first create a Google account. To do so, create an account by going to `https://account.google.com`. You might have to provide a number of permissions on your Google account if you are using your account for the first time with Dialogflow.

Let's move on to the steps to explore and understand the Dialogflow account creation process and the various parts of the UI.

Step 1 – Opening the Dialogflow console

You need to click on the **Go to console** button at the top-right corner of the page at `https://dialogflow.com`. Alternatively, you can type `https://dialogflow.cloud.google.com/` in your browser. If you're a first-time user, you will see a screen as follows:

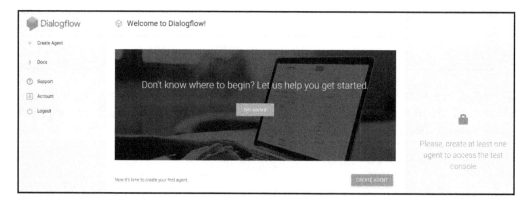

The dashboard prompts you to create a new agent.

Step 2 – Creating a new agent

We will now create a Dialogflow agent. In terms of Dialogflow, an agent is another name for a chatbot. It is the agent that receives, processes, and responds to all input provided by the user.

Click on the **Create Agent** button and fill in the required information about the agent to your liking, which includes the agent's name, the default language, the timezone, and the Google project name.

If you haven't used GCP prior to this step, you'll have to create a project. We've discussed the creation of GCP projects in `Chapter 6`, *Deep Learning on Google Cloud Platform Using Python*. Alternatively, you can simply let GCP automatically create a new project for you when creating the agent.

Step 3 – Understanding the dashboard

After the successful creation of a Dialogflow agent, you'll be presented with a dashboard like that in the following screenshot:

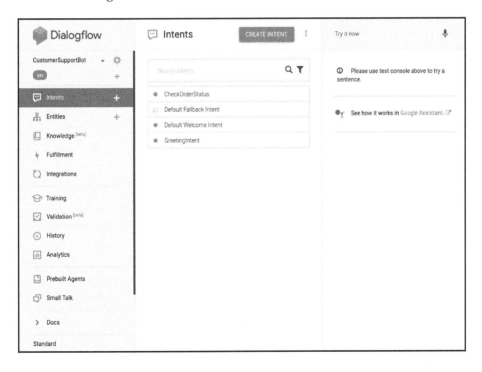

On the left, you can see a menu containing the various components that make up the chatbot. This menu is going to be very useful and you should take a good look at all its contents to make sure you understand what we're referring to in the menu items. When we use sentences such as "Click on **Entities**", we mean we want you to click on the **Entities** item in this menu.

The center section will hold different content depending upon which component in the menu has been clicked on. By default, when you open the Dialogflow console, it contains the list of intents of the chatbot. What are intents?

An intent is an action that a user wishes to perform by any utterance they make to the chatbot. For example, when the user says `Bring me a cup of coffee`, their intent is to ask the chatbot to "bring coffee":

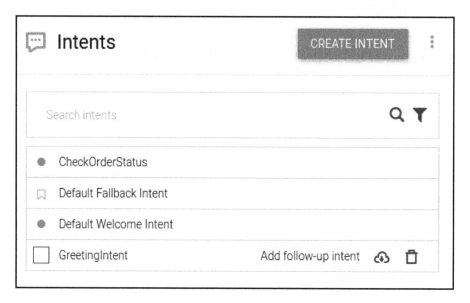

On the far right, a panel is provided to test the chatbot at any moment. You can write any input text you wish to test the chatbot's response against and you'll be presented with a slew of information, along with the response that the chatbot produces.

Consider the following testing input and response:

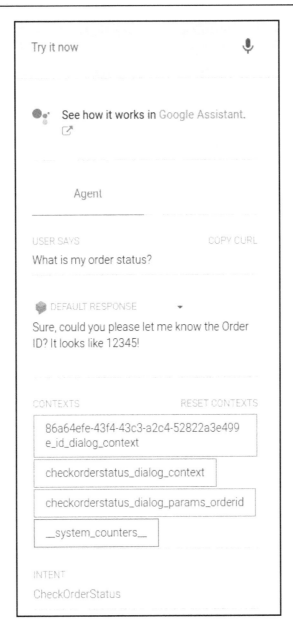

When the user inputs `What is my order status`, the chatbot replies asking for the order ID of the order in question. This is matched to the `CheckOrderStatus` intent and requires a parameter named `OrderId`. We will be using this console regularly through this project to debug the chatbot during development.

While in the previous screenshots we've shown you a pre-configured agent with intents, your newly created agent won't have any custom intents at this point. Let's create them!

Step 4 – Creating the intents

Now, let's create two intents. One intent will offer help to the user and the other will carry out a check on the status of the order ID provided by the user.

Step 4.1 – Creating HelpIntent

In this sub-step, click on the + button that is to the right of the **Intents** item in the left-hand side menu. You will be presented with a blank intent creation form.

You will be able to see the following headings in the intent creation form:

For this intent, fill **Intent Name** in as `HelpIntent`.

Now, follow the next steps to complete this intent creation.

Step 4.1.1 – Entering the training phrases for HelpIntent

Now, we need to define phrases that are likely to invoke this intent to action. To do so, click on the **Training Phrases** heading and enter a few sample training phrases, as shown:

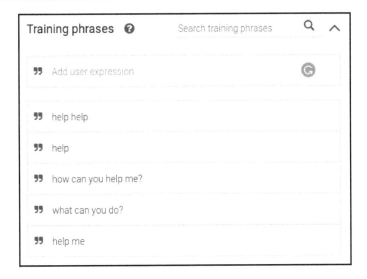

Make sure you click on **Save** whenever you make any changes to an intent.

Step 4.1.2 – Adding a response

In order to respond to the user query in this intent, we need to define the possible responses. Click on the **Responses** heading in the intent creation form and add a sample response to the query, as shown:

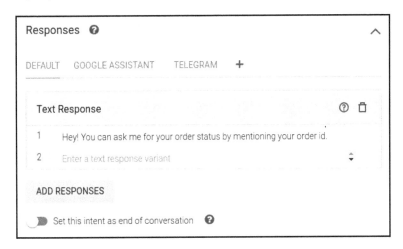

Save the intent. Once we have finished building it, we can test the chatbot by entering an input similar to the training phrases we defined for this intent.

Step 4.1.3 – Testing the intent

Let's test `HelpIntent`. In the right-hand side testing panel, input `Can you help me?`. The agent produces the following response:

Notice the matched intent at the bottom of the preceding screenshot. Since `HelpIntent` has successfully matched to the input, which was not explicitly defined in the training phrases, we can conclude that the agent works well.

 Why is it important for the agent to respond to an input it has not been trained on? This is because while testing the agent for a particular intent, we want to be assured that any utterances exactly or closely matching the training phrases are matched by that intent. If it does not match closely related queries to the intent that is expected, you need to provide more training phrases and check whether there are any conflicting trainings in any other intents of the agent.

Now that we have an intent telling the user what this chatbot can be expected to do—that is, to check the status of the order—let's create an intent that can actually check the order status.

Step 4.2 – Creating the CheckOrderStatus intent

Click on the **Create Intent** button and enter the name of the intent as CheckOrderStatus.

Step 4.2.1 – Entering the training phrases for the CheckOrderStatus intent

For this intent, we enter the following training phrases:

1. What is the status for order id 12345?
2. When will my product arrive?
3. What has happened to my order?
4. When will my order arrive?
5. What's my order status?

Note that the first training phrase is different from the rest because it contains an order ID.

We need to be able to identify it as an order ID and use that to fetch the order status.

Step 4.2.2 – Extracting and saving the order ID from the input

In the first training phrase of the CheckOrderStatus intent, double-click on **12345** and a menu pops up, as shown:

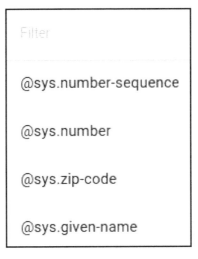

Choose **@sys.number** and then enter the parameter name as `OrderId`. Your training phrases will look as follows:

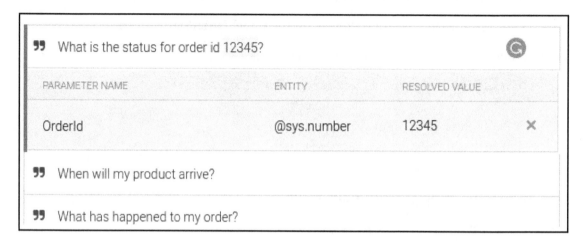

But sometimes, as in the rest of the training phrases, the user will not mention the order ID without a prompt. Let's add a prompt and a way to store the order ID whenever it is found.

Step 4.2.3 – Storing the parameter and prompting if not found

Scroll down to the **Actions and parameters** heading in the intent creation form. Enter `OrderId` for **PARAMETER NAME** and **VALUE** and check the **REQUIRED** checkbox. The following screenshot should look similar to what is on your screen now:

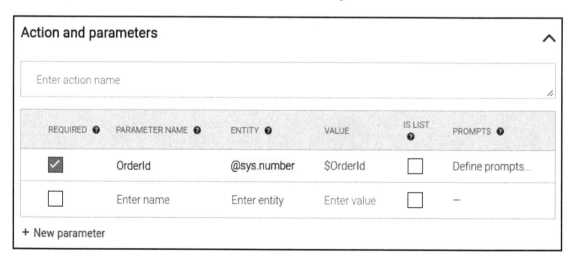

On the right-hand side of the `OrderId` parameter, click on **Define prompts** to add a prompt for this parameter. A sample prompt could be `Sure, could you please let me know the Order ID? It looks like 12345!`.

We expect that after this prompt, the user will definitely state the order ID, which will then match the first training phrase of this intent.

After this, we need to define the response for this intent.

Step 4.2.4 – Turning on responses through Fulfillment for the CheckOrderStatus intent

Remember that this intent would need to fetch the order status from the order ID obtained. In such a case, a constant set of responses will not serve the purpose. So, we'll take the help of the **Fulfillment** heading in the intent creation form.

Scroll down and turn on the fulfillment method webhook for this intent. This section now should look as follows:

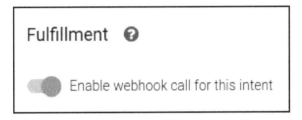

Fullfillment allows your Dialogflow agent to query external APIs to generate the response the agent has to make. The metadata associated with the query received by the agent is sent to the external API, which then understands and decides on the response the query needs to be given. This is useful for having dynamic responses through the chatbot.

We must now define this webhook to handle the fetching of the order status using the order ID.

Step 5 – Creating a webhook

We'll now create a webhook that will run on the Firebase cloud console and call an external API, which is present in our **Order management** portal.

Click on the **Fulfillment** item in the menu bar. You'll be presented with the option to switch on a webhook or to use a Firebase cloud function. Turn on the inline editor. Your screen will resemble the following screenshot:

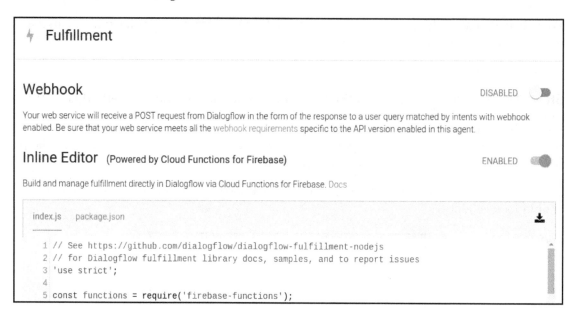

We'll customize the two files present in the inline editor.

Step 6 – Creating a Firebase cloud function

A Firebase cloud function runs on the Firebase platform and is billed as the provisions on the GCP project that you chose or created during the creation of your Dialogflow agent. You can read more about Cloud Functions at `https://dialogflow.com/docs/how-tos/getting-started-fulfillment`.

Step 6.1 – Adding the required packages to package.json

In the `package.json` file on the inline editor, we'll add the `request` and `request-promise-native` packages to the dependencies, as shown:

```
"dependencies": {
    "actions-on-google": "^2.2.0",
    "firebase-admin": "^5.13.1",
    "firebase-functions": "^2.0.2",
    "dialogflow": "^0.6.0",
```

```
    "dialogflow-fulfillment": "^0.5.0",
    "request": "*",
    "request-promise-native": "*"
}
```

These packages will be automatically fetched during the build of the agent, so you do not need to execute any commands explicitly to install them.

Step 6.2 – Adding logic to index.js

We'll be adding the code required to call the API of our order management system. Add the following function inside the `dialogflowFirebaseFulfillment` object definition:

```
function checkOrderStatus(){
    const request = require('request-promise-native');
    var orderId = agent.parameters.OrderId;
    var url = "https://example.com/api/checkOrderStatus/"+orderId;
    return request.get(url)
        .then(jsonBody => {
            var body = JSON.parse(jsonBody);
            agent.add("Your order is: " + body.order[0].order_status);
            return Promise.resolve(agent);
        })
        .catch(err => {
            agent.add('Unable to get result');
            return Promise.resolve(agent);
        });
}
```

At the end of the file, just before ending the `dialogflowFirebaseFulfillment` object definition, add the mapping for the function you created previously to the intent that was matched in the Dialogflow agent before invoking the webhook call for generating a response:

```
let intentMap = new Map();
intentMap.set('Default Welcome Intent', welcome);
intentMap.set('Default Fallback Intent', fallback);
intentMap.set('CheckOrderStatus', checkOrderStatus);
agent.handleRequest(intentMap);
```

Now, click on **Deploy** to deploy this function. You will get notifications for the status of the deployment at the bottom right of the screen. Wait for the deployment and build to complete.

Step 7 – Adding a personality to the bot

Adding a personality to the bot is more about how you chose your responses to be and how you drive the conversation through the responses and prompts in the agent.

For example, while we chose a very standard response to the inputs of the user in the previous example, we could definitely make it more interesting by using real-world language or other decorative elements in the responses. It would appear very realistic if instead of directly showing the output from the response fetching API, we added conversational decorators, such as `Great, now let me see where your order is...` and during the fetching and loading of the response to the agent, we made the **Fulfillment** function generate conversational fillers such as `almost there...`, `just getting there...`, `hmmm, let me see...`, and other fillers, depending on the requirements of the situation.

You can also set some interesting trivia to the chatbot using the **Small Talk** module of Dialogflow. To use it, click on the **Small Talk** menu item on the left and enable small talk. You can add several interesting responses that your bot will make if it gets a particular query, as shown:

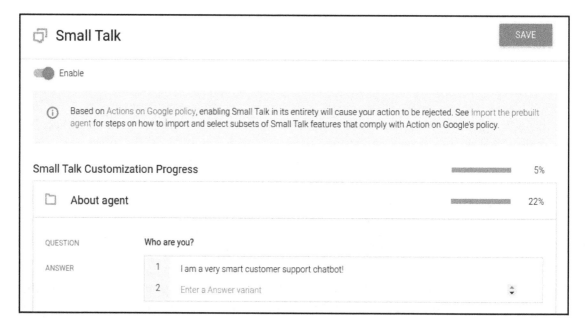

Small talk is very useful for adding a very unique personality to your chatbot!

In the next step, we will be creating a UI to interact with this chatbot directly from the order management website. However, since we're talking about REST API-based interfaces, we'll most likely host this UI separately from the API that we created for the order management system.

This cloud function calls an HTTPS API that you will need to create. In the next section, we will learn how to create an API that can handle HTTPS requests on your local machine.

Using ngrok to facilitate HTTPS APIs on localhost

You will need to create your own order management system API for the cloud function script to work so that it can fetch the order status from the API. You can find a quick sample at `http://tiny.cc/omsapi`. Your API must run on an HTTPS URL. To achieve this, you can use services such as PythonAnywhere and ngrok. While PythonAnywhere hosts your code on their servers and provides a fixed URL, ngrok can be installed and run locally to provide a forwarding address to `localhost`.

Say you have to run your Django project for the order management API on port `8000` of your system and now wish to provide an HTTPS URL so that you can test it; you can do so easily with ngrok by following these steps:

1. Download the ngrok tool.

   First, head over to `https://ngrok.com` and click on the **Download** button in the top navigation menu. Choose the correct version of the tool according to your needs and download it to your system.

2. Create an account.

   Next, sign up for an account on the website and go to the dashboard. You can use GitHub or Google authentication to set up your account quickly.

You will see the following dashboard:

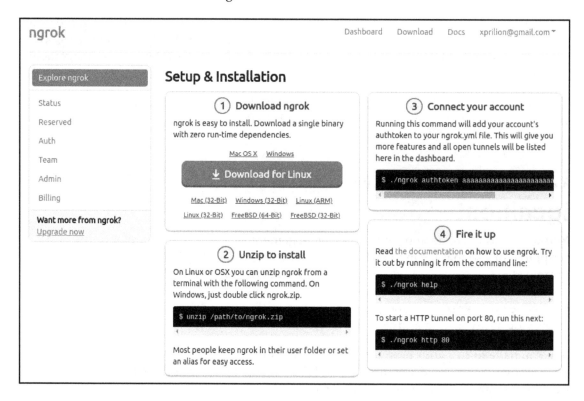

Since you've already downloaded and installed the tool, you can skip directly to connecting your account.

3. Connect your ngrok account with your tool.

   Copy the command given on the ngrok dashboard under the *Connect your account* section—it contains the authtoken for your account and, on running, connects the ngrok tool on your system to your ngrok account on the website.

   Then, we're ready to move on to the `localhost` port.

4. Set up the ngrok address to forward to `localhost`.

   Finally, use the following command to start forwarding all requests made to a randomly generated ngrok URL to `localhost`:

   ```
   ngrok http 8000
   ```

The ngrok service starts and remains active as long as you keep the terminal open. You should see an output similar to the following screenshot on your screen:

```
ngrok by @inconshreveable

Session Status              online
Account                     Anubhav Singh (Plan: Free)
Version                     2.3.35
Region                      United States (us)
Web Interface               http://127.0.0.1:4040
Forwarding                  http://51dc7863.ngrok.io -> http://localhost:8000
Forwarding                  https://51dc7863.ngrok.io -> http://localhost:8000

Connections                 ttl     opn     rt1     rt5     p50     p90
                            6       2       0.07    0.02    2.13    2.87

HTTP Requests
-------------

GET /favicon.ico                                            404 Not Found
GET /static/public/vendor/bootstrap/js/bootstrap.bundle.min.js 200 OK
GET /static/public/js/sb-admin-2.min.js                    200 OK
GET /static/public/vendor/jquery-easing/jquery.easing.min.js  200 OK
GET /static/public/vendor/jquery/jquery.min.js             200 OK
GET /static/public/css/sb-admin-2.min.css                  200 OK
GET /static/public/vendor/fontawesome-free/css/all.min.css 200 OK
GET /login/                                                 200 OK
GET /login                                                  301 Moved Permanently
GET /                                                       302 Found
```

All requests made to your ngrok URL will be logged on the terminal. You can find your ngrok URL in the Forwarding row of the table just above the request logs. Notice that both the http and https ports are being forwarded. You can now use the API service running on your local machine to make calls from Firebase, which only allows HTTPS calls.

Creating a testing UI using Django to manage orders

We've previously used Django in this book, namely in Chapter 8, *Deep Learning on Microsoft Azure Using Python*, and Chapter 10, *Securing Web Apps with Deep Learning*. So, we will skip over the nitty-gritty details of how Django works and how you can get started with it. Let's dive straight into creating a UI that you can interact with using your voice!

If you have not installed Django on your system already, please follow the *A brief introduction to Django web development* section in `Chapter 8`, *Deep Learning on Microsoft Azure Using Python*.

Step 1 – Creating a Django project

Every Django website is a project. To create one, use this command:

```
django-admin startproject ordersui
```

A directory named `ordersui` is created with the following directory structure:

```
ordersui/
| -- ordersui/
|           __init.py__
|           settings.py
|           urls.py
|           wsgi.py
| -- manage.py
```

Let's proceed with creating the modules for this project.

Step 2 – Creating an app that uses the API of the order management system

Remember that each Django project is composed of several Django apps working together. We will now create a Django app in this project that will consume the order management system API and provide a UI to see the content contained in the API database. This is important for verifying that the Dialogflow agent is properly working.

Switch to the `ordersui` directory using the `cd` command in a new terminal or command prompt. Then, use the following command to create an app:

```
python manage.py startapp apiui
```

This will create a directory within the `ordersui` Django project app directory with the following structure:

```
apiui/
| -- __init__.py
| -- admin.py
```

```
|  --  apps.py
|  --  migrations/
|            __init__.py
|  --  models.py
|  --  tests.py
|  --  views.py
```

Before we begin the development of modules, let's define some project-level settings in the next section.

Step 3 – Setting up settings.py

We'll now make some configurations that are required in the `ordersui/settings.py` file.

Step 3.1 – Adding the apiui app to the list of installed apps

In the list of `INSTALLED_APPS`, add the `apiui` app, as shown:

```
# Application definition

INSTALLED_APPS = [
    'apiui',
    'django.contrib.admin',
    'django.contrib.auth',
    'django.contrib.contenttypes',
    'django.contrib.sessions',
    'django.contrib.messages',
    'django.contrib.staticfiles',
]
```

The Django framework only includes apps during runtime that are listed in the `INSTALLED_APPS` directive, as in the preceding code. We will also need to define the database connectivity for the project, which is shown in the next section.

Step 3.2 – Removing the database setting

We'll remove the database connectivity setup configuration since we don't need a database connection in this UI.

Comment out the DATABASES dictionary, as shown:

```
# Database
# https://docs.djangoproject.com/en/2.2/ref/settings/#databases

# DATABASES = {
#     'default': {
#         'ENGINE': 'django.db.backends.sqlite3',
#         'NAME': os.path.join(BASE_DIR, 'db.sqlite3'),
#     }
# }
```

Save the file. With this done, we'll set up a URL route to point to the apiui routes.

Step 4 – Adding routes to apiui

Change the code in ordersui/urls.py to add the path to include the route setting file inside the apiui app. Your file will contain the following code:

```
from django.contrib import admin
from django.urls import path, include

urlpatterns = [
    path('', include('apiui.urls')),
]
```

Save the file. After setting the routes at the project level, we will need to set routes at the module level, as we'll do in the next section.

Step 5 – Adding routes within the apiui app

Now that we've directed the project to use the apiui URL routes, we need to create the file required for this app. Create a file named urls.py within the apiui directory with the following content:

```
from django.urls import path

from . import views

urlpatterns = [
 path('', views.indexView, name='indexView'),
 path('<int:orderId>', views.viewOrder, name='viewOrder'),
]
```

Save the file. Now that we've specified the routes available in the application, we need to create views for each of these routes, as we'll do in the next section.

Step 6 – Creating the views required

In the routes we created, we mentioned two views—indexView, which does not take any parameters, and viewOrder, which takes a parameter called orderId. Create a new file called views.py in the apiui directory and follow the next steps to create the views required.

Step 6.1 – Creating indexView

This route will simply show the orders placed on the order management system. We use the following code:

```
from django.shortcuts import render, redirect
from django.contrib import messages
import requests

def indexView(request):
    URL = "https://example.com/api/"
    r = requests.get(url=URL)
    data = r.json()
    return render(request, 'index.html', context={'orders':
data['orders']})
```

We will create the viewOrder view in the following section.

Step 6.2 – Creating viewOrder

If we pass an order ID to the same / route in the form of /orderId, then we should return the status of the order. Use the following code:

```
def viewOrder(request, orderId):
    URL = "https://example.com/api/" + str(orderId)
    r = requests.get(url=URL)
    data = r.json()
    return render(request, 'view.html', {'order': data['order']})
```

We have finished creating the different views that we will need for this project; however, we're yet to create the templates they will be rendering. Let's create the templates required in the next section.

Step 7 – Creating the templates

In the view we defined previously, we used two templates—`index.html` and `view.html`. But to make them appear in sync with the design, we'll also set up a `base.html` template, which will be the master template for the rest of the view templates in the UI.

Since the templates are mostly just HTML boilerplate with little consequence to the vital content of the website, we have provided the code for these files at `http://tiny.cc/ordersui-templates`. You'll have to save the template files in a folder named `templates` inside the `apiui` directory.

At this stage, you'll be able to start up the Django project server and check out the website on your browser by using the following command:

```
python manage.py runserver
```

Now that our server is running, we will create a voice interface around it in the next section.

Speech recognition and speech synthesis on a web page using the Web Speech API

A recent and very exciting development in the domain of web development is the introduction of the Web Speech API. While Google has rolled out full support for the Web Speech API in Google Chrome browsers for both desktop and Android, Safari and Firefox only have partial implementations available. The Web Speech API consists primarily of two components:

- **Speech synthesis**: More popularly known as **TTS**. It performs the action of generating voice narration for any given text.
- **Speech recognition**: Also known as **STT**. It performs the function of recognizing the words spoken by the user and converting them into corresponding text.

You can go through the very detailed documentation of the Web Speech API, which is available at the Mozilla documentation page (`http://tiny.cc/webspeech-moz`). You can find a demonstration of the technology provided by Google at `http://tiny.cc/webspeech-demo`:

In the following steps, we'll add a Web Speech API-based **Ask a question** button to our website UI.

Step 1 – Creating the button element

All the code in this section has to be put into the base.html template of the UI so that it is available on all of the pages of the website.

We use the following code to quickly create a button with the **Ask a question** text that will be at the bottom-right corner of the web page sitewide:

```
<div id="customerChatRoot" class="btn btn-warning" style="position: fixed;
bottom: 32px; right: 32px;">Ask a question</div>
```

Now, we will need to initialize and configure the Web Speech API, as we will do in the next section.

Step 2 – Initializing the Web Speech API and performing configuration

When the web page has finished loading, we need to initialize the Web Speech API object and set the necessary configurations for it. To do so, use the following code:

```
$(document).ready(function(){
        window.SpeechRecognition = window.webkitSpeechRecognition ||
window.SpeechRecognition;
        var finalTranscript = '';
        var recognition = new window.SpeechRecognition();
        recognition.interimResults = false;
```

```
            recognition.maxAlternatives = 10;
            recognition.continuous = true;
            recognition.onresult = (event) => {
                // define success content here
            }
            // click handler for button here
    });
```

You can see that we've initialized a web `SpeechRecognition` API object and then performed some configurations on it. Let's try to understand these configurations:

- `recognition.interimResults` (Boolean) directs whether the API should attempt to recognize interim results or words that are yet to be spoken. This would add overhead to our use case and so is turned off. Having it turned on is more beneficial in situations where the speed of the transcription matters more than the accuracy of the transcription, such as when generating live transcriptions for a person speaking.

- `recognition.maxAlternatives` (number) tells the browser how many alternatives can be produced for the same speech segment. This is useful in cases where it is not very clear to the browser what was said and the user can be given an option to choose the correct recognition.

- `recognition.continuous` (Boolean) tells the browser whether the audio has to be captured continuously or whether it should stop after recognizing the speech once.

However, we've not yet defined the code that is executed when a result is received after performing STT. We do so by adding code to the `recognition.onresult` function, as shown:

```
            let interimTranscript = '';
            for (let i = event.resultIndex, len = event.results.length; i
    < len; i++) {
                let transcript = event.results[i][0].transcript;
                if (event.results[i].isFinal) {
                    finalTranscript += transcript;
                } else {
                    interimTranscript += transcript;
                }
            }
            goDialogFlow(finalTranscript);
            finalTranscript = '';
```

The preceding block of code creates an interim transcript while the user is speaking, which is continually updated as more words are spoken. When the user stops speaking, the interim transcript is appended to the final transcript and passed to the function handling the interaction with Dialogflow. After the response is received from the Dialogflow agent, the final transcript is reset for the next voice input from the user.

Notice that we've sent the final recognized transcript of the user's speech to a function named `goDialogFlow()`. Let's define this function.

Step 3 – Making a call to the Dialogflow agent

Once we have the text version of the user's speech-based query, we will send it to the Dialogflow agent, as shown:

```
function goDialogFlow(text){
            $.ajax({
                type: "POST",
                url:
"https://XXXXXXXX.gateway.dialogflow.cloud.ushakov.co",
                contentType: "application/json; charset=utf-8",
                dataType: "json",
                data: JSON.stringify({
                    "session": "test",
                    "queryInput": {
                    "text": {
                        "text": text,
                        "languageCode": "en"
                        }
                    }
                }),
                success: function(data) {
                    var res = data.queryResult.fulfillmentText;
                    speechSynthesis.speak(new
SpeechSynthesisUtterance(res));
                },
                error: function() {
                    console.log("Internal Server Error");
                }
            });
        }
```

You'll observe that when the API call succeeds, we use the SpeechSynthesis API to speak out the result to the user. Its usage is much more simple than the SpeechRecognition API and so is the first of the two to appear on Firefox and Safari.

Notice the API URL used in the preceding function. It might look weird currently and you might wonder where we obtained this URL from. What we did was essentially skip the requirement of setting the Dialogflow agent service account configurations using the terminal, which is always local to the system the script is working on and is so difficult to transport.

To obtain a similar URL for your project, follow along with the following steps; otherwise, skip *step 4* and move directly on to *step 5*.

Step 4 – Creating a Dialogflow API proxy on Dialogflow Gateway by Ushakov

Head over to `https://dialogflow.cloud.ushakov.co/`. You'll be presented with an interface, as shown:

Dialogflow Gateway facilitates the interactions between your voice UI and the Dialogflow agent. This is very useful in situations where our project is hosted as a static website. Dialogflow Gateway provides simplified API wrappers around the Dialogflow API and is very easy to use.

You'll have to create an account to get started with Dialogflow, shown in the next section.

Step 4.1 – Creating an account on Dialogflow Gateway

Click on **Get Started** to begin the account creation process on the platform. You'll be asked to sign in with your Google account. Make sure you use the same account that you used to create the Dialogflow agent previously.

Step 4.2 – Creating a service account for your Dialogflow agent project

We previously discussed in detail how to create a service account for GCP projects in `Chapter 6`, *Deep Learning on Google Cloud Platform Using Python*. Create a new service key for the project linked to your Dialogflow agent, as shown:

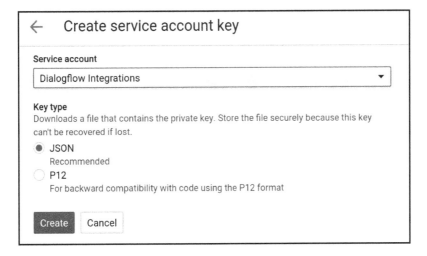

Once the key has been created successfully, a dialog box will pop up, telling you that the key has been saved to your computer, as shown:

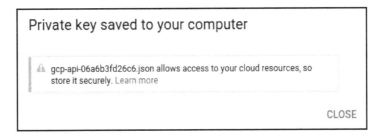

The service account credentials are downloaded to your local system in the form of JSON, with the name as shown in the preceding screenshot.

Now, we will use this service account credentials file to connect Dialogflow Gateway to our Dialogflow agent.

Step 4.3 – Uploading the service key file to Dialogflow Gateway

On the Dialogflow Gateway console, you'll find the **Upload Keys** button. Click on it to upload your generated service account key file. Once uploaded, the console will display your Dialogflow API proxy URLs, as shown:

We'll use the Gateway URL in the function we defined previously.

Step 5 – Adding a click handler for the button

Finally, we add a `click` handler to the **Ask a question** button so that it can trigger the speech recognition of the user input and the synthesis of output from the Dialogflow agent.

Within the document `ready` function defined in *step 2*, add the following `click` handler code:

```
$('#customerChatRoot').click(function(){
    recognition.start();
    $(this).text('Speak!');
});
```

Now, when the microphone starts listening for the user input, the button text changes to **Speak!**, prompting the user to start speaking.

Try testing the website on your setup and see how accurately you can get it to work!

Summary

In this chapter, we combined several technologies to come up with an end-to-end project that demonstrates one of the most rapidly growing aspects of applying deep learning to websites. We covered tools such as Dialogflow, Dialogflow Gateway, GCP IAM, Firebase Cloud Functions, and ngrok. We also demonstrated how to build a REST API-based UI and how to make it accessible using the Web Speech API. The Web Speech API, although presently at a nascent stage, is a cutting-edge piece of technology used in web browsers and is expected to grow rapidly in the coming years.

It is safe to say that deep learning on the web has huge potential and will be a key factor in the success of many upcoming businesses. In the next chapter, we'll explore some of the hottest research areas in deep learning for web development and how we can plan to progress in the best way.

Appendix: Success Stories and Emerging Areas in Deep Learning on the Web

It is often important to know what others have been doing with any technology to understand the scale of its applicability and the return of investment that it can promise. This chapter illustrates some of the most famous websites whose product was based heavily upon leveraging the power of deep learning. This chapter also discusses some key research areas in web development that can be enhanced using deep learning. This chapter will help you to delve even deeper into the fusion of web technologies and deep learning and will motivate you to come up with your own intelligent web applications.

The chapter consists of two main sections:

- Success stories of organizations such as Quora and Duolingo that have been applying deep learning in their products
- Some key emerging areas in deep learning, such as reading comprehension, audio searching, and more

Let's get started!

Success stories

In this section, we will take a brief look at some products/companies that used AI at their core to boost their business growth. It's worth noting here that it is not important that your entire product or service is based on any AI technique or algorithm; only having AI in a small portion of it or for a specific feature is enough to boost your product's usefulness and hence the widespread usage of your product by customers. Sometimes, you may not even have AI present in any of the product's features, and instead, you might only use it to perform data analysis and come up with expected trends to make sure your product conforms to the upcoming trends. Let's take a look at what worked for these companies as they made it large.

Quora

Before Quora, there had been a plethora of question-and-answer websites and forums. At one point in time in the history of the internet, online forums were seen as something that could no longer be improved; however, Quora came up with a few tweaks that were enabled using deep learning to help them rapidly outperform other forums. The following are the tweaks that they implemented:

- They enabled contributors to request an answer to any question as soon as it was published using the Ask to Answer feature. This made it easier for the questions to reach the relevant subject experts, who gave answers rapidly and made the platform more responsive and accurate.
- They blocked out poorly written questions and answers using **natural language processing** (**NLP**). This brought in the concept of automoderated forums with high-quality content.
- The determination of tags and related articles for any given question–answer thread made the discovery of similar questions easy. This made Quora users spend a lot of time reading answers to similar questions to theirs just to find new information in each of them.
- The Quora Digest newsletter was a highly curated collection of articles, based on the user's interests, that almost always succeeded in bringing the user back to the platform:

Quora at one point in time became (and is still counted among) the most addictive social platforms on the internet. They took a simple question-and-answer website and used deep learning to transform it into an amazing platform. You can check out the platform at `https://quora.com`.

Duolingo

Learning a new language has always been a tough feat. When Duolingo came onto the market in 2012, it brought with it a term that was beginning to grow in importance and scope—artificial intelligence. They converted something as mundane as memorizing words and grammar rules into minigames that would respond differently to each user. The Duolingo AI took into account the temporal nature of the human mind. They formulated research on how quickly a person is likely to forget the words he/she has learned. They called this concept half-life regression and used it to reinforce the knowledge of the words it predicted that the user would have forgotten at any given point of time.

This worked immensely in their favor and made Duolingo one of the most popular apps on mobile app stores. Their website is also a classic example of unorthodox designs that were well received. You can learn more about Duolingo at `https://duolingo.com`.

Spotify

Audio players have existed for a very long time, but no one had what Spotify brought to the table. Spotify used deep learning to determine which songs a user would like to hear at any given point of time. Over the years, their AI has progressed in leaps and bounds, suggesting entire playlists according to the recently played songs of the user. The rapid rise of Spotify has inspired a huge number of products that attempt to do the same and are trying to catch up with the popularity of Spotify.

Spotify also introduced a very powerful feature—searching for a song based on an audio sample. It was an instant hit feature; many users downloaded Spotify just because they could not remember the name of a nice song they were listening to wanted to find its name out quickly. You simply had to record the audio of a song playing nearby and feed it to Spotify to know the song that was playing.

Google Search/Photos

While image storage on the cloud was an existing solution offered by companies such as Dropbox, Google Photos revolutionized the cloud image storage space by bringing AI into the equation. Google Photos has been adopted by billions of people worldwide because of its amazing features, such as the following:

- **Face recognition:** This feature was present in an earlier Google product named Picasa, which is considered to be the precursor to Google Photos.
- **Wizard:** Google Photos automatically determines which photos were taken at the same event or occasion. It then tries to create movies about the related pictures or simply touches upon the images to make them appear better. Sometimes, Google Photos also creates animated GIFs with photos that appear to be in a sequence.
- **Recognition of documents and memes:** Google Photos suggests that its users archive old documents, screenshots, and memes. This is very helpful in saving device storage:

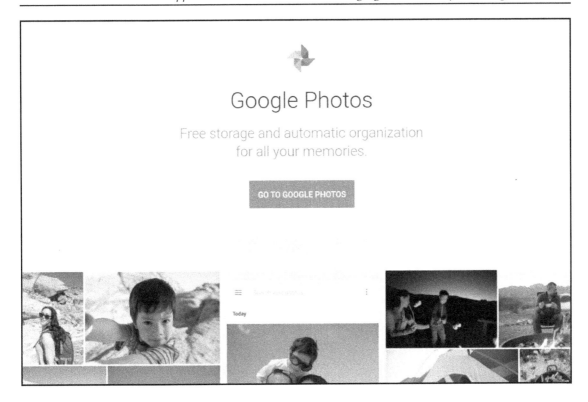

Google Photos is a market leader in terms of personal online galleries because of its usage of deep learning behind the curtain. If you would like to learn more about it, visit `https://photos.google.com`.

In this section, we took a look at a few products that have been greatly impacted by deep learning. In the next section, we will be seeing some of the emerging areas where deep learning seems to bring a lot of positive results.

Key emerging areas

In the previous sections, we saw how several companies have incorporated deep-learning-based techniques in order to improve their products. In this section, we will be discussing some of the areas that are currently being heavily researched, and we will see how impactful they are through the lens of web development.

Audio search

Suppose you are in a pub and you like the song being played by the live band. In your mind, you know that you have already heard that song before, but you are unable to recollect the name of the song. Wouldn't it be nice if you could have a system that would listen to the song and search for its name? Welcome to the world of audio search engines!

There are a number of existing audio search engines available out there, with Sound Search (which is offered by Google Assistant) being one of the most popular ones. You might also want to check out Shazam. In the following screenshot, you can see a sample audio search result produced via Sound Search:

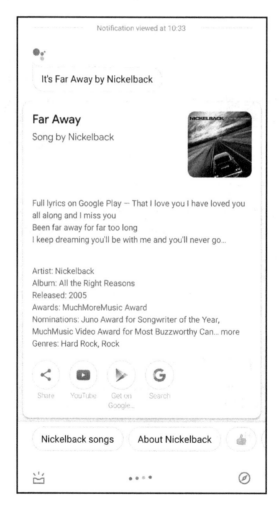

For a system to perform an audio search based on the audio signal it is receiving, the system first needs to process the signal, which is known as audio signal processing. The system then compares that processed signal with its existing database of tens of thousands of songs. Before the signal is even compared to an existing database, it is given a particular representation using a neural network, which is often referred to as a fingerprint; however, this is still an active area of research, and I highly encourage you to read the article at `https://ai.googleblog.com/2018/09/googles-next-generation-music.html` for a more detailed overview of these techniques.

Reading comprehension

Have you ever wished that a search engine would give you the answer to your search query instead of finding suitable links to resources that might contain the answer to your search query? Well, it's now possible for a system to achieve this if it is programmed with reading comprehension. Let's look at the following screenshot to see what this means:

If you notice carefully, we did not even phrase the statement *Sachin Tendulkar's father* as a question. Modern systems are capable enough to infer properties like this by themselves.

Now, to be able to appreciate the depth of a system (or a machine) that has reading comprehension, say that you wanted to find an answer to your question after performing a web search. This is the multistep process that you would need to go through:

1. You start by formulating the search query with the relevant keywords and the search engine performs the search.
2. The search engine then gives you a list of relevant documents for the given search query.
3. You go through those documents, organize the information present in them according to your understanding, and then you come to a conclusion.

There are still a number of steps that are manual in nature, and the question still gets raised—can we design a system that would automate the process of finding that suitable answer for us? Existing search engines give us a list of relevant documents for given search queries, but are not sufficient to develop systems that can actually produce answers to the search queries by themselves. Briefly, such a system would need to do the following:

1. Follow the structure of the relevant documents.
2. Make sense out of the contents present in those documents.
3. Come to a final answer.

Let's simplify the problem a bit. Let's say that for a given question, we already have a list of relevant passages and now we need to develop a system that would actually make sense out of those passages and give us a definite answer for the given question. In reading comprehension systems, neural networks typically learn to capture a deep semantic relationship between the given questions and the relevant passages and then they formulate the final answers.

As you might have already figured out, search engines such as Google Search, Bing, and so on already come with the capability of reading comprehension.

Detection of fake news on social media

With social media booming at a very rapid pace, there is never a dearth of news. Social media has easily become one of the prime sources of news for us; however, its authenticity is often not ensured. Not every news article that you stumble across on social media is genuine, and it is safe to say that a vast number of them are fake. The after-effects of this phenomenon can be really very alarming, and it can indeed lead to acts of abuse, violence, and so on.

There are a handful of organizations and agencies that are trying to fight with this and make people aware of the authenticity of news articles. This task can be very tedious given the amount of news that we see daily on social media. So, the question now becomes can we leverage the power of machine learning to automatically detect fake news? This is, in fact, an active area of research and there are no substantial applications that are known to tackle this at a large scale.

However, the following are some research studies conducted by various groups where they have used classical machine learning and deep learning approaches:

- *Detecting Fake News in Social Media Networks*: `https://www.sciencedirect.com/science/article/pii/S1877050918318210`
- *Fake News Detection on Social Media using Geometric Deep Learning*: `https://arxiv.org/abs/1902.06673`

You are encouraged to check out the survey paper at `https://arxiv.org/pdf/1812.00315.pdf`, which provides a comprehensive guide on various fake news detection techniques and also discusses related research on the subject. On the other hand, a German startup named Varia (`https://www.varia.media/`) is trying to solve the problem of fake news in a unique way. Instead of detecting the authenticity of the news, they are providing different perspectives of certain news items. In other words, they are providing perspective as a service. To know more about it, you should definitely check it out at `https://alpha.varia.media/`.

Summary

In this final chapter of this book, we have tried to inspire you to build your next deep learning project and use it on a web platform. You might be interested in the stories of more such companies that transformed their businesses using AI and ruled the market space. If you take a look at almost every website you visit, they will all use elements of AI and deep learning on them in some way, be it in the form of recommendation systems or advertisements (which are again promotional recommendation systems). We then covered the upcoming topics in the field of deep learning, which are looking for implementation on websites in the very near future. It would be amazing if you could come up with a service based on any of these topics!

Other Books You May Enjoy

If you enjoyed this book, you may be interested in these other books by Packt:

Hands-On Machine Learning with TensorFlow.js
Kai Sasaki

ISBN: 978-1-83882-173-9

- Use the t-SNE algorithm in TensorFlow.js to reduce dimensions in an input dataset
- Deploy tfjs-converter to convert Keras models and load them into TensorFlow.js
- Apply the Bellman equation to solve MDP problems
- Use the k-means algorithm in TensorFlow.js to visualize prediction results
- Create tf.js packages with Parcel, Webpack, and Rollup to deploy web apps
- Implement tf.js backend frameworks to tune and accelerate app performance

Hands-On Web Scraping with Python
Anish Chapagain

ISBN: 978-1-78953-339-2

- Analyze data and information from web pages
- Learn how to use browser-based developer tools from the scraping perspective
- Use XPath and CSS selectors to identify and explore markup elements
- Learn to handle and manage cookies
- Explore advanced concepts in handling HTML forms and processing logins
- Optimize web securities, data storage, and API use to scrape data
- Use Regex with Python to extract data
- Deal with complex web entities by using Selenium to find and extract data

Leave a review - let other readers know what you think

Please share your thoughts on this book with others by leaving a review on the site that you bought it from. If you purchased the book from Amazon, please leave us an honest review on this book's Amazon page. This is vital so that other potential readers can see and use your unbiased opinion to make purchasing decisions, we can understand what our customers think about our products, and our authors can see your feedback on the title that they have worked with Packt to create. It will only take a few minutes of your time, but is valuable to other potential customers, our authors, and Packt. Thank you!

Index

K

Keras neural network
  compiling 100
  training 100
Keras
  arrays, reshaping for processing with 98
  used, for creating neural network 99, 100
kernel 78

L

layers 118
lemmatization 326
library
  versus application programming interfaces
    (APIs) 140
linear neuron
  anatomy 44
linear neurons
  about 46
  anatomy 44, 45, 46
Long Short-Term Memory (LSTM) 278
LSTM-based model
  building, for authenticating users 275
  building, for authentication validity check 275,
    276, 277, 278, 279

M

Machine Learning (ML), terminologies
  bias and variance 15, 16
  generalization error 17
  overfitting 16, 17
  test set 15
  train set 15
  training error 17
  underfitting 16, 17
  validation set 15
Machine Learning (ML), types
  reinforcement learning (RL) 13, 14
  semi-supervised learning 14
  supervised learning 12
  unsupervised learning 13
Machine Learning (ML)
  about 8, 10, 11
  fundamentals 11

terminologies 14
  types 11, 12
Machine Learning APIs
  URL 217
malicious user detection 274, 275
middlewares
  reference link 126
ML model
  comparison and selection 24
  deployment 25
  monitoring 25
ML modeling
  about 21, 22
  model evaluation 22
  training 22
  tuning 23
ML systems 5
ML workflow
  about 18
  data preparation 19
  data retrieval 19
ML, deploying in production with tools
  about 301
  Airflow 305, 306
  AutoML 307
  creme 301, 302, 303, 304, 305
MNIST dataset of handwritten digits
  about 90, 91
  exploring 91, 92
  functions, creating to read images files 92, 93
  functions, creating to read label files 94
  summary 95
modal 71
model deployment 25
model evaluation 22
models 118
multilayer perceptron (MLP) 46

N

Natural Language Processing (NLP)
  about 165, 322, 324, 360
  Bag of Words (BoW) 326, 327
  corpus 325
  lemmatization 326
  parts of speech 325

CPSIA information can be obtained
at www.ICGtesting.com
Printed in the USA
BVHW010233120620
581397BV00007B/256